Attacking Faulty Reasoning

A Practical Guide to Fallacy-Free Arguments

Fifth Edition

T. Edward Damer
Emory & Henry College

THOMSON
™
WADSWORTH

Australia • Canada • Mexico • Singapore • Spain • United Kingdom • United States

ABOUT THE AUTHOR

T. Edward Damer is Professor of Philosophy, the Rowlett Chair of Creative Studies, and Chair of the Division of Visual and Performing Arts at Emory & Henry College in Virginia.

Publisher/Executive Editor: *Holly J. Allen*
Acquisitions Editor: *Steve Wainwright*
Technology Project Manager: *Julie Aguilar*
Assistant Editors: *Lee McCracken, Anna Lustig*
Marketing Manager: *Worth Hawes*
Marketing Assistant: *Annabelle Yang*
Permissions Editor: *Kiely Sexton*

Print Buyer: *Lisa Claudeanos*
Production Service: *Scratchgravel Publishing Services*
Copy Editor: *Mary Anne Shahidi*
Cover Designer: *Bill Stanton*
Compositor: *Scratchgravel Publishing Services*
Printer: *Webcom*

For more information about our products, contact us at:

**Thomson Learning Academic
Resource Center
1-800-423-0563**

For permission to use material from this text or product, submit a request online at

http://www.thomsonrights.com

Any additional questions about permissions can be submitted by email to

thomsonrights@thomson.com

Library of Congress Control Number: 2003116808

ISBN: 0-534-60516-8

**Thomson Wadsworth
10 Davis Drive
Belmont, CA 94002-3098
USA**

Asia
Thomson Learning
5 Shenton Way #01-01
UIC Building
Singapore 068808

Australia/New Zealand
Thomson Learning
102 Dodds Street
Southbank, Victoria 3006
Australia

Canada
Nelson
1120 Birchmount Road
Toronto, Ontario M1K 5G4
Canada

Europe/Middle East/Africa
Thomson Learning
High Holborn House
50/51 Bedford Row
London WC1R 4LR
United Kingdom

Latin America
Thomson Learning
Seneca, 53
Colonia Polanco
11560 Mexico D.F.
Mexico

Spain/Portugal
Paraninfo
Calle/Magallanes, 25
28015 Madrid, Spain

Contents

VI   FALLACIES THAT VIOLATE THE RELEVANCE CRITERION   78

VII   FALLACIES THAT VIOLATE THE ACCEPTABILITY CRITERION   104

Preface

This text is designed to help students construct and evaluate arguments. More specifically, its purpose is to help students recognize when they have constructed or encountered a good or successful argument for a particular action or belief. This skill is reinforced in every section, beginning with the first four chapters that focus on the criteria of a good argument and continuing through each of the five major chapters on specific fallacies and the final chapter on writing the argumentative essay.

Scattered throughout the text are 13 distinct principles or guides for participants in rational discussion. These principles represent virtually everything a person needs to know to engage responsibly in the evaluation and construction of arguments and to participate fairly and effectively in a rational discussion of controversial issues.

One of the most difficult things for most of us to do is to know when to end a debate or discussion on an issue and to make a decision about what to do or believe. The key is to recognize when an argument is good enough for a reasonable person to embrace its conclusion. This book provides a simple and effective method for doing so by means of the five criteria of a good argument, which constitute the basis for my own theory of fallacy.

THEORY OF FALLACY

Most treatments of fallacies are not informed by any theory of fallacy. They simply list fallacies as things not to do. The approach of this book, however, is different. According to my own theory of fallacy, a fallacy is a violation of one or more of the five criteria of a good argument. The fallacies are categorized in the text by the criterion of a good argument that they violate. These five categories deal with (1) the structural demands of a well-formed argument, (2) the relevance of the argument's premises, (3) the acceptability of the argument's premises, (4) the sufficiency of the premises to support the conclusion of the argument, and (5) the effective rebuttal of the strongest arguments against the argument or the position it supports.

By its careful treatment of the criteria of a good argument, this book helps the reader to recognize when the argument is a successful one. The approach is clear and uncomplicated, and the reader should come away from the study of the text with a well-developed, lifelong skill in assessing and formulating arguments.

The 60 fallacies treated in the book are organized in Chapters V through IX by the criterion violated, with one chapter devoted to each criterion. An extended discussion of each fallacy explains and illustrates exactly how the fallacy violates the criterion.

In most cases, each specific fallacy is defined with a single sentence; at the end of the text, the Glossary of Fallacies brings all these definitions together in one place for easy reference. Several examples follow a discussion of each fallacy. Unlike those in many other textbooks, these examples are realistic, practical and typically as current as the most recent family disagreement, campus discussion, or letter to the editor. Most of the examples are about real issues or common situations, although they have been simplified and separated from other issues in order to illustrate clearly the features of a particular fallacy.

Following the treatment of each fallacy is a unique "Attacking the Fallacy" section, which makes specific suggestions for dealing constructively with particular fallacious arguments when they are encountered. But here, as is the case throughout the book, the emphasis is more on resolving issues than on pointing out flaws in arguments.

USE OF THE TEXT

Students should be able to read and absorb the material on the specific fallacies in Chapters V–IX with very little assistance. The material in the first four chapters may require more class discussion.

At the end of each major section on specific fallacies and at the end of each chapter, the student is given practice assignments in identifying fallacious pieces of reasoning. The reader is asked not only to identify the fallacy by name, but also to explain how the specific piece of reasoning violates one of the criteria of a good argument. Sample answers and explanations are found at the end of the book.

In other assignments, students are asked to bring to class examples of reasoning from current magazines, newspaper editorials, letters to the editor in newspapers and magazines, speeches, lectures, conversations, and advertisements. Class time can be spent assessing the merit of these student-submitted arguments by applying the five criteria discussed in the first four chapters and identifying specific patterns of faulty reasoning discussed in the other chapters. Students are also asked to strengthen these submitted arguments or to devise better arguments for alternative views, as well as to construct their own arguments in support of a position on self-chosen current controversial issues. These submitted arguments can then be evaluated by all class members.

NEW FEATURES IN THE FIFTH EDITION

A new and fifth criterion is added to the other four criteria of a good argument. The new criterion judges an argument in terms of its formal structure and introduces the reader to some of the deductive fallacies, such as the fallacies of inconsistency and the most common conditional and syllogistic fallacies: Incompatible Premises, Contradiction Between Premise and Conclusion, Denying the Antecedent, Affirming the Consequent, False Conversion, Undistributed Middle Term, and Illicit Distribution of an End Term. The new criterion provides an important tool of argument evaluation that was missing from former editions. The begging-the-question fallacies are transferred to this category and treated as "formal" fallacies. These newly treated fallacies are brought together in a new chapter entitled "Fallacies That Violate the Structural Criterion."

To make room for the seven new "formal" fallacies, seven of the less commonly committed "informal" fallacies have been eliminated or combined with other fallacies. The total number of fallacies treated in the text thus remains the same. Playing to the Gallery now combines Appeal to Pity, Use of Flattery, and Assigning Guilt by Association. Leading Question is combined with Question-Begging Language, and three fallacies are entirely eliminated: Fallacy of Novelty, Inference from a Name or Description, and Fallacy of Impossible Precision.

A short chapter on writing an argumentative essay in now included in the text. The guidelines for writing an argumentative essay incorporate ideas from the Code of Conduct, the criteria of a good argument, and various strategies suggested throughout the text.

This new edition includes a great number of skill-building written and oral assignments. The "guide questions" in the fourth edition have been eliminated in favor of questions that ask the students to analyze real arguments they have recently encountered. At the end of each chapter students are given assignments that ask them to do increasingly more difficult tasks in their analyses of these "found" arguments. Students are also asked to analyze more extended examples of good and bad arguments and to construct and/or look for their own examples of each fallacy.

There are minor changes to the names and descriptions of a number of the fallacies. The names are now more user friendly in that they comply, where possible, with ordinary language. In fact, I have attempted throughout this new edition to use nontechnical language as much as possible. In the treatment of the new formal fallacies, for example, only the barest minimum of technical language is employed. In new introductions to each of the twelve divisions of fallacies, each of the 60 fallacies is introduced to the reader without reference to its technical name.

The section on the acceptability criterion of a good argument and a number of other sections have been completely rewritten in the interest of clarity, while dated and confusing examples in the texts and in the assignments have been replaced by more current and less confusing ones.

ACKNOWLEDGMENTS

Several people have been especially helpful in the preparation of this fifth edition. Lawrence Habermehl, professor of philosophy at American International College in Massachusetts and Ben Letson, my colleague in philosophy at Emory & Henry College, both read the revised text and made helpful suggestions. My youngest son, Taylor Bradford-Damer Stone, not only proofread the text but was always willing and able to solve those frustrating word-processing problems that I encountered throughout the revision.

Introduction

It seems as if very few people are really interested in the study of logic, because, as philosopher Charles Peirce suggested many years ago, every person "conceives himself to be proficient enough in the art of reasoning already."[1] It is interesting to note, however, that we "proficient" reasoners rarely recognize in others a similar proficiency. Few arguments other than our own are regarded as genuinely good ones, and it is sincerely believed that what the *rest* of the world needs is "to study a little logic."

Those who make the effort "to study a little logic" will no doubt improve their ability to think correctly and to express that thinking more clearly. One of the current terms for such a skill is "critical thinking." One philosopher has defined critical thinking as "a process, the goal of which is to make reasonable decisions about what to believe and what to do."[2] To do such reflective thinking, students of logic need to learn not only the techniques of distinguishing bad arguments from good ones but also how to construct good arguments.

REASONS FOR USING GOOD ARGUMENTS

There are a number of practical reasons why it is important to formulate quality arguments and to expect others to do the same. First, and most important, good arguments help us to make better personal decisions. Indeed, there is reason to believe that those who use rational criteria in all aspects of their lives have a better chance of success in achieving their goals or completing their projects.

---

[1]Charles Sanders Peirce, "The Fixation of Belief," in *Collected Papers of Charles Sanders Peirce*, ed. Charles Hartshorne and Paul Weiss (Cambridge, MA: The Belknap Press of Harvard University Press, 1934), Vol. 223.

[2]Robert H. Ennis, *Critical Thinking* (Upper Saddle River, NJ: Prentice-Hall, Inc., 1996), p. xvii.

Second, good arguments promote our general interest in holding only those views that we have reason to believe are true or defensible ones. If we demand good arguments of ourselves, that demand will lead us to new and better ideas, reinforce the strength of our present beliefs, or expose weaknesses that might lead to qualification or abandonment of those beliefs.

Third, the use of good arguments raises the level of thinking and discussion in social, business, and personal contexts. Such arguments are usually more effective in trying to convince others of a point of view than are methods such as fear, intimidation, or emotional bribery. At least they have a more permanent effect.

Fourth, focusing on the quality of an argument is a way to resolve personal disputes or to settle conflicts, for by attending to the merit of each other's arguments, discussants are able to discover strengths that make a position more convincing or weaknesses that make it less so.

Finally, good arguments play an important role in helping us to make difficult moral decisions. Not only do they help us to decide what positive action to take but also to avoid actions with harmful consequences. False beliefs, to which fallacious arguments sometimes lead, blur our moral vision and often result in actions that cause considerable harm to others. Since we are all responsible for the consequences of our actions, it is important that we base our beliefs and decisions on the conclusions of good arguments.

If good or fallacy-free arguments are so important, then why should one spend time studying bad or fallacious arguments, or, more specifically, the fallacies in this book? We should do so because the ability to discriminate between fallacious and nonfallacious patterns of reasoning is a necessary condition for good reasoning. A person cannot construct good arguments if he or she does not know the difference between a good one and a bad one.

GOALS OF THE TEXT

The primary purpose of this book, then, is to assist students in becoming better thinkers by giving attention to some of the most common errors in our ordinary ways of thinking. However, because little constructive purpose is served by simply learning to identify errors, it is my hope that the skills that may be developed in recognizing bad reasoning may help to generate habits of good reasoning. In other words, focusing attention on errors should help one to construct good or fallacy-free arguments.

A second purpose of this book is to suggest some concrete ways of challenging the faulty reasoning of others. If one is conscientious in this task, it is usually possible to confront one's verbal opponents with their faulty reasoning without creating ill feeling. The strategies that are suggested for each fallacy in the "Attacking the Fallacy" sections are designed to get reasoning back on the right track—that is, to turn faulty reasoning into good reasoning. Indeed, they are designed to assist faulty arguers in doing what they allegedly wish to do—to effectively demonstrate the truth of a claim or the rightness of an action.

The strategies may also help to alleviate another problem created by faulty reasoning—the feeling of helplessness often experienced when one is the target of such reasoning. This experience results from simply not knowing any effective way to address the error in question. Familiarity with some of the most common errors in reasoning is a defense against being misled or victimized by others. The suggestions accompanying the treatment of each fallacy will assist one in gaining control of such situations by not only exposing the error, but also redirecting the discussion toward constructive ends.

One of the main goals of an education is to develop the ability to discover and to defend reliable ideas about ourselves and our world. A careful study of this practical guide to fallacy-free arguments should be of help in accomplishing that aim. And because it is likely that the book will expose some of the careless and defective ways that you yourself have defended ideas in the past, you may soon come to believe that not only the rest of the world, but you too, may need "to study a little logic."

I
A Code of Intellectual Conduct

While the primary focus of this text will be the construction of good or fallacy-free arguments, it is important to spell out some basic rules of behavior that an intellectually mature person would be expected to follow when constructing and assessing arguments for use in a rational discussion of disputed issues. The principles that constitute this "code of conduct" are actually a summary of the criteria of a good argument and other elements of effective discussion and argumentation that are addressed more fully throughout the text. The code, as a whole, provides us with two very important standards of behavior.

AN EFFECTIVE PROCEDURAL STANDARD

First, it represents the kind of intellectual behavior that is most often successful in resolving the issues that divide us. The code of conduct, then, is simply a formalizing of effective ways of dealing rationally with difficult issues. The type of thinking that is effective in settling disputes, confirming judgments, and/or revising beliefs is usually conducted in accordance with such principles. Indeed, researchers in speech communication have discovered *empirically* that discussions that follow procedural ground rules similar to these are more successful in settling issues than those that do not. My experiences as an arguer and my experimentation with these principles in my own college classes over the last several years have yielded the same gratifying results.

AN IMPORTANT ETHICAL STANDARD

Second, the code of conduct represents an important ethical standard. While it may seem a bit odd to suggest that failure to carry on a discussion in accordance with the principles outlined here is immoral, it is surely not strange to suggest that one ought to argue fairly. Insofar as a spirit of fair-mindedness demands of all participants in rational discussion a commitment to the same minimal standards of intellectual behavior, these rules clearly take on an ethical dimension. Consider how often we find ourselves in situations in which our verbal opponent refuses to abide by what we regard as the rules of the game. This not only shuts down the discussion, but more important, it prevents the issue at stake from being decided or at least further explored. In such situations we frequently become indignant toward our opponent, and our demand for compliance with certain ground rules is more than a mild irritation; it has decidedly moral overtones. We clearly expect fair play on the part of others, and we obviously should expect no less of ourselves.

A CODE OF CONDUCT FOR EFFECTIVE DISCUSSION

One who wishes (1) to earn the respect of fellow arguers, (2) to avoid committing the most common errors in reasoning, (3) to construct the strongest possible arguments for one's views, (4) to escape any charge of unfairness, and (5) to do one's part in resolving those conflicts concerning issues that matter, should make each of the following principles a part of his or her intellectual style.

1. The Fallibility Principle

Each participant in a discussion of a disputed issue should be willing to accept the fact that he or she is fallible, which means that one must acknowledge that a thorough examination of the issue may reveal that one's own initial view is not the most defensible position on the question.

2. The Truth-Seeking Principle

Each participant should be committed to the task of earnestly searching for the truth or at least the most defensible position on the issue at stake. Therefore, one should be willing to examine alternative positions seriously, look for insights in the positions of others, and allow other participants to present arguments for or raise objections to any position held with regard to any disputed issue.

3. The Clarity Principle

The formulations of all positions, defenses, and attacks should be free of any kind of linguistic confusion and clearly separated from other positions and issues.

4. The Burden of Proof Principle

The burden of proof for any position usually rests on the participant who sets forth the position. If and when an opponent asks, the proponent should provide an argument for that position.

5. The Principle of Charity

If a participant's argument is reformulated by an opponent, it should be expressed in the strongest possible version that is consistent with the original intention of the arguer. If there

*is any question about that intention or about implicit parts of the argument, the arguer should be
given the benefit of any doubt in the reformulation.*

6. The Structural Principle

*One who argues for or against a position should use an argument that meets the funda-
mental structural requirements of a well-formed argument, using premises that are compatible
with one another, that do not contradict the conclusion, that do not assume the truth of the conclusion, and that are not involved in any faulty deductive inference.*

7. The Relevance Principle

*One who presents an argument for or against a position should attempt to set forth
only reasons that are directly related to the merit of the position at issue.*

8. The Acceptability Principle

*One who presents an argument for or against a position should attempt to use reasons
that are likely to be accepted by a rationally mature person and that meet standard criteria of
acceptability.*

9. The Sufficiency Principle

*One who presents an argument for or against a position should attempt to provide rea-
sons that are sufficient in number, kind, and weight to support the acceptance of the conclusion.*

10. The Rebuttal Principle

*One who presents an argument for or against a position should attempt to provide an
effective rebuttal to all serious challenges to the argument or the position it supports and to the
strongest arguments for viable alternative positions.*

11. The Resolution Principle

*An issue should be considered resolved if the proponent for one of the alternative posi-
tions successfully defends that position by presenting a structurally sound argument that uses
relevant and acceptable premises that together provide sufficient grounds to support the conclusion and provides an effective rebuttal to all serious challenges to the argument or position at
issue. Unless one can demonstrate that these conditions have not been met, one should accept the
conclusion of the successful argument and consider the issue, for all practical purposes, to be
settled. In the absence of a successful argument for any of the alternative positions, one is obligated to accept the position that is supported by the best of the good arguments presented.*

12. The Suspension of Judgment Principle

*If no position comes close to being successfully defended, or if two or more positions
seem to be defended with equal strength, one should, in most cases, suspend judgment about the*

issue. If practical considerations seem to require an immediate decision, one should weigh the relative risks of gain or loss connected with the consequences of suspending judgment and decide the issue on those grounds.

13. The Reconsideration Principle

If a successful or at least good argument for a position is subsequently found by any participant to be flawed in a way that raises new doubts about the merit of that position, one is obligated to reopen the issue for further consideration and resolution.

The first three of these principles are commonly regarded as standard principles of intellectual inquiry. They are almost universally understood as underlying our very participation in serious discussion.

THE FALLIBILITY PRINCIPLE

Each participant in a discussion of a disputed issue should be willing to accept the fact that he or she is fallible, which means that one must acknowledge that a thorough examination of the issue may reveal that one's own initial view is not the most defensible position on the question.

To employ the fallibility principle in discussion is consciously to accept the fact that you are fallible—that is, that you may very well be wrong in your view, or at least not in possession of the most defensible view on the matter in dispute. If you refuse to accept your own fallibility, you are, in effect, saying that you are not willing to change your mind, no matter what—even if you hear a better argument. This is strong evidence that you do not intend to play fairly. Consequently, there is no real point in pursuing the discussion any further, for there is little likelihood that any significant progress will be made. An admission of fallibility, however, is a positive sign that you really are interested in the kind of honest inquiry that may lead to a fair resolution of the issue.

The assumption of mutual fallibility is a crucial first step for serious discussants to take. Unfortunately, this move is rarely made in discussions of religion and politics, which is probably the reason that so little progress is made in those important areas of dispute. It is, however, the standard principle of inquiry among scientists, philosophers, and most other academics. In fact, these truth-seekers would probably argue that it is a necessary condition of intellectual progress.

If there is any doubt about the appropriateness of accepting the fallibility principle, take any issue about which people hold a number of alternative and conflicting opinions. For example, consider the area of religion. Since each of the hundreds of conflicting theological or ecclesiastical positions is different in some respect from all the others, we know before we begin any examination of those positions that only one of them has the possibility of being true—and even that one may be seriously flawed. So it turns out that not only is it *possible* that our own religious position is false or indefensible, it is *probable* that it is.

It is likely, of course, that our own position is more defensible than many of the others—especially if we have spent time developing and refining it in accordance with the available evidence and the tools of reason. Nevertheless, out of all of the conflicting religious positions currently held, many of which are vigorously defended by good minds, it is *unlikely* that only our position will be the correct one. Although we may believe that our own view is the most defensible one, we must keep in mind that others believe the same thing about their views—and only one of us, at best, can be right.

Several years ago at a conference on critical thinking, a panelist defined a critical thinker as "a person who by force of argument had changed his or her mind about an important issue at least once during the last year." He went on to say that it is highly unlikely that any person would just happen to be correct on every position held on important matters. On the contrary, given the great number of issues that divide us and the large number of different positions on each of those issues, it is more likely that a person would turn out to be wrong on more issues than he or she would be right.

The most convincing evidence of the fallibility of human opinions comes from the history of science. We are told by some of science's historians that virtually every knowledge claim in the history of science has been shown by subsequent inquiry to be either false or at least seriously flawed. And if this is true of the past, it may be true as well of present and future claims of science, even in spite of the more sophisticated techniques of inquiry used by modern science. Moreover, if such observations can be made about an area of inquiry with well-developed evidential requirements, it seems reasonable to assume that nonscience claims would suffer an even worse fate. In the face of such findings, we should at least be intellectually humbled enough to be less than certain about our claims to truth.

The important point here is that an admission of fallibility is a clear indication that we are consciously prepared to listen to the arguments of others. Although it is not easy to admit honestly that a firmly held position may not be true, it is a discussion-starter unlike any other. It not only calms the emotional waters surrounding the treatment of issues about which we feel deeply, but it has the potential for opening our ears to different and better arguments. We may even become critical thinkers—that is, persons who change our minds by the force of those arguments.

If you are skeptical about how effectively this tactic works, be the first to confess your own fallibility. At least make it clear that you are willing to change your mind. Your opponents will surely enter the confessional right behind you, if only to escape intellectual embarrassment. If they refuse to do so, you will at least know the futility of any further conversation about the matter at issue.

THE TRUTH-SEEKING PRINCIPLE

Each participant should be committed to the task of earnestly searching for the truth or at least the most defensible position on the issue at stake. Therefore, one should be willing to examine alternative positions seriously, look for insights in the positions of others, and allow other participants to present arguments for or raise objections to any position held with regard to any disputed issue.

The truth-seeking principle has gone hand in hand with the fallibility principle since the time of Socrates, who taught that we come to true knowledge only by first recognizing our own ignorance or lack of knowledge. The search for truth then becomes a lifelong endeavor, which principally takes the form of discussion, wherein we systematically entertain the ideas and arguments of fellow seekers after truth, while at the same time thoughtfully considering criticisms of our own views.

Since, as we have seen, it is not likely that the truth is now in our custody, all of our intellectual energies expended in discussion should be directed toward finding it or at least finding the most defensible position possible for the present time. That position, of course, is the position that is supported by the strongest or best argument encountered.

If the truth were already held, there would obviously be no use in any further discussion. To those who might claim that a discussion could at least be used to convince others of what *we* already know to be the truth, it should be pointed out that the "others" are probably making the same assumptions about the views that they now hold. Hence, it is unlikely that any "truth" will be changing hands. If we really are interested in finding the truth, it is imperative not only that we assume that we may not now have the truth, but that we listen to the defenses of alternative positions and encourage criticism of our own arguments.

There are some issues, of course, about which we have already done the hard work of investigation. For example, we may have thoroughly examined an issue, listened to and found seriously wanting the arguments on the other side, and entertained and found weak and nondamaging the criticisms of our position. In such a situation, we should not give the impression that we have an open mind about the issue. Neither should we carry on a pseudodiscussion. We have two other alternatives. If we really are tired of the issue and anticipate little or no possible evidence that might change our mind, we should admit that to our opponent and perhaps skip the discussion. But if we genuinely believe that we might have missed something that could cause us to alter our position, then, by all means, we should enter the debate as an honest seeker. The outcome may be that we convince our opponent of our position, but we should enter the debate only if we ourselves are willing to be turned around by the force of a better argument.

In our better moments we probably all want to hold only those opinions that really are true, but the satisfaction of that interest comes at a price—a willingness to look at all available options and the arguments in support of them. Otherwise, we might miss the truth completely. The problem, of course, is that most of us want the truth to be what we now hold to be the truth. We want to win, even if we have to cheat to do it. For example, we may want our child to be the smartest kid on the block, but to declare our child the contest winner before objectively examining the test score of every other child in the neighborhood is simply dishonest.

Real truth-seekers do not try to win by ignoring or denying the counter-evidence against their positions. Real winning is finding the position that results from playing the game in accordance with the rules. To pronounce yourself the winner before playing the game or by refusing to play by the rules fails to advance the search for truth and is in the end self-defeating.

THE CLARITY PRINCIPLE

The formulations of all positions, defenses, and attacks should be free of any kind of linguistic confusion and clearly separated from other positions and issues.

Any successful discussion of an issue must be carried on in language that is understood by all the parties involved. Even if what we have to say is perfectly clear to ourselves, others may not be able to understand us. A position or a criticism of it that is expressed in confusing, vague, ambiguous, or contradictory language will not only fail to reach those toward whom it is directed, it will contribute little to resolving the issue at hand.

Perhaps the most difficult problem in achieving clarity is being able to concentrate clearly on the main issue at stake. In informal discussion it is not easy to keep focused on the central issue. Controversial issues usually have many related features, and all of them may be important to deal with. To be successful, however, we must usually deal with issues one feature at a time. Each party to the dispute must therefore exercise great care in trying to keep other interesting yet distracting issues from clouding the discussion.

Finally, there is a special hell prepared for those who attempt to end a discussion by smugly suggesting that "our disagreement is just a matter of semantics." Such people are more villainous than benign, because they thereby contribute to the failure to resolve what is probably an important matter. Linguistic confusion is not the place to stop a discussion; it is usually the starting place from which we need to move forward. We must not let the potential resolution of an issue that matters to us falter on the rock of verbal confusion.

ASSIGNMENTS

A. Discuss in class some of the obstacles to adopting the "Code of Conduct for Effective Discussion" as a means to resolving conflicts in our practical lives.

B. In class, choose a controversial topic on which the class is more or less evenly divided. Divide into two groups, face each other in the classroom, and attempt to achieve some consensus on the topic by employing the principles in the "Code of Conduct for Effective Discussion." Your professor can serve as the moderator of the discussion.

II

What Is an Argument?

AN ARGUMENT IS A CLAIM SUPPORTED BY OTHER CLAIMS

The kind of faulty reasoning addressed in this book is that which is found in arguments. The term "argument" here does not refer to a bitter dispute or heated exchange, but to the use of statements that are already believed to be true to support the truth or acceptability of another statement. *An argument, then, is a group of statements, one or more of which (the premises) support or provide evidence for another (the conclusion).*

The premises of an argument are those statements that together constitute the grounds for affirming the conclusion. They are of many types. Some premises are conclusions of previous arguments, while others may be definitions, principles, or rules that are supportive of or relevant to the truth of the conclusion. Statements of fact, personal observation, expert testimony, or common knowledge may also be used to support a particular conclusion.

If a claim or position is being asserted and no other explicit or implicit statement is used to support it, then the spoken or written material in question is not an argument. It may express an opinion or take a position on an issue, but it is not an argument unless that opinion or position is defended with at least one piece of evidence or some statement of support. Arguments are aimed at the goal of demonstrating the truth or falsity of particular claims by presenting evidence that may convince others to accept those claims.

One of the most difficult tasks in evaluating arguments is that of identifying which of several statements in a piece of writing or discourse is the conclusion. The conclusion of an argument should be the statement or claim that has at least one other statement in support of it. The conclusion of an argument should not be confused with the main point in the material being examined. Most editorials and letters to the editor, for example, have a point to make, but many of them are not arguments. Since no reasons are given for the position taken, there is nothing to conclude. The letter or editorial is simply a series of unsupported claims or points. If you are uncertain about whether there is a conclusion lurking about, look for a statement that is supported by at least one other statement. That claim is likely to be the conclusion.

In some arguments, there may be more than one statement that is supported by others. These other supported statements may be some of the argument's premises, which are themselves conclusions supported by so-called subpremises. To distinguish between the supported premise and the conclusion of the argument, it will be necessary to determine which supported statement also seems to be the primary thesis being defended in the passage. It is possible, of course, that there is more than one argument being presented. If that is the case, you should examine each argument separately.

DISTINGUISHING ARGUMENT FROM OPINION

Many people have difficulty understanding the difference between an argument and the expression of a personal belief or opinion. They use the words "argument" and "opinion" interchangeably. Sometimes when I ask students for an argument for their belief or position on an issue, they give me their opinion about that issue rather than an argument. In other words, they simply tell me what they believe. But if we follow the principles suggested in this text, a belief should be the conclusion of an argument. The very word "conclusion" suggests that it is an opinion or judgment resulting from some process of rational reflection on the evidence.

While it is true that all of our claims are opinions, the important question is whether our opinions are supported or unsupported. An argument is a *supported* opinion. When students criticize an argument by saying of its conclusion something like, "Well, that's just his (or her) opinion," I remind them that an opinion expressed as the conclusion of an argument is not "just an opinion"; it is a *supported* opinion, and any criticism of that opinion should be aimed at the quality of the argument supporting it.

The expression of personal opinion is one of the most common forms of verbal exchange, and since reasons for our opinions are often not requested, we are unaccustomed to defending them and are even lulled into thinking that reasons are not required. "Everyone is entitled to his or her own opinion," it is often said. That is true, but the question here is not whether one has the right to express an opinion; it is a question of what opinions deserve our acceptance. If an opinion is not accompanied by reasons to support it, it is not possible to determine whether it merits our acceptance.

Most of us enjoy exchanging our opinions with others, but rarely do our opinions change unless arguments are presented. And since some of our opinions are in conflict with each other and with the opinions of others, it is obvious that some of our opinions are false and therefore need to be changed. For example, if there are two opposing opinions about some matter, probably only one of those opinions merits acceptance. If the views happen to contradict each other, only one of them can be true, for we know that contradictory claims cannot both be true. But which one is true? That question can be answered only by looking at the quality of the argument presented on behalf of each view.

THE BURDEN OF PROOF PRINCIPLE

The burden of proof for any position usually rests on the participant who sets forth the position. If and when an opponent asks, the proponent should provide an argument for that position.

Just as a person is generally held accountable for his or her own actions, one who makes a positive or negative claim about something has what is called the burden of proof. In many cases, of course, one does not have to supply such proof, for we are not always challenged to defend our claims. But if the claimant is asked "Why?" or "How do you know that is true?" he or she is logically obligated to produce reasons in behalf of the claim.

An exception to this rule is a situation in which the claim in question is well established or noncontroversial. In such a case, the burden of proof might rest on the one who wishes to *challenge* that claim.

A good discussion is not simply a verbal contest in which opinions are traded between opposing parties. A good discussion will include arguments in support of any opinion found by one of the participants to be questionable. Many opinions, of course, are shared by the parties involved and thus require no defense in a particular context. However, the central claims at issue in a dispute will almost always require some support.

If one had to defend not only the basic claim but also each of the premises, each of the statements in support of the premises, and each of the statements in support of the statements of support, one would be involved in an infinite chain of proofs—an obviously impractical task. But one at least has the responsibility to provide evidence for the main thesis and for any questionable premise, if asked to do so.

This is as it should be. Indeed, we follow this procedure in our basic social institutions. If a pharmaceutical firm wishes to market a new drug, it has the burden of proving to the Food and Drug Administration that the drug is safe and effective. Our legal system places the burden of proof in a criminal case on the one who does the accusing, the prosecutor. We would permit neither the drug manufacturer nor the prosecutor to get by with simply expressing an opinion on the matter at issue. Neither should we allow others to get by without defending their opinions, especially about important or controversial issues.

To ask others to accept your claim without any support, or to shift the burden of proof to them by suggesting that your position is true unless they can prove otherwise, is to commit the fallacy of "arguing from ignorance," for you are, in this way, making a claim based on no evidence at all. Indeed, you are basing the claim on the absence of evidence—that is, on ignorance. You can see the absurdity of such a move by taking any highly questionable claim and arguing that the claim is true in the absence of any counterevidence. For example, you could argue that it is true that your great-grandfather died of AIDS unless someone can prove otherwise, or that it is true that pornography causes sex crimes, unless someone can prove that it doesn't. In this way you fail to take responsibility for your own claims and even attempt to get your opponents to do your work for you. Moreover, since negative claims are notoriously difficult to establish, you are attempting to set yourself up for a "win" by default. But in the argument game, there are no wins by default, for the merit of any position is only as good as the argument given in support of it.

We do not want to give the impression, of course, that a good discussion must be carried on with the formal style of the courtroom. When the mutual interest of the parties is in finding the truth or the best solution to a problem, it is not unusual for all participants to assume the task of both defending and evaluating any claim presented. This approach is sometimes a good one, because it is more natural and often saves time, but no one should believe that the burden of proof no longer rests on the shoulders of those who make controversial claims, nor that it can be shifted without blame to others.

It should perhaps be pointed out that "proof," in the context in which it is being used here, does not mean absolute, knockdown proof. It does not even mean, for example, "beyond a reasonable doubt," as required of the prosecutor in a criminal trial. When a tobacco industry representative recently argued that "they have not yet proved any connection between the smoking of cigarettes and health problems," I presume that he was using the term with a meaning that is close to that kind of proof required in a criminal trial. Such proof, however, is not likely to be found for any claim typically encountered in informal discussion.

To satisfy the burden of proof required by the principle is to try to present what appears to be a good, or fallacy-free, argument in behalf of a claim. In most contexts, this kind of proof would probably resemble the kind of proof offered not in criminal courts but in civil courts. In other words, the argument would not have to prove the claim "beyond a reasonable doubt" but try to meet the burden of proof with what is called "the preponderance of the evidence." If the argument is a good argument it should at least do that.

In some contexts, practical considerations allow for a legitimate way of avoiding the burden of proof. For example, if you claim that since you have no reason to believe that a particular claim is true, it is therefore false, you have actually made a claim for which you now have the burden of proof—a task for which you might not be presently inclined or prepared. A careful distinction, however, should be made between asserting that "I have no reason to believe that X is true" and asserting that "X is false." The first does not entail the second. Each is a distinct claim. The first explains why one is not now prepared to affirm or deny the claim; the second is a negative claim for which one must assume the burden of proof. In the absence of a thorough investigation of the issue, the best response in dealing with a questionable claim might be simply to say that you have no reason to believe the claim rather than to deny it.

A practical way to deal with the "denial" option would be to simply act as if the negative claim were true, without making the denial—especially if you do not have the time, energy, or inclination to defend it. For example, you may not be prepared to prove that ghosts do not exist; but if, on the basis of the available evidence, you do not believe that they do, you could simply act as if they do not, without denying their existence. Most people who do not believe in God do not call themselves atheists; they simply act as if God does *not* exist. They may be neither interested in nor able to take on the burden of proving that God does not exist by calling themselves atheists. This is a practical way of contending daily with one's world without having to defend every belief or assumption on which one acts.

THE STANDARD FORM OF AN ARGUMENT

Once a person has satisfied the burden of producing reasons in support of a claim, we are then in a position to evaluate his or her argument. The first step in doing so is to reconstruct the argument into what is called a standard form. Whether this extraction of the argument from its original context is done mentally or in writing, it is an important part of the process of evaluating effectively the quality of the argument. A standard format that exhibits the logical structure of an argument is as follows:

Since (premise),
> which is a conclusion supported by (subpremise),

and (premise),
> which is a conclusion supported by (subpremise),

and (premise),

and (rebuttal premise),

Therefore, (conclusion).

One will seldom encounter an argument in so clear a form, but any argument can be reconstructed in a manner similar to this by an orderly separation of the premises from the conclusion. Contrary to what might be inferred from the standard model, the number of premises may vary from one to as many as is thought to be necessary to establish the truth of the conclusion. And it may be the case that not all—or even any—of the premises will be supported ones. One will also sometimes find that a premise, and maybe even the conclusion, is unstated but understood from the context. These missing parts should be carefully "spelled out" when the argument is put into standard form. When supplying missing parts it is helpful to enclose them in parentheses, so that it will be clear that the supplied parts did not appear in the original argument.

When reconstructing an argument one will often encounter what is called a subargument, wherein a subpremise is used to support one of the premises of the main argument. In the standard form reconstruction, one should indicate *not* that such evidence is directly supportive of the conclusion but that it supports one of the premises that support that conclusion.

Unfortunately, only a few encountered arguments contain what might be called a rebuttal premise. This important feature of an argument is an attempt to answer anticipated objections to the argument or to the position that it supports. A good argument must contain an effective rebuttal to those objections and/or to the arguments for viable alternative positions.

When reconstructing an argument into standard form, it is entirely appropriate to exclude irrelevant matter found in the original material that you believe was clearly not intended to be a part of the argument, but which for some reason the arguer wanted to include. Material that you think is irrelevant to the truth of the conclusion, but which the arguer apparently thinks *is* relevant, should be included. Additional or related arguments in the material should be reconstructed separately, ignored, or saved for another day.

Let us now take a sample argument and reconstruct it into the standard format. Consider the following letter to the editor of a local newspaper.

> Dear Editor:
> Your article about AIDS in yesterday's (October 2) newspaper fails to recognize how wrongheaded we are in our attempt to understand AIDS. For those who are willing to listen, the Bible makes it very clear what causes AIDS. God hates homosexual behavior. He does not, of course, hate the homosexual. God loves all human beings. After all, He created them. But homosexual behavior is a sin, and God punishes the sinner. The scientists can do all the research they want, but they are not going to find out what causes AIDS by looking in the laboratory.

A reconstruction of this argument might look like this:

> Since homosexual behavior is disapproved by God, (premise)
>> which is a conclusion supported by passages in the Bible, (subpremise)
>
> and God punishes those who commit acts that He disapproves of (premise)
>> (which is also supported by the passages in the Bible) (implicit subpremise)
>
> (and AIDS is clearly associated with homosexual activity), (implicit premise)
>
> and since science has not found any other cause for the disease and will find none, (rebuttal premise)
>
> ---
>
> Therefore, AIDS is a form of divine punishment for homosexual activity. (conclusion)

As can be seen, this reconstruction has eliminated material that is irrelevant to the argument, such as "He does not, of course, hate the homosexual . . ." and reference to the earlier newspaper article. The premise that homosexual behavior is disapproved by God is supported by the subpremise referring to passages in the Bible. The premise that God punishes sinners is implicitly supported by the same evidence. Because that evidence is implicit, it is enclosed in parentheses. The next premise (in parentheses) expresses an unstated but clear assumption that AIDS is a disease that is connected to homosexual activity. The rebuttal premise anticipates the response of the scientific community that it will find the cause of AIDS through its investigation and makes the claim that science has yielded no positive results about the causes of AIDS. Therefore, the only conclusion to draw is that AIDS is a divine punishment for homosexual behavior.

The question of whether this argument is a good one is, of course, not the issue here. The important thing is that we are now able to see its structure clearly and are thus in a position to examine its merits.

The assumption that an argument presented for any position should be one that is capable of being reconstructed into a commonly accepted or standard argument form leads us to the next principle in our code of intellectual conduct.

THE PRINCIPLE OF CHARITY

If a participant's argument is reformulated by an opponent, it should be expressed in the strongest possible version that is consistent with the original intention of the arguer. If there is any question about that intention or about implicit parts of the argument, the arguer should be given the benefit of any doubt in the reformulation.

Once an argument has been reformulated, the question then becomes a matter of whether it has been reconstructed fairly. To ensure fairness, one should allow the arguer to correct or even refine it further, so that it will be the best possible version of the argument that is under scrutiny.

If you are the one who is reconstructing your opponent's argument, you should make every effort to be as careful as possible to formulate the argument that you think he or she actually intended to make. While you need not turn it into a different or better argument than it is, you should give the arguer the benefit of any doubt that you may have about his or her intention. This means that you should be willing to supply any unstated or implicit parts of the argument, to eliminate any obviously irrelevant clutter, and maybe even to use words that are clearer or more precise than those used in the original argument. You should not, however, try to improve the argument by supplying premises that are neither explicitly nor implicitly present.

Cleaning up an argument by restating it in its most economical form can save considerable time in the evaluation process. When there is some question about whether an argument should be construed in what is probably a stronger version, the principle of charity suggests that the arguer be given the benefit of any doubt. Besides, if the argument is attacked in a weaker form, it is likely to be subsequently amended by the arguer to conform to the stronger version. Ultimately, then, one will still have to address the stronger form.

Once the strongest version of an opponent's argument has been put into standard form, with all extraneous material cleared away, its faulty character may be quite transparent. Indeed, the defects may be so obvious that the arguer might even accuse you of distorting his or her argument. To help avoid such a charge, you might ask the arguer to confirm the correctness of your work before you call attention to any flaw. The arguer's complementary act of fairness is not to wrongly accuse you of distorting his or her argument, simply because your reformulation of it exposes its weaknesses.

If the argument's defects are clearly exposed by putting it into standard form, the arguer may be inclined to start amending it right away in order to turn it into a better argument. If you are feeling especially charitable, you might even want to lend a helpful hand to the process.

It should be clear by now that good discussion in general and argumentation in particular impose an ethical requirement. But there is also a practical reason for being fair with one another's arguments. If we create a straw man to attack, we will not only waste time and risk losing our intellectual integrity, we will also quite possibly fail to achieve the very goals the discussion was designed to serve. If we are really interested in the truth or the best answer to a problem, then we will want to evaluate the best version of any argument set forth in support of one of the options. Hence, if we don't deal with the best version now, we will eventually have to do so, once an uncharitable version has been corrected by its author or others. We would do well, then, to be fair with it in the first place.

DEDUCTIVE VERSUS INDUCTIVE STRENGTH OF ARGUMENTS

A fair appraisal of an argument sometimes depends on an understanding of the difference between an inductive and a deductive argument, because the category to which an argument may belong suggests something important about its relative strength. A correctly formed *deductive argument* is one whose form is such that the conclusion follows with logical necessity or certainty from the premises. In other words, if the premises are true, the conclusion must also be true. Another way of describing the relationship between the premises and the conclusion of a valid (or correctly formed) deductive argument would be to say that it is impossible for such an argument to have true premises and a false conclusion. One could not accept the premises and deny the conclusion without contradicting oneself. For example:

> Since all senators in the U.S. Senate are at least 35 years old,
>
> and John Morgan is a U.S. senator,
>
> ---
>
> Therefore, John Morgan is 35 years or older.

The conclusion of this or any deductive argument simply spells out what is already implicit in the premises. If one can get others to accept the crucial premises, which already include the conclusion, then the arguer's work is done. The argument is indeed so strong that its conclusion cannot be denied.

A very effective strategy that is sometimes employed in argumentation is that of constructing an argument in this deductive way, so that the conclusion is, in effect, accepted when the crucial premise is accepted. One would then have a foolproof argument for one's claim. Moral arguments are often presented in this deductive form. Consider the following example:

> Since sexist practices are wrong,
>
> and the use of male-dominated language is a sexist practice or tradition,
>
> ---
>
> Therefore, the use of male-dominated language is wrong.

If the arguer can get his or her opponent to accept the first premise, there is little likelihood that the conclusion can be denied. This is not to say that there cannot be any disagreement about the factual claim made in the second premise, or even that there cannot be any dispute about the meaning of sexism. The point is that the crucial and most controversial premise here is most likely to be the first one, and if it is accepted, the deal, in effect, is closed.

An *inductive* argument is one in which the premises are supposed to provide some evidence for the truth of the conclusion. However, the conclusion of an inductive argument does not follow with logical necessity or certainty from the premises, even if all the premises are true, because the conclusion is not already contained in any of the premises. Therefore, in contrast to a deductive argument, the truth or acceptability of relevant premises in an inductive argument does not force or guarantee the truth of its conclusion. For example:

> Since John Morgan is the most popular Democrat in the Senate,
>
> and he is personally very charming and articulate,
>
> and he has moved to a politically moderate position on most issues,
>
> and he always easily wins reelection to his Senate seat,
>
> and he is in great demand on the speaking circuit,
>
> and he is often mentioned by prominent journalists and other Democrats as a possible presidential candidate,
>
> ---
>
> Therefore, Senator John Morgan will be chosen by the Democrats as their next presidential candidate.

The conclusion of this or any inductive argument is at best only probable, because the conclusion makes a claim that goes beyond the evidence provided in the premises. It is quite possible that an inductive argument might fail to take into account crucial information that would be relevant to the truth of the conclusion. For example, if Senator Morgan is uncertain or even negative about running for the presidency, that fact could obviously affect the truth of the argument's conclusion.

Most of the arguments that we encounter in our everyday world will be inductive arguments. For that reason, most of them will not exhibit the kind of force that a deductive argument would have. Nevertheless, it is sometimes possible to reformulate an inductive argument in such a way that it takes on the form and the power of a deductive one. Consider the following inductive argument:

> Since you underreported your income on your income tax form,
>
> and many of us would say that such underreporting is cheating the government,
>
> and persons who underreport their income may cause taxes to be raised for all of us,
> _____
>
> Therefore, it was wrong for you to have underreported your income on your tax form.

All of these premises would probably be accepted as true, but the conclusion does not necessarily follow from the premises as stated. It is possible to accept the premises but reject the conclusion. However, if we change this argument into a deductive one and use a premise that is likely to be accepted that implicitly contains the conclusion, acceptance of the conclusion would be guaranteed. For example:

> Since stealing is morally wrong,
>
> and underreporting your income on the tax form is a case of stealing from the government,
>
> and you underreported your income on your tax form,
> _____
>
> Therefore, it was morally wrong for you to have underreported your income on your tax form.

If one were to reformulate the original inductive argument in this deductive form, it would be a much more powerful argument, because if the premises of this deductive formulation of the argument are accepted as true, the conclusion must be accepted also.

MORAL ARGUMENTS HAVE A MORAL PREMISE

We have already noted that moral questions lend themselves to the deductive form of argument, which means that moral arguments could be appropriately construed as being among the strongest of arguments. Nevertheless, many participants in moral discussion assume that disputes involving moral issues cannot be settled by argument. Moral judgments are mere personal opinions, they contend, and there is no way to say that one opinion is any better than another. We reject this assumption, for we believe that value claims should be treated like any other kind of claim. Indeed, if this were not so, there would be very little for many of us to discuss, for it is these value issues that engage our most serious intellectual interest and activity.

Moral claims that are not defended with any relevant evidence are indeed rightly categorized as mere opinions. However, a moral opinion ceases to be a mere opinion whenever it is the conclusion of a moral argument.

The parts of a moral argument are very much like those of any other kind of argument. For example, factual and definitional premises, which form a part of most arguments, are important features of moral arguments as well. A properly constructed moral argument, however, has at least one essential feature not found in nonmoral arguments. *A moral argument has a moral premise*, which is usually expressed with the help of moral words like "ought," "should," "right," "wrong," "good," "bad," "moral," or "immoral." Examples of moral premises would be "One *should* treat other people with respect" and "It is *wrong* to discriminate against a person on the basis of gender."

A moral premise provides a general principle, rule, or standard for behavior from which a particular moral conclusion can be drawn. In other words, it provides a warrant to move the argument forward to a particular moral judgment. Without such a moral premise, no moral conclusion can be drawn, for it is not logically appropriate to move in an argument from a factual claim, a so-called "is," to a moral claim, a so-called "ought." To do so is to commit the so-called "is-ought" fallacy. The only legitimate logical moves are from factual claims to factual claims, a feature of most arguments, or from moral claims to moral claims, the unique feature of moral arguments.

A moral argument, then, moves from a moral premise, along with other premises, to a moral judgment or conclusion. This means that when constructing or evaluating moral arguments, one should always keep in mind that a moral judgment about a particular action or policy that is part of an argument's conclusion must be based on a more general moral principle that is one of the argument's premises. If the principle is a controversial one or one not likely to be accepted by those to whom the argument is addressed, the arguer will need to supply a good subargument in support of that premise. The arguer will also probably need to show why the principle or rule would apply in the present case. For example, if someone argued that it would be wrong for a student to study from an "advance" copy of a logic exam, one of the premises would have to be some more general moral claim like "cheating is wrong." To make the premise a relevant one, the argument should also include a premise that would show the connection between the rule against cheating and studying from an advance copy of the exam. The argument might be standardized as follows:

Since cheating is wrong, (moral premise)

and studying from an advance copy of a logic exam is a form of cheating, (connection between the moral premise and the moral judgment in question)

Therefore, studying from an advance copy of a logic exam is wrong. (moral judgment)

Notice that this argument has the form and strength of a deductive argument. If one accepts the premises, one cannot rationally deny the conclusion. Hence, it can be reliably maintained that if an argument's moral premise is clearly expressed and adequately defended, and the argument is presented in a deductive form, moral arguments can be among the strongest of the arguments we encounter.

MAKING THE MORAL PREMISE EXPLICIT

Unfortunately, in most moral arguments the crucial moral premise is not clearly or explicitly stated. If we follow the principle of charity in our reconstruction of moral arguments, we should, of course, acknowledge any implicit moral premise and then attempt to spell it out clearly as part of the reconstructed argument.

Making explicit an implicit moral premise serves at least two important purposes in the construction and evaluation of moral arguments. First, it points directly to the crucial issue or principle that divides those involved in a moral dispute. Second, reflection on the articulated moral premise often triggers ideas about possible legitimate exceptions to that general principle and/or conflicts between it and other relevant moral principles. Such considerations will often lead to a possible reconsideration of its use in the argument in question. Let us try to illustrate this point with the following moral argument:

> We ought to register all handguns in the country and allow only those who have a documented need to carry them. There is just too much killing going on in this country. Children get hold of guns, no matter how careful we adults are, and accidents happen.

Our first task is to reconstruct this argument into standard form, which might look something like this:

> Since the easy availability of handguns contributes to many accidental deaths, (premise)
>
> and the availability of handguns contributes to many other unnecessary deaths as well, (premise)
>
> and it is impossible for adults totally to prevent unauthorized access to guns from minors and other violence-prone people, (premise)
>
> (and we ought to do whatever would reduce the number of accidental and unnecessary deaths), (implicit moral premise)
>
> (and registration of handguns with limitations set on those who may carry them would reduce the number of those deaths), (connection between the moral premise and the moral judgment at issue)
>
> ———————————————————————————
>
> Therefore, we ought to register all handguns and allow only those with a documented need to carry them. (moral judgment)

As can be seen, the crucial premise in this reconstructed argument is the moral premise. However, that premise was not explicit in the original argument. We have spelled it out, so that it may be carefully examined. Since most opponents would probably not disagree with the factual premises in this argument, the only seriously disputed question has to do with the acceptability of the moral premise. And since the argument has a deductive form, an acceptance of that premise will entail an acceptance of the moral judgment as well. But is the moral premise acceptable?

Making the premise explicit has clearly exposed where real disagreement might lie. Opponents may have very different views about the acceptability of this moral premise, and these differences must be resolved if the issue is to be settled. Moreover, the articulation of the moral premise may cause even the arguer to reconsider whether he or she really wants to use it in the argument. For example, would the arguer wish to apply the same general principle that "we ought to do whatever would reduce the number of accidental and unnecessary deaths" to the use of automobiles, which might entail the judgment that automobiles, since they kill accidentally and unnecessarily, should be restricted to those with a documented need? Would the arguer want to apply the same principle to the use of swimming pools or to horseback riding, both of which cause accidental and unnecessary deaths, but are available to all? Are these legitimate exceptions to the general principle? If so, why could not general access to guns be a legitimate exception? In any case, it should be clear that it is the articulation of the moral premise that can help us to do the serious work of evaluating moral arguments.

Because so many of the matters of real concern to us center on controversial moral issues, it is important to know how to construct and evaluate moral arguments effectively. Indeed, you will soon discover that moral arguments will command the greatest portion of your time and energy in the world of arguments. Therefore, you should not shy away from using your whole arsenal of argumentative skills when dealing with them.

ASSIGNMENTS

A. Bring an example of an argument to class and explain why it is an argument and not just an opinion. Reconstruct the argument into standard form. Label each of the parts of the reconstructed argument.

B. Bring to class a written advertisement for a product or service. To what extent does it qualify as an argument?

C. Find or construct an example of a moral argument and reconstruct it into standard form. Give special attention to making the moral premise explicit. Label each of the parts of the argument.

III
What Is a Good Argument?

A GOOD ARGUMENT MUST MEET FIVE CRITERIA

There are five criteria of a good argument. A good argument must be structurally well-formed, and it must have premises that are relevant to the truth of the conclusion, premises that are acceptable, and premises that together constitute sufficient grounds for the truth of the conclusion. It must also have premises that anticipate and provide an effective rebuttal to all reasonable challenges to the argument or to the position which it supports and to arguments on behalf of viable alternative positions. An argument that meets all of these conditions is a good one, and its conclusion should be accepted. If an argument fails to satisfy these conditions, it is probably a flawed one.

Some faulty arguments, of course, are less flawed than others, just as some good arguments are better than others. An assessment of the quality of an argument is almost always a judgment call, for the criteria lend themselves to a wide range of application. There are degrees of relevance, just as there are degrees of acceptability, sufficiency of grounds, and effectiveness of rebuttal. However, there are a number of specific guidelines available for applying these criteria that may be helpful in improving our ability to assess accurately the quality of an argument. In this chapter the important features of each of these criteria will be carefully explained.

THE STRUCTURAL PRINCIPLE

One who argues for or against a position should use an argument that meets the fundamental structural requirements of a well-formed argument, using premises that are compatible with one another, that do not contradict the conclusion, that do not assume the truth of the conclusion, and that are not involved in any faulty deductive inference.

A necessary condition of a good argument is that it be structurally sound. It must look and work like an argument should. In other words, it should be formed in such a way that the conclusion either follows *necessarily* from the premises, in the case of deductive arguments, or follows *probably* from the premises, in the case of inductive arguments.

A good argument should also provide reasons to believe that the conclusion deserves our acceptance. Since most discussions begin *without* the argument's conclusion being accepted by all participants, the goal of the arguer is to use reasons that are more likely to be accepted than the conclusion. If those premises are then accepted and they do in fact lead to the conclusion, it is more likely that the conclusion will also be accepted.

For this reason, a good argument should not use premises that make the same claim as or assume the truth of the conclusion. An argument structure that uses such a premise is referred to as "begging the question." An example of this "question-begging" device is as follows: "One shouldn't vote for oneself in a fraternity election, because it just isn't appropriate to do that sort of thing." The reason given for the conclusion is no different from the claim at issue. Even though deductive logicians remind us that a question-begging argument actually meets the formal requirements of deductive logic and is therefore a valid one, we believe that the demands of a well-formed argument go beyond the demands of validity. A question-begging argument violates the very nature of an argument, since an argument, by definition, is a claim supported by at least one *other* claim. However, an argument that begs the question provides no *other* claim in support of its conclusion; it is therefore structurally flawed.

There are also other formal or structural features of arguments that can render them fatally flawed. One such feature is that of premises that are not compatible with one another. According to the rules of deductive logic, an argument that has incompatible or inconsistent premises is one from which any conclusion, no matter how outrageous, can be validly drawn. The very possibility that these premises may yield such an absurd result demonstrates the argument's flawed character. If no *acceptable* conclusion can be drawn, an argument that contains such premises cannot even function as an argument—let alone a good one. The same is true of an argument with a conclusion that contradicts a premise. Since a conclusion that contradicts another claim in the same argument violates the law of noncontradiction (not both A and not-A), an argument that contains such a conclusion is not a structurally sound or well-formed one.

Finally, there are well-established rules of deductive logic that apply to hypothetical and syllogistic reasoning. Violating any one of them would create a structural flaw in a deductive argument. For example, one rule states that one cannot exchange or convert the subject and predicate terms in a universal statement and assume the same truth value for the converted statement; for while it is true that "all potatoes are vegetables," it is not true that "all vegetables are potatoes." Hence, it would violate a logical rule to move from the original claim to the converted one. Since the violation of this or any other deductive rule creates a situation in which no conclusion should or could be rationally drawn, any argument that violates one of these rules would be structurally flawed.

The first requirement of a good argument, then, is that it meet the structural requirements of a well-formed argument, using premises that do not assume the truth of the conclusion, that are compatible with one another, that do not contradict the conclusion, and that are not involved in the violation of any of the rules of deductive logic.

THE RELEVANCE PRINCIPLE

One who presents an argument for or against a position should attempt to set forth only reasons that are directly related to the merit of the position at issue.

The premises of a good argument must be relevant to the truth or merit of the conclusion. There is no reason to waste time assessing the truth or acceptability of a premise if it is not even relevant to the truth of the conclusion.

A premise is relevant if its acceptance provides some reason to believe, counts in favor of, or has some bearing on the truth or merit of the conclusion. A premise is irrelevant if its acceptance has no bearing on, provides no evidence for, or has no connection to the truth or merit of the conclusion.

In most cases the relevance of a premise is also determined by its relation to the other premises, although in some cases additional premises may be needed to make the relevance of another premise more apparent. Most of us are familiar with the case of the attorney who convinces an initially skeptical judge that a seemingly irrelevant question or piece of testimony is relevant by introducing other evidence or testimony.

An important first step in the reconstruction of another's argument, then, is to check it for any obvious irrelevancies. In the context of informal discussion, we usually encounter quite a number of sometimes colorful yet irrelevant pieces of material. Most of these features are not intended to be a part of the argument and can therefore be safely ignored. It is, however, sometimes difficult to know whether an arguer intends a particular claim to be a relevant reason for believing the conclusion to be true or whether the claim serves some other purpose, such as providing important background information for understanding the context of the issue under review. If the latter is true, it is not a part of the argument and should not be included as a part of its reconstruction. If the former is true, it should definitely be included, even if subsequent evaluation may show it to be irrelevant.

In the terms of traditional logic, the premises of an argument are relevant if the conclusion in some sense follows from the premises. If the argument is a *deductive* one, the conclusion necessarily follows from the premises if the argument is patterned after a logically correct or valid form. In such cases, the premises are obviously relevant to the conclusion, because the conclusion of a correctly formed deductive argument simply spells out what is already implicit in the premises.

If the argument is an *inductive* one, the conclusion follows from the premises if those premises support or tend to confirm the truth of the conclusion. However, determining whether the premises of an inductive argument *strongly* or *adequately* support the truth of its conclusion depends also on how well those premises meet the *other* criteria of a good argument.

There are a number of typical ways that arguments fail to conform to the relevance principle. Some arguments use reasons that are simply emotional appeals, such as appealing to pity and to fear. Other arguments draw the wrong conclusion from the evidence or use the wrong evidence to support the conclusion. Appeals to common opinion and to questionable authorities are other ways to use irrelevant information to support a conclusion. All arguments with these features clearly violate the relevance criterion.

There are several questions that one may want to ask in an effort to determine whether a particular premise or reason is relevant. First, would the premise's being true in any way make one more likely to believe that the conclusion is true? If the answer is yes, the premise is probably relevant. If the answer is no, the premise is probably not a relevant one. Second, does the premise seem to have any connection to whether or not the conclusion is true? For example, could the premise be true and the conclusion be no more likely to be true than false—or no more likely to be a good thing to do than not to do? If so, then it makes no difference whether the premise is true or false, which is another way of saying that the premise is irrelevant. Finally, even if the premise is true, should it be a consideration in the determination of whether or not the conclusion of the argument is true? For example, does the fact that a new movie has enjoyed the greatest box office success in history be a consideration in the determination of the quality of the film? If the answer is no, then a premise that asserts that claim is an irrelevant one. If the answer is yes, which is unlikely in this case, then the premise should be regarded as relevant.

THE ACCEPTABILITY PRINCIPLE

One who presents an argument for or against a position should attempt to use reasons that are likely to be accepted by a rationally mature person and that meet standard criteria of acceptability.

The third test by which we determine the quality of an argument is whether the reasons set forth in support of the conclusion are acceptable. A reason is acceptable if it is the kind of claim that would be accepted by a rational person in the face of all the relevant evidence available.

The term "acceptable" is preferable to the more traditional term "true" for several reasons. First, the notion of acceptability stems from the very nature of argumentative interchange. In most argumentative situations, the key to achieving agreement on the conclusion is gaining acceptance of the premises. One who presents an argument is usually trying to get a skeptic or an opponent to accept a particular conclusion. The arguer typically starts with premises that the skeptic is likely to accept or that a rational person ought to accept. Upon acceptance of the premises, assuming that other criteria of a good argument are satisfied, the opponent is logically led to the acceptance of the conclusion.

Second, since it is notoriously difficult to establish the absolute truth of any statement, it would be an impractical requirement of a good argument that its premises must be true in any absolute sense. Indeed, if such a condition were enforced, there would be very few good arguments. The most that we can legitimately expect is what a reasonable person would *accept* as true.

Third, an analysis of our language suggests that in many ordinary contexts, what we typically mean by the word "true" would be more appropriately expressed by the phrase "accepted as true." Consider, for example, the contradictory testimony from courtroom witnesses, each of whom is allegedly telling "the truth, the whole truth, and nothing but the truth." A better way to describe what is happening there is that each witness is presumably telling what he or she *accepts* as true.

Fourth, even if a premise were true in the absolute sense, it may be unacceptable to a particular audience because that audience may not be in a position to determine its truth. For example, the evidence for a premise may be inaccessible to them in that it is too technical for them to understand. The truth of the premise would therefore not add anything to the practical force of the argument. An argument can be a good one only if the premises are *accepted* or *recognized* as true.

For all these reasons, the notion of "acceptability" rather than "truth" seems to be the more appropriate way of understanding this third criterion of a good argument. It is very important, however, that we not give the impression that a premise is acceptable simply because one accepts it or can get others to accept it. We know too well how easy this is, especially if one is preaching to the saved, to the immature, or to the easily tricked. Neither does "acceptable" simply refer to what one finds it comfortable or easy to believe. And most certainly it does not mean whatever happens to be accepted. It has to do with what a reasonable person *should* accept. A claim is acceptable only if it would be the kind of claim accepted by a rationally mature person using generally agreed-upon standards of acceptability.

What seems rational to some people, of course, does not always seem rational to others. For that reason, we suggest a number of specific guidelines that should be helpful in determining what is or is not an acceptable claim. Guidelines that provide standards for determining what claims we *should* accept are called the "criteria of acceptability," and guidelines that help us determine what claims we *should not* accept are called the "conditions of unacceptability." One who takes on the task of assessing the acceptability of premises should carefully follow such standards, just as in criminal cases lawyers and judges must be guided by rules of evidence.

Criteria of Acceptability

A premise should be *acceptable* to a rationally mature person if it expresses any of the following:

1. A claim that is a matter of undisputed common knowledge.

2. A claim that is confirmed by one's own personal experience or observation.

3. A claim that is adequately defended in the context of the argument or at least capable of being adequately defended by some other accessible source.

4. An uncontroverted eyewitness or personal testimony.

5. An uncontroverted claim from a relevant authority.

6. The conclusion of another good argument.

7. A relatively minor claim that seems to be a reasonable assumption in the context of the argument.

A claim that is virtually undisputed by the community of competent inquirers is one that a rationally mature person *should* accept. The question, then, becomes whether there is any serious dispute about the claim in question. Although 98 percent of the American people believe or accept the claim that God exists, the question of whether God exists *is* in serious dispute by competent scholars. In contrast, there is no serious dispute about whether aspirin tends to reduce fever.

A rationally mature person should also accept a claim that is confirmed by his or her own experience or observation. And even though one might not have the evidence present in the argumentative context, it is reasonable to accept a claim that could be easily defended by reference to a readily accessible authoritative source.

Personal or eyewitness reports are more problematic. Experience tells us that there is good reason to be skeptical about many first-person reports. However, if the personal report is not contradicted by any other person, by one's own personal experience, or by credible counterevidence, there is no reason not to accept it. The same is true for a claim made by a relevant authority. Unless there is some reason to challenge an authority's claim, it should be regarded as acceptable.

According to the resolution principle in the code of conduct, we should also be willing to accept the conclusion of a good argument. If that conclusion is used as a premise in another argument, there is no reason not to accept it.

Finally, there are many somewhat minor claims that we encounter as premises in arguments about which we have no evidence either for or against. If we have no reason to question them, we should probably be willing to accept them, if they seem to be reasonable assumptions in the context. While we cannot say they are true, we may as a practical matter accept them as true in the absence of contrary evidence. To treat them as acceptable moves the discussion along.

Conditions of Unacceptability

A premise should *be unacceptable* to a rationally mature person if it expresses any of the following:

1. A claim that contradicts credible evidence, a well-established claim, or a legitimate authority.

2. A claim that is inconsistent with one's own personal experience or observations.

3. A questionable claim that is not adequately defended in the context of the argument or not capable of being adequately defended in some other accessible source.

4. A claim that is self-contradictory or linguistically confusing.

5. A claim that is based on a usually unstated but highly questionable assumption.

The first three of these conditions look like negative versions of the first three criteria of acceptability. They are restated in this way because they present a special difficulty in assessing the acceptability of claims. A claim that is inconsistent with credible evidence, a well-established claim, a legitimate authority, or one's own experience, or is not defended in the context of the argument, may ultimately be found to be an acceptable one. However, until the conflict is resolved by further inquiry, the claim in question should not be regarded as acceptable.

There are some claims, however, that probably could not be defended by available evidence or by reference to an accessible source. For example, suppose that an arguer claimed that "thirty percent of all divorces are the result of people getting married too young." If the arguer then claimed that "in order to stabilize the institution of marriage in the society, states should raise the minimum age at which persons can marry," it would be a conclusion based on an unacceptable premise; since we can think of no available source or any evidence that could possibly be obtained with the kind of mathematical precision claimed. Because the premise clearly conforms to one of the conditions of unacceptability, it should be treated as an unacceptable premise.

A claim that is self-contradictory or expressed in language that is confusing is not acceptable, for we obviously cannot accept a claim that we do not understand. In Chapter VII, "Fallacies That Violate the Acceptability Criterion," an entire section is devoted to the most common ways that confusing language contributes to the unacceptability of a premise and to the unacceptability of any conclusion that premise supports.

One should also not accept a claim that is based on a so-called unwarranted assumption, wherein a premise implicitly uses a questionable assumption to support the claim at issue. For example, if an arguer claims that "Dan must be a good singer, because he is a member of a very good-sounding choir," he or she has used as an unstated premise the unwarranted assumption that "what is true of the whole is true of each of its parts." Since that assumption is an unacceptable one, the claim that rests on it would also be unacceptable. A second section of fallacies in Chapter VII addresses those premises that implicitly use the most common of these unwarranted assumptions.

The premises of an argument, then, should be regarded as acceptable if each of them conforms to at least one of the criteria of acceptability and if none of them conforms to one of the conditions of unacceptability.

THE SUFFICIENCY PRINCIPLE

One who presents an argument for or against a position should attempt to provide reasons that are sufficient in number, kind, and weight to support the acceptance of the conclusion.

Once one has examined an argument for the relevance and the acceptability of the premises, there is still plenty of work to do. Relevant and acceptable premises do not necessarily a good argument make. An argument must also meet the demands of the sufficiency criterion. There must be a sufficient number of relevant and acceptable premises of the appropriate kind and weight in order for an argument to be good enough for us to accept its conclusion.

This is perhaps the most difficult criterion to apply, because we have no clear guidelines to help us determine what constitutes sufficient grounds for the truth of a claim or the rightness of an action. Each argumentative context seems to be different and thus creates different sufficiency demands. For example, what constitutes sufficient grounds for voting for one of two opposing candidates for political office is very different from what might be sufficient grounds for buying rather than leasing a car.

The feature of the sufficiency criterion that is most difficult to apply is the assignment of weight to each piece of supporting evidence. Indeed, disagreement over this issue probably causes most of the problems in informal discussions. What one participant regards as the most important piece of evidence, another may regard as trivial by comparison with other considerations. It is therefore not likely that we will come to closure in our disputes until we come to some kind of agreement about what weight to give to critical kinds of relevant and acceptable evidence used in support of our conclusions.

Some sciences have well-developed sufficiency criteria in place. Statisticians, for example, have determined what constitutes a proper sample from which to draw defensible conclusions. Witness the accuracy of most election predictions. But in informal discussion, it is sometimes very difficult to determine what constitutes sufficient grounds. The application of the criterion in some areas of discussion, such as morality, politics, and religion, leaves much to be desired. Each area of inquiry seems to have its own, even if fuzzy, standard of sufficiency. Not only the amount of evidence but also the kind and weight of evidence required seem peculiar to each context.

The only comfort we can offer in this situation is to suggest that the more experience we have in evaluating arguments, the more likely it is that we will have a feel for what constitutes sufficient evidence in a particular context. A small child thinks that a sufficient reason for granting his or her every wish is that he or she wants it granted. But parents and most college students, I assume, are experienced enough to know that such an argument does not provide sufficient grounds for giving the child everything that he or she desires. Experience teaches us that certain kinds of evidence *do* provide sufficient grounds for conclusions in some arenas. For example, polling data taken by objective polling services do provide sufficient grounds for drawing conclusions about which political candidate is likely to win and which television shows are being watched.

There are many specific ways in which arguments may fail to satisfy the sufficiency criterion. For example, the premises may provide evidence that is based on too small a sample or on unrepresentative data. The evidence may be simply anecdotal—that is, based entirely on the personal experience of the arguer or a few people of his or her acquaintance. The evidence could also be based on a faulty causal analysis of a situation. Perhaps the most common way of violating this criterion is found in arguments in which crucial evidence is simply missing.

There are several questions to ask when applying the sufficiency test to a particular argument. First, are the reasons that are given, even if they are relevant and acceptable, enough to drive one to this particular conclusion? Second, is additional evidence of the same kind needed to support the conclusion? Third, is the evidence presented flawed by some kind of faulty causal analysis? Finally, is there some key or crucial evidence that is simply missing from the argument that must be included as one of the premises in order for one to accept the argument's conclusion?

THE REBUTTAL PRINCIPLE

One who presents an argument for or against a position should attempt to provide an effective rebuttal to all serious challenges to the argument or the position it supports and to the strongest arguments in support of viable alternative positions.

Meeting the demands of the rebuttal principle is perhaps the most difficult of all argumentative tasks. It is the weakest part of my own arguments and of the arguments of my students, children, wife, friends, relatives, and colleagues. Since an argument is usually being presented against the background that there is another side to the issue, a good argument must meet that other side head-on. *An argument is not a good one if it does not anticipate and effectively rebut, or successfully blunt the force of, criticisms of the argument and of the position that it supports.* A complete argument would even rebut the arguments mustered in behalf of viable alternate positions on the issue in question.

Most reasonably clever people can devise what appears to be a good argument for whatever it is that they want to believe or want us to believe. For example, virtually every jury in a criminal trial is impressed by the quality of the prosecutor's argument. If that were the only argument heard, nearly all juries would convict the accused. It is the defense attorney's rebuttal and the prosecutor's response to that rebuttal that give the jury the whole picture and the proper basis for decision.

If you look at most controversial issues and the arguments in their behalf, you will notice that the opposing arguments often meet the first four criteria of a good argument. They are structurally sound, and they each have relevant, acceptable, and a sufficient number of premises. This suggests that almost any argument can be made to look good if it does not engage the principal challenges to its strength. Therefore, the ultimate key to distinguishing between a good and a not-so-good argument is to determine how well the rebuttal criterion is met.

The fact that arguments can be more or less equally attractive as long as they are devoid of rebuttal premises may partly explain why so many people are skeptical about the ability of arguments to settle controversies. It all seems to come out even. But it is not likely that there can be *good* arguments in support of both sides of opposing or contradictory positions, because at least one of the arguments presented will not be able to satisfy the rebuttal criterion. Probably only one of them will be able to *effectively* answer the challenges of the other. Otherwise, we could find ourselves in a situation in which each of two contradictory positions would merit our acceptance. But we cannot logically or practically tolerate such a situation. It simply cannot be the case, for example, that a particular abortion is both wrong and not wrong. The solution to this dilemma of "double truth" is therefore to be found by determining which of the arguments can more effectively meet the most serious challenges to its own position or can damage the strongest arguments for the other position.

What should be regarded as a serious challenge? It is one that reasonable people, following all the guidelines suggested in the code of conduct and the text, would regard as appearing forceful enough on the surface to require some answer. Even if the arguer thinks that there is an effective response to the criticism, he or she should treat it as a serious challenge, if for no other reason than to ultimately convince its holder and others of its weakness. Indeed, a good argument would anticipate the most obvious challenges and use the rebuttal premise to blunt their force. It not only shows that one has done one's homework, but it disarms the critic in advance. The alleged "big guns" are rendered ineffective before they are fired.

What would be an effective response? It is one that a reasonable person, following all the guidelines suggested in the code of conduct and the text, would accept as destroying or at least seriously damaging the force of the criticism or counterargument. In other words, an effective response to a serious challenge is one that should cause a reasonable person to no longer regard the challenge as a serious one.

The rebuttal should be the primary driving force behind the formation of every argument. In this way one will have a constant reminder that an argument is not finished until one has finished off the criticisms and counterarguments. But, unfortunately, the rebuttal premise is the most frequently neglected feature of arguments. There are perhaps several reasons why this element is missing from most of our arguments. First, we can't think of any effective answers to the challenges to our position, so we just keep quiet about them. Second, we don't want to mention the contrary evidence for fear that our position will be weakened by bringing it to the attention of our opponents. Finally, we are so convinced by our own position that we really don't believe that there is another side to the issue. Whatever the reason, an argument that lacks this feature cannot be a good one, for in order for us to be properly convinced of anything, we must first look at all the evidence. And we have not looked at all the evidence until we have looked at the contrary evidence.

There are several ways that arguments can fail to meet the rebuttal criterion. Several diversionary tactics are commonly used by those wishing to avoid the responsibility of rebuttal. For example, arguments that misrepresent the criticism, bring up trivial objections or a side issue, or resort to humor or ridicule are using devices that clearly fail to make effective responses. The same can be said of those arguments that ignore or deny the counterevidence against the position defended. Finally, there are those who try to avoid responding to a criticism by attacking the critic instead of the criticism. All of these approaches are clear violations of our obligation to respond honestly to the arguments of our opponents.

There are several questions that one must ask and answer in applying the rebuttal principle to an argument. First, what are the strongest arguments against the position being defended? Second, does the argument address the counterarguments effectively? Third, what potentially serious weaknesses in the argument for the position might be recognized by an opponent? Fourth, does the argument itself recognize and address those possible weaknesses? Finally, does the argument show why arguments for alternative positions on the issue are flawed or unsuccessful?

In summary, it is our position that an argument that violates any one of these five principles of a good argument is a flawed one. Yet, the fact that it is flawed does not mean that it could not be turned into at least a better argument by amending it.

MAKING ARGUMENTS STRONGER

We have a number of suggestions for making arguments stronger. You will notice that almost all of our advice for improving the quality of arguments comes directly from explicit or implicit standards embodied in the five criteria. More specific recommendations for strengthening arguments are made in the sections on individual fallacies throughout the rest of the text.

1. Find ways to give additional support to weak or questionable premises.

2. Substitute less controversial premises if they will do the job required.

3. Add additional or missing premises if needed to give sufficient grounds for the conclusion.

4. Soften, if necessary, any absolute claims made in the premises in a way that might make them more acceptable.

5. Restate premises in their clearest and most economical form.

6. Spell out any implicit premises that have important roles in the argument.

7. Recast the argument in a more orderly form so that it can be followed more easily.

8. Declare which are the weakest points in the argument, not only to demonstrate your objectivity but also to blunt the force of your opponent's counterfire.

9. Clear up any vague or confusing language used.

10. Take out irrelevant matters that tend to clutter the argument.

11. Introduce as much deductive character to the argument as the subject matter will allow.

12. Be as exhaustive in your rebuttal as the context calls for.

Some arguments, of course, cannot be improved on, not because they are good enough already, but because they defend views for which good arguments are not likely to be found. Our commitment to the search for truth demands that we not spend time and energy trying to make a hopelessly weak or bad argument a trifle less weak— unless, of course, we are attorneys who are required by our profession to give the best defense possible in the service of our clients.

APPLYING THE CRITERIA TO ARGUMENTS

The attention we have given to the five criteria of a good argument and the general suggestions for improving not-so-good arguments should give us a very clear picture of what a good argument looks like. We should therefore be ready to apply these criteria to some sample arguments.

The first step in evaluating arguments is to become mentally prepared. We must remember that the issue is not whether one is inclined to believe the conclusion. The primary question in evaluating arguments is whether one should believe the conclusion on the grounds provided by the argument. Even if the conclusion might be true, the argument presented might not authorize our acceptance of it.

Let us put the criteria of a good argument to work in evaluating arguments that might be found in some of the following Letters to the Editor.

> **Letter A**
> Dear Editor,
> I think that Governor Morgan is doing a great job, in spite of all his Republican critics. Just last week, Nancy Stone said in a news confer-ence that she thought Governor Morgan was one of the best gover-nors in the South and that he was doing an excellent job dealing with the complex problems of the state. And she should know! She's the state chair of the Democratic party.

Let us first put this argument into standard form. This means that we must first identify the conclusion and then find the premises that are used to support that conclusion, along with any supporting statements for those premises. The other or ex-traneous material can then be ignored. The reconstructed argument about Governor Morgan would look something like this:

> Since Nancy Stone, the chair of the Democratic party, says that the Democratic governor is doing a good job,
> _____
> Therefore, Governor Morgan is doing a good job.

Our next step is to test the reformulated argument against the five criteria of a good ar-gument. Since there appear to be no structural problems with this argument, let us be-gin with the criterion of relevance. As we have indicated previously, there is no reason to waste time assessing the acceptability of a premise if it is not even relevant to the truth of the conclusion.

Stated in its most economical form, the argument before us gives only one rea-son for the positive assessment of the governor's performance in office. That premise fails to meet the criterion of relevance. Since the chair of the governor's party is likely to be less than objective in her assessment of his effectiveness, her statement must be seen as irrelevant, for the testimony of a biased authority cannot count in favor of the truth of a claim. Perhaps an excellent argument could be constructed for the conclusion in question, but that is not the issue at this point. The issue is whether the argument being examined is a good one. Our evaluation says that it is not, because its only premise is irrelevant.

Letter B

Dear Editor,
The seat-belt law is unfair and a clear abuse of governmental authority. By not wearing a belt we are not endangering anyone but perhaps ourselves. In some cases, wearing seat belts can actually endanger your life. Recently, in an accident in Jackson County, the vehicle hit a tree and was crushed except for a small space underneath the steering wheel. Since the driver broke the seat-belt law, his life was saved when he was thrown to the floor of the car.

Reconstructing this argument will take a little more effort than the first one. Even though the writer claims that the government has no right to require us to use seat belts, no reason is given in support of that claim. Hence, it cannot be the conclusion of this argument—unless we want to be more than charitable. The only claim that is supported within the argument is the one that wearing a seat belt can be dangerous and should not be required. The reconstructed argument would probably look like this:

(Since laws should not require things that endanger our lives)

and wearing seat belts can endanger our lives

> because one man's life was saved because he was not wearing his seat belt,

---

(Therefore, we should not be required by law to wear seat belts.)

The Principle of Charity requires us to grant that the first premise and the conclusion are implicit. For that reason, we have enclosed them in parentheses to indicate that they were not explicitly stated but are understood as part of our reconstruction of the argument. We believe the argument exhibited in this form actually looks better than the original one, but that does not mean that it is a good argument.

How well does it meet the criteria of a good argument? The argument seems to be structurally well-formed, and the premises seem clearly relevant to the truth of the conclusion. The first premise also seems to be acceptable, for it is a commonly accepted view by reasonable people that the government should not pass laws that endanger our lives. But the second premise clearly fails to meet the acceptability criterion, because it is a questionable claim that is not adequately supported in the context and also conflicts with credible evidence to the contrary.

The subargument for the second premise is also problematic. The anecdotal evidence given in support of the premise that seat belts endanger our lives is hardly sufficient grounds for such a claim. The argument also fails to meet the rebuttal criterion, for it makes no attempt to effectively answer the arguments on the "buckle-up" side of this issue. The seat-belt argument fails at least three criteria of a good argument, and it is therefore not a good argument.

Letter C

Dear Editor,

I am a resident of the Monroe District in Washington County. I am very thankful to have someone of Supervisor Alice Morton's intellect, dedication, and experience who not only is willing to serve, but also has the time to devote to all the citizens of this county.

I called Mrs. Morton at home the other night and learned that she had been out of town for two days on Washington County business. On other occasions when I wanted to speak with her, I found her working in the county offices.

My understanding is that someone is running against her for the Monroe district seat. I don't want to trade Mrs. Morton, who has proven ability and experience, for someone who could not possibly bring to the office of supervisor the expertise and devotion that we citizens now enjoy.

Most of us would probably agree that the unstated conclusion of this argument is that we should all vote for the incumbent in the upcoming election. The rest of the reconstruction would be as follows:

Since Alice Morton is experienced,

and she is devoted to the citizens of the county,

and she is willing and has time to serve,

and she works hard,

and she is intelligent,

and no other person in the Monroe district could do a better job in the office of supervisor,

---

(Therefore, district residents should vote for Alice Morton.)

This argument satisfactorily meets the basic structural demands of a good argument. It is also the case that all of the premises presented in this argument seem to be relevant to the issue of choosing county representatives, and since Ms. Morton is an incumbent, the first premise is unquestionably an acceptable one. The next four premises are fairly standard descriptions of people running for local office, so there is probably no good reason not to find them acceptable. Even though some of these premises may be questioned with regard to the adequacy of supporting evidence, these are probably not crucial issues in the argument. The sixth or last premise, however, is highly questionable. Indeed, it is so overstated that it is unlikely that any support for it could be found. This would perhaps not matter if the premise were not so crucial. But the question of the merits of rival political candidates is one of the crucial issues in an argument defending one of them. The sixth premise, then, is one that is not adequately defended and is therefore unacceptable.

To the arguer's credit, the sixth premise is also probably an attempt to rebut the argument against the election of Ms. Morton, but it is hardly an effective one. The argument therefore fails the rebuttal criterion as well.

Perhaps the most serious problem with the argument, however, is its violation of the sufficient grounds criterion. As noted earlier, the context of an argument often determines what constitutes sufficient grounds for a claim. In this case, sufficient grounds for taking the action of voting for a particular political candidate would at least include information about the goals and ideas of the person whose candidacy is being supported. In this argument, however, such matters are totally absent. For this and for the other reasons given, this argument is not a good one.

Letter D

Dear Editor,

The American Heart Association is debating whether to fund a proposed study that would involve drowning 42 dogs at the State University. The University's College of Medicine received permission to use stray dogs from the local pound to determine whether the Heimlich maneuver could be used to save drowning victims.

Dr. Heimlich himself has denounced the proposed study as a "needless experiment" and as one that "must be classified as cruelty." Others have stated that a dog's windpipe and diaphragm are not comparable to those of humans and therefore cannot be used in determining whether mouth-to-mouth resuscitation or the Heimlich maneuver would be preferable. Concerned readers should urge the American Heart Association to reject the study.

Although the arguer wants readers to contact the American Heart Association with their concerns, no specific reasons are given for that action, so we can infer that it is not the argument's conclusion, even though one might take that action if convinced of the actual conclusion. The substantive conclusion is that the American Heart Association should not approve the proposed study. The reformulated argument looks like this:

Since the proposed study by the State University's College of
Medicine involving dogs would not help to determine whether the
Heimlich maneuver could be used effectively for drowning victims,

> because some people have said that a dog's breathing apparatus
> is different from that of humans,

and Dr. Heimlich himself has said that such an experiment would be needless and cruel,

(and experiments that are cruel and not useful in any way should not be performed),

---

(Therefore, the American Heart Association should not fund the experiment with the Heimlich maneuver involving dogs.)

The conclusion is clear, although it is not explicitly stated. Support for the first premise does not pass the relevance criterion, because the testimony is from an unidentified source. Since we don't know whether the "others" are experts in physiology, we don't know whether their testimony about a dog's breathing apparatus should count in favor of the premise or even be taken seriously. Even if the testimony were relevant, it would probably not be acceptable; for it is difficult to believe that personnel from the College of Medicine, who submitted the grant proposal, would not know whether there is a crucially relevant physiological difference between dogs and humans that might make the proposed experiment worthless.

The implicit third premise is acceptable because it appears to be a self-evident principle. It is at least one that most rationally mature people would accept. The second premise may be acceptable as well, but it probably carries very little real weight in the argument; for we are not told why Dr. Heimlich thinks the experiment is "needless."

We have, then, one relevant and acceptable self-evident premise and one premise with very little weight in the argument. Together they do not constitute sufficient grounds for embracing the conclusion. The argument could possibly have been saved from being severely flawed if it had effectively rebutted the implicit claim of the College of Medicine that the experiment was a worthwhile one. But, as previously stated, criticism of the proposal should be regarded as irrelevant because of its questionable source. The argument, as presented, is not a good one.

Letter E

Dear Editor,

I am concerned about the consequences of changing the Constitution simply because we don't like how the Supreme Court has interpreted it. More specifically, I am concerned about the efforts of some to amend the Constitution to prohibit the burning of the American flag. The Court has said that burning the flag can be seen as an expression of free speech and that free speech is protected by the First Amendment.

I love my country and the flag that represents it in official ways, and I don't like to see anybody use the flag in a disrespectful way. I am even upset when I see some people use it as a shirt or bathing suit. But I love the freedom that we have in this country even more, and that includes the freedom to criticize the country in whatever peaceful way we choose. I would not choose to do it by burning the flag and I wish that others would not do so either, but criticizing the country or its policies is a right guaranteed by our Constitution. If we start changing the Constitution to limit the freedom to express opinions in this way, it is not unlikely that some will soon want to limit it in other ways as well, such as prohibiting people from expressing a negative opinion about the country in a federal office building or spitting on a copy of the Declaration of Independence. Would we then have to pass additional amendments to prohibit those actions? Such an outcome would not be good for a healthy democracy.

Some people say very hateful, false, and hurtful things about our president and other leaders, but they have the right to do that. Even though I might not like some of the things that critics do to express their disagreement, I am not aware of any way in which the country is seriously damaged by these expressions. In some ways it is actually strengthened, because positive changes in policy and leadership come about as a result of criticizing the status quo, however that is done.

Just as we try to teach people to show respect for others, we can teach them to respect the flag. But sometimes they show respect for neither. However, we do not want to put people in jail just because they do not always show the respect that we think they should.

The conclusion of this argument is never explicitly stated, but it is exceedingly clear that the writer is opposed to amending the Constitution to prohibit flag burning. Here is how a reformulation of this argument might look:

Since the Constitution guarantees freedom of speech,

and the Supreme Court has ruled that burning the flag can be interpreted as an expression of free speech,

and having the unrestricted freedom to express our opinions is more important than restricting the peaceful method or the content of that expression,

and a constitutional restriction on free speech by restrictions on flag burning could lead to other constitutional amendments to restrict free speech,

> because there are many distasteful ways to criticize or show disrespect for the country,

and a string of such constitutional restrictions would not be good for a healthy democracy,

and criticizing the country by burning the flag or even by other distasteful methods does not do any serious damage to the country but actually strengthens it,

> because it is through criticism of our country, however it is expressed, that we make positive changes,

and we would not want to punish people for showing disrespect for the flag,

> because it is unlikely that we would punish them for showing disrespect for other people,

---

(Therefore, we should not amend the Constitution to prohibit burning of the flag.)

This is a structurally well-formed argument, and all of the premises in this argument seem to be relevant to whether or not it would be a good idea to amend the Constitution with regard to the issue of flag burning. And since the first two premises are matters of undisputed fact, there should be no question about their acceptability.

Since there is little question about the importance of the principle of free speech in a democracy, rational persons would probably find the third premise to be an acceptable one. Most of us, including the defenders of the amendment, would also probably accept the view expressed in the fourth and fifth premises, that there are other equally distasteful expressions of free speech that some would want to restrict, but we would not regard such an outcome as a desirable one for a healthy democracy.

The last two premises are attempts to rebut the main arguments of the defenders of the amendment. The sixth premise addresses the view that burning the flag does damage to the country in some way, but since there is no obvious damage that has been identified, a simple denial of the claim may be sufficient in this argument. The burden of proof that there *is* damage is on those who claim that it occurs. However, this premise and its subpremise defend the view that criticism, however it is expressed, often serves a public good, and it would be difficult to find fault with that claim. The second rebuttal premise and its subpremise try an analogy that may be the weakest part of the argument, but it may still play a positive role. They challenge the defenders of the amendment by pointing out since we are not likely to punish those who show disrespect for other human beings, it seems odd to want to punish people for showing disrespect for an inanimate object.

This well-formed argument uses relevant and acceptable premises that appear to be of the right kind and number to support the conclusion. It also does an effective job of rebutting the main arguments of the defenders of the other side of the issue. For these reasons, we would assess this argument as a good one.

Our involvement in the process of *evaluating* arguments encourages the *construction* of good arguments by constantly reminding us of the criteria of a good argument. Just as a prosecutor or defense attorney gets a clear picture of what the law requires by participating in the process of dealing with those who violate it, one can come to understand what is required of good arguments by becoming sensitive to the great number of ways that they can go wrong. Moreover, in many cases, a criticism of an argument is an implicit construction of a better argument for the same view or a different argument for an alternative view. The very process of evaluating is therefore constructive.

Constructing a good argument for a position on an issue in dispute is a giant step forward toward coming to agreement or resolving disagreement. However, one of the hardest tasks in rational discussion is that of knowing when and how to end a discussion and to consider an issue settled.

THE RESOLUTION PRINCIPLE

An issue should be considered resolved if the proponent for one of the alternative positions successfully defends that position by presenting a structurally sound argument that uses relevant and acceptable premises that together provide sufficient grounds to support the conclusion and provides an effective rebuttal to all serious challenges to the argument or position at issue. Unless one can demonstrate that these conditions have not been met, one should accept the conclusion of the successful argument and consider the issue, for all practical purposes, to be settled. In the absence of a successful argument for any of the alternative positions, one is obligated to accept the position that is supported by the best of the good arguments presented.

If the purpose of rational discussion is ultimately to decide what to do or believe, then coming to closure should happen more often than it does. There are many good arguments out there, and if good arguments resolve issues, why are not more issues resolved by them? For example, since the flag-burning amendment argument just discussed was found to be a good one, should that not settle the issue? Other issues, such as the effect of cigarette smoking on health, the creationism/evolution debate, and questions of gender and racial bias should also be settled. The arguments have been made, and they are good ones, but the debates go on. How much more discussion is needed, just because some refuse to recognize the force of a successful argument?

Unfortunately, very few controversial issues ever come to rational resolution. If you have doubts about this, then ask yourself when was the last time you allowed the force of argument to change your mind about an important issue—even though changing one's mind in the face of a successful argument should not be a difficult thing to do for a genuine truth-seeker.

So why does it not happen? Why are issues not resolved? There are probably a number of reasons. It could be that one of the parties to the dispute has a blind spot—that is, he or she simply cannot be objective about the particular issue at hand. Or maybe he or she has been rationally but not psychologically convinced by the discussion. Another possible explanation is that one or more of the parties in the dispute have been rationally careless or at least guilty of not thinking as clearly as they should. It is even possible that one of the parties has a hidden agenda—an issue to defend other than the stated one. Or maybe the parties involved are simply not being honest with themselves, for they may want to win the argument more than they want to find a solution to the problem. Finally, perhaps the parties are in what might be called "deep disagreement"—that is, they are divided on the issue because of fundamental underlying assumptions that have yet to be explored.

Unfortunately, none of these explanations is a justification for not resolving our disputes. Indeed, each explanation rests on an identifiable feature of uncritical thinking or is a violation of at least one of the principles in the code of intellectual conduct to which we should be rationally committed.

It is possible, of course, that some matters are left unresolved for more respectable reasons. Perhaps the evidence available is regarded as presently too skimpy to lead to a conclusion, or perhaps one of the parties is still looking for an effective counterargument that he or she thinks is out there. There may even remain serious disagreement over whether an argument presented has indeed been successful.

These are all reasons that may make one less confident in adopting the conclusion of one of the arguments presented, but since few arguments are ever found to be totally successful, one is obligated to accept the position that is supported by the best of the good or near-successful arguments presented. Otherwise, since one can always claim that there has been no absolute proof presented, one could leave unresolved forever virtually every issue discussed. Besides, we have tried to show that there are objective criteria available to determine the quality of an argument. Judges and juries do it routinely, and there is no reason why the rest of us cannot do it as well. We are not saying that there is one monolithic logic to which all discussion participants must bow down; we are simply saying that there are more objective ways of evaluating arguments than some are willing to admit.

THE SUSPENSION OF JUDGMENT PRINCIPLE

If no position comes close to being successfully defended, or if two or more positions seem to be defended with equal strength, one should, in most cases, suspend judgment about the issue. If practical considerations seem to require an immediate decision, one should weigh the relative risks of gain or loss connected with the consequences of suspending judgment and decide the issue on those grounds.

If the appropriate evidence is so lacking that one has no good basis for making a decision either way, it may be quite appropriate to suspend judgment on the matter and wait until there is more of a basis for decision. This alternative should not, however, be seen as a clever way to avoid the psychological fright of making a difficult decision or of moving into unfamiliar territory.

The same might be said of the second condition for suspending judgment—the equal strength of the arguments. This situation is actually a very rare phenomenon, for one argument is almost always better than the others if judged by the objective standards available.

Some issues, of course, do not permit suspension of judgment. If the decision is a forced or momentous one, such as deciding whether to have an abortion, one has to decide on the grounds of the practical consequences of *not* making the decision.

THE RECONSIDERATION PRINCIPLE

If a successful or at least good argument for a position is subsequently found by any participant to be flawed in a way that raises new doubts about the merit of that position, one is obligated to reopen the issue for further consideration and resolution.

No argument may be regarded as permanently successful. There is always the possibility that new evidence will come to light that will raise new doubts about a position held on what were thought to be good grounds. Under these conditions, further examination is always appropriate. Pride in good or successful arguments past should not become an obstacle to reopening the issue in the present if conditions warrant it. The principles of fallibility and truth-seeking are as important at this point as they were in the original inquiry.

The new doubts, however, should not be the same old doubts in new clothing. Reopening the issue should come only as a consequence of uncovering new or reinterpreted evidence not considered in the earlier treatment of the issue. Otherwise, the reexamination of the issue is the worst form of the violation of the resolution principle—simply a device to continue to haggle over the same ground.

ASSIGNMENTS

A. Submit an argument that you have read or heard within the last week that defends a position on a current controversial social, political, moral, religious, or aesthetic issue. You may find such arguments in "Letters to the Editor" in newspapers or magazines, in editorials, op-ed pieces, speeches, advertisements, classroom lectures, and conversations with fellow students. Cut out, photocopy, or reconstruct the argument from its source and tape it on a separate page from your typewritten analysis of it. The original argument can then be photocopied and used in class for discussion and further analysis. Using the Principle of Charity and your own words, reformulate the argument into standard form, distinguishing the premises from the conclusion, making it the clearest argument possible consistent with the premises given or implied. Supply in parentheses any implicit premises or implicit conclusion. Using the procedure employed in "Applying the Criteria to Arguments" in this chapter, point out any violations of the criteria of a good argument and then suggest how the premises might be altered to strengthen the argument. Evaluate the overall quality of the argument on a 5-point scale (excellent, good, fair, poor, or bad).

B. Bring to class an argument in support of a position on a controversial issue that you have heard or read recently and found to be persuasive. Attempt to explain why it was persuasive. Did it meet all the criteria of a good argument?

C. Discuss in class the reasons why we all seem to have difficulty in following the Resolution Principle. If an argument meets all the criteria of a good argument, should its conclusion be accepted by all participants in the discussion? Evaluate the "flag-burning" argument in this chapter to determine if it meets all the criteria of a good argument. If not, which of the criteria does it fail to meet? If you conclude that it does not violate any of the criteria, are you prepared to accept its conclusion? Why or why not?

What Is a Fallacy?

A FALLACY IS A VIOLATION OF A CRITERION OF A GOOD ARGUMENT

A fallacy is a violation of one of the criteria of a good argument. Any argument that fails to satisfy one or more of the five criteria is a fallacious one. Fallacies, then, stem from a structural flaw in the argument, from the irrelevance of a premise, from the unacceptability of a premise, from the insufficiency of the combined premises of an argument to establish its conclusion, or from the failure to give an effective rebuttal to the most serious challenges to its position or to the argument in support of it.

This understanding of the notion of fallacy arose from my own study of arguments and is not a common one. Several years ago I began to notice that the arguments that do not work—that is, fail to bring others to the conclusion being defended—are arguments that violate one or more of the criteria of a good argument. I also observed that each of the commonly committed fallacies likewise violates one or more of the criteria and shares some common features with other patterns of reasoning that violate the same criterion. A new theory of fallacy soon emerged, which defined a fallacy as a pattern of reasoning that exhibits a violation of one of the criteria of a good argument. This view of fallacy, then, is not limited to the named fallacies that one might find on a list somewhere. Because it is tied to the criteria of a good argument, it is inclusive of both named and unnamed flaws in reasoning.

Logicians who have given particular attention to the fallacies have usually focused on grouping them into categories based on the shared properties of the mistakes. For them, it appears that a fallacy is simply something to avoid in argumentation—it is just one of those items on a list of things that you shouldn't do. I believe that such an approach suffers from being unrelated to the nature of good arguments, is negative in tone, and is devoid of any connecting link between the fallacies.

It is my view that a properly developed theory of fallacy is the key to the construction of good arguments. A fallacy, then, is much more than something to avoid in argumentation. Properly understood, a fallacy is connected to the notion of a good argument. My own theory of fallacy, which is based on the criteria of a *good argument*, helps one not only to recognize a poor argument but, more important, to know what a good argument looks like. It is therefore positive in tone, it is directly related to the nature of good arguments, and it connects all of the fallacies together as violations of one or more of the five criteria of a good argument.

Fallacies are mistakes in reasoning that typically do not seem to be mistakes. Indeed, part of the etymology of the word "fallacy" comes from the notion of deception. Fallacious arguments usually have the deceptive appearance of being good arguments. That perhaps explains why we are so often misled by them. Such deceptiveness, of course, may be unintentional on the part of the arguer. But it really doesn't matter whether the mistake was intended or not; a mistake is a mistake, regardless of the arguer's intention.

In most cases, fallacies are mistakes made by those who construct or present arguments for our consideration. However, those to whom such arguments are addressed may also be guilty of faulty reasoning if they accept the conclusion of a faulty argument. If they accept the bad argument as a good one, they are, in effect, making the same argument and thus bear the same responsibility for its problems. Similarly, a person who accepts the conclusion of a good argument is, in effect, making the same argument and should be recognized as a good thinker.

NAMED VERSUS UNNAMED FALLACIES

To be able to identify a particular pattern of fallacious reasoning by name serves an important function. If a mistake in reasoning is so common that a name has been assigned to it, we should be considerably more confident about our assessment of its faulty character when we encounter it in an argument. It is intellectually reassuring to discover that particular kinds of reasoning have been specifically identified by experts in argumentation as fallacious, even to the point of having been assigned a name.

To say of an argument simply that it is "illogical" or that "something seems wrong with it" is not very helpful in eliminating its problems. It is analogous to the situation of one who does not feel well, goes to a physician, and is told "You're sick!" If a medical problem is to be treated effectively, one must first diagnose the problem. If the physician is well acquainted with the symptoms of particular diseases, he or she is more likely to identify the patient's problem correctly and to respond to it appropriately.

If a problem in reasoning is to be treated effectively, we must first diagnose the problem. This diagnosis entails specifying precisely what makes the argument fallacious. If we are well acquainted with the features of particular faulty patterns of reasoning, we are more likely to identify the mistake correctly and to respond to it effectively.

It should be clear by now that a fallacy does not have to have a name in order to be a fallacy. In fact, most of the fallacies that one will encounter in real-life arguments will not be named. Neither is it necessary to know the names of fallacies in order to assess the merit of an argument. Indeed, our evaluations of the five "Letters to the Editor" in the previous chapter, you may have noticed, were carried out with little reference to any particular or named fallacy—although some of the mistakes found there did have names. It has therefore been demonstrated that it is not necessary to know or to remember the names of particular fallacies in order to evaluate the merit of an argument. It is entirely sufficient to be able to recognize features of the argument that may violate one or more of the five criteria of a good argument, although recognizing the mistakes by name or by identifiable pattern will often make the task easier. Nevertheless, even if you forget every named fallacy that will be addressed in this text, the theory of fallacy exhibited here is broad enough to give you a lifelong skill in evaluating arguments, simply by knowing the five criteria.

ORGANIZATION OF THE FALLACIES

The organization of the fallacies in this book, as we have explained, is dictated by the criteria of a good argument. Each type of fallacy treated here is a species of a structural flaw, an irrelevant premise, an unacceptable premise, insufficient grounds, or a failure to provide an effective rebuttal. Some of these fallacies, however, share some common features and can be grouped into subclasses. For example, there are a number of begging-the-question fallacies, all of which commit the same basic error, even though each does so in a distinguishable way.

Each of the commonly committed fallacies is assigned to a subclass or category of fallacies under each of the criteria. Generally, the begging-the-question fallacies, the fallacies of inconsistency, and the fallacies of deductive inference belong to the class of structurally flawed arguments. The fallacies of irrelevance and irrelevant emotional appeals belong to the class of irrelevant premise. The fallacies of linguistic confusion and unwarranted assumption fall into the general class of unacceptable premise. The fallacies of missing evidence and causal fallacies are categorized in the class of insufficient grounds. *Ad hominem* fallacies, fallacies of diversion, and fallacies of counterevidence are in the category of ineffective rebuttal. (See the table on the following page.)

A particular fallacy, of course, may fail to meet more than one of the criteria. In such cases, the mistake in reasoning should be construed as properly belonging to the category that seems to describe best the error's most serious infraction of the rules of good reasoning. A good example is the so-called *ad hominem* fallacies. Arguments that employ these fallacies are arguments directed toward some feature of the arguer rather than the arguer's argument. Claims made about the arguer, even if true, would not count for or against the truth of the conclusion; such claims are usually irrelevant and should not be included in a good argument. The *ad hominem* fallacies, then, might be categorized as a violation of the criterion of irrelevance. But the more important error committed by one who attacks the arguer rather than his or her argument is that of using a tactic that avoids addressing the substance of the argument encountered. Hence, it would be more appropriate to construe the fallacy as a case of ineffective rebuttal.

Each of the next five chapters is devoted entirely to one of the five ways arguments can go wrong. Even though the fallacies are grouped in terms of some common features among them, careful attention is focused on each individual fallacy. Each one is given a precise definition. In most cases, this definition is restricted to one or two sentences. Although the definition could be memorized, it is more important that readers understand and translate it into their own words—as long as those words capture the distinctive features of the fallacy. Several examples are given for each fallacy, along with some suggestions about how one might respond to those who use such faulty patterns of reasoning.

THEORY OF FALLACY

Structure	Relevance	Acceptability	Sufficiency	Rebuttal
Begging-the-Question Fallacies Arguing in a Circle Question-Begging Language Complex Question Question-Begging Definition *Fallacies of Inconsistency* Incompatible Premises Contradiction Between Premise and Conclusion *Fallacies of Deductive Inference* Denying the Antecedent Affirming the Consequent False Conversion Undistributed Middle Term Illicit Distribution of an End Term	*Fallacies of Irrelevance* Irrelevant or Questionable Authority Appeal to Common Opinion Genetic Fallacy Rationalization Drawing the Wrong Conclusion Using the Wrong Reasons *Irrelevant Emotional Appeals* Appeal to Force or Threat Appeal to Tradition Appeal to Self-Interest Playing to the Gallery	*Fallacies of Linguistic Confusion* Equivocation Ambiguity Misleading Accent Illicit Contrast Argument by Innuendo Misuse of a Vague Expression Distinction Without a Difference *Unwarranted Assumption Fallacies* Fallacy of the Continuum Fallacy of Composition Fallacy of Division False Alternatives Is-Ought Fallacy Wishful Thinking Misuse of a Principle Fallacy of the Mean Faulty Analogy	*Fallacies of Missing Evidence* Insufficient Sample Unrepresentative Data Arguing from Ignorance Contrary-to-Fact Hypothesis Fallacy of Popular Wisdom Special Pleading Omission of Key Evidence *Causal Fallacies* Confusion of a Necessary with a Sufficient Condition Causal Oversimplification *Post Hoc* Fallacy Confusion of Cause and Effect Neglect of a Common Cause Domino Fallacy Gambler's Fallacy	*Fallacies of Counterevidence* Denying the Counterevidence Ignoring the Counterevidence *Ad Hominem Fallacies* Abusive *Ad Hominem* Poisoning the Well Two-Wrongs Fallacy *Fallacies of Diversion* Attacking a Straw Man Trivial Objections Red Herring Resort to Humor or Ridicule

No special effort is made to preserve the traditional names for the fallacies studied. For example, traditional Latin names are maintained in only two cases—the *post hoc* fallacy and the abusive *ad hominem* fallacy—because of the relative familiarity of these terms in ordinary discourse. In general, I have tried to assign names that give some indication of the actual character of the argument error, and for that reason I have abandoned some of the traditional nomenclature.

ATTACKING THE FALLACY

A number of strategies may be used effectively to attack faulty reasoning, whenever it is encountered. Specific strategies for particular fallacies are offered throughout the book. However, three general lines of attack deserve special attention.

The first is the method of allowing the argument to self-destruct. Sometimes the easiest way of attacking an argument is to reconstruct the argument into standard form and then let the argument destroy itself by having its flawed character clearly exposed. Consider the following argument expressed in a recent conversation.

> **Jason:** I think that the college orchestra's performance of Mahler's symphony was terrible.
> **Dave:** Why do you say that?
> **Jason:** Because the way they played it was not the way the composer intended it at all.

A simple reconstruction of this argument will immediately expose its flawed character—almost without further comment.

> (Since orchestral performances of a composer's work that are not in line with the composer's original intention cannot be good ones),
>
> and this orchestra's performance was not in line with composer Mahler's intention,
>
> ───────────────────────────────
>
> Therefore, this was not a good performance.

Even though the arguer was clearly using the principle found in the first premise to justify his conclusion, once it is stated as starkly as it is here, it will probably seem so clearly unacceptable that even the arguer may want to withdraw it. The reason that few people would regard it as a justifiable or acceptable principle is that most of us have come to expect and appreciate a performing artist's own unique interpretation of a creative work. Hence, the first premise, once it is made explicit, would not be an acceptable one, and since the conclusion is based exclusively on that questionable claim, the argument cannot be a good one.

A second way of attacking faulty reasoning is the counterexample method, which is a quick and easy way to challenge an unacceptable premise. For instance, if someone claims that a particular product is good or better because it is new or different, the claim is based on an implicit yet unacceptable assumption that whatever is new or different is better. You could demonstrate that the premise is false by pointing to an obvious counterexample to the claim, such as the fiasco experienced by Coca-Cola several years ago when it came out with the "New Coke." It was new, but by consumer reaction, not better. What you are establishing by a counterexample is that the claim in question is not necessarily or always true, which is usually a good enough reason to find it unaccept-able in a particular case. Although the counterexample approach is risky, since every claim usually has some legitimate exceptions, it is typically very effective.

A third way of attacking faulty reasoning is perhaps the most imaginative and effective of the strategies. It is called the "absurd example method" and shares some of the features of the other two. This method is a way of demonstrating faulty patterns of reasoning without appealing to technical jargon or rules. It is particularly effective with people unfamiliar with or unimpressed by the special names and distinc-tions logicians use.

If you wish to demonstrate the flaw in your opponent's argument by using the absurd example method, you simply construct an argument of your own that has the same form or pattern as the faulty argument of your opponent. Construct your argu-ment, however, so that it leads to an obviously false or even absurd conclusion. Since a good argument cannot yield an obviously false conclusion, your opponent should be able to understand, with a little help from you, that your argument is flawed. Once you point out that there is no essential difference in the pattern of reasoning exhibited in both arguments, your opponent will be compelled logically to acknowledge the faulty nature of his or her argument as well.

This method is especially effective when dealing with a deductive argument. Suppose that an opponent uses an argument that commits the fallacy of "undistributed middle term":

> Paul must be a Marxist. Why? Well, he is an atheist, and everybody
> knows that Marxists are atheists.

In standard form, the opponent's argument looks like this:

> Since all Marxists are atheists,
>
> and Paul is an atheist,
> _____
>
> Therefore, Paul must be a Marxist.

The absurd example method of attack can easily demonstrate that the form of this argu-ment is flawed—without resort to technical jargon:

> All library books are made out of paper,
>
> Patti's kite is made out of paper,
> _____
>
> Therefore, Patti's kite is a library book.

The same pattern of reasoning exhibited in the first argument renders an absurd conclu-sion in the second, and since that is not possible in a correctly formed deductive argu-ment with true premises, the pattern of reasoning must be structurally flawed.

This method of attack can be used with almost any kind of fallacy, but let us now use it on the more subtle so-called "fallacy of the continuum." Suppose that an op-ponent argued in the following manner:

> The fetus is a human being at birth. Right? And it certainly did not
> suddenly become a human being at delivery. In other words, it would
> be silly to say that a fetus is a human being at birth and not a human

being a minute earlier or an hour before that or a day or a month before that. At no time would you be able to say rationally that the fetus suddenly became a human being. So the fetus has to be just as much a human being at conception as it is at delivery.

To demonstrate the faulty character of this kind of reasoning, construct another argument of the same form as that of the original argument, but with an obviously false conclusion. For example:

An atmospheric temperature of 100° F is regarded as hot. Right? And it certainly did not suddenly become hot at 100° F. In other words, it would be silly to insist that a temperature that is one degree, or five, or ten degrees less than 100° F is not hot. And at no time would you be able to say rationally that at some particular point during a period in which the temperature moves from 0° F to 100° F that the temperature suddenly becomes hot, one could conclude that at 0° F it is just as hot as it is at 100° F.

If your opponent does not see the similarity of the two arguments, which makes the original argument as flawed as the absurd example, it may be necessary to reconstruct the argument into standard form:

Human Being Argument

(Since contraries or extremes, connected by small intermediate differences, are very much the same),

and it would be arbitrary to insist that at some particular point between the extremes they become different,

and conception and delivery are extremes connected by small intermediate differences,

and a fetus is a human being at delivery,

Therefore, a fetus is a human being at conception.

Temperature Argument (Absurd Example)

(Since contraries or extremes, connected by small intermediate differences, are very much the same),

and it would be arbitrary to insist that at some particular point between the extremes they become different,

and the temperatures of 0° F and 100° F are extremes connected by small intermediate differences,

and a temperature of 100° F is hot,

Therefore, a temperature of 0° F is hot.

The most serious problem with the temperature argument is that the conclusion comes directly from the highly questionable assumptions expressed in the first two premises. Yet those same premises appear implicitly in the original argument. If they lead to such an absurd conclusion in one argument (the absurd example), it is rational to infer that they cannot be used to reach an acceptable conclusion in another (the original argument). Hence, the original argument is also fatally flawed, although its conclusion does not appear as ridiculous as the conclusion in the absurd example.

This method serves as a graphic demonstration of the faulty character of the opponent's argument. I am not saying that the conclusion is false. I am simply saying that this particular argument should not lead one to that conclusion, because it follows a pattern of reasoning that has been shown to be seriously flawed.

It is often difficult to produce an example of an absurd argument spontaneously, so it might be wise to keep examples in mind for most of the named fallacies. In many of the "Attacking the Fallacy" sections following the discussion of each fallacy, particular examples are supplied for such a purpose.

The absurd example method of confronting others with their mistakes in reasoning is not easy to master. It requires considerable practice, imagination, and a thorough understanding of the most common patterns of faulty reasoning. You will find, however, that this method is sometimes easier and more effective than trying to use technical language to try to explain to your opponent the sometimes complex nature of the particular fallacy that he or she has committed.

RULES OF THE GAME

Argumentation, like sports and many other activities, must be conducted in accordance with certain ground rules. In this case, however, the rules I have in mind are not the rules governing effective rational discussion. We have already provided 13 principles for that purpose. The ground rules I am referring to here are the rules of good sportsmanship. If you wish to maintain friendly relationships with your verbal opponents, and if you hope ultimately to win your point with the least amount of embarrassment and bitterness, I suggest you use the following guidelines.

First, don't be a fallacy monger. Some people, with a little knowledge of fallacious reasoning, develop a kind of obsession with identifying fallacies in the utterances of others. They sniff suspiciously at every argument and point of debate. Such pouncing on others often creates alienation. Several students have reported to me that while taking my course in logic, they experienced considerably more difficulty in relating to their friends, parents, and other professors. Perhaps these difficulties stem from a kind of fallacy mongering, wherein one attempts to point out, in a pedantic fashion, all the fallacies in even the most casual comments of friends and acquaintances.

Second, confront an opponent with fallacious reasoning only when you are convinced that an unwarranted conclusion has been reached as a result of violating one or more of the criteria of a good argument and/or in order to explain why you find the conclusion of the argument unacceptable. To point out questionable features of an argument that have no significant bearing on the basic thrust of the argument may only delay the progress of the debate and divert attention away from the point at issue.

Third, be aware that sometimes a fallacy is not a fallacy. In other words, what might appear to be a fallacy may very well not be one at all in certain contexts. As we pointed out earlier, the very reason that we are misled by fallacious reasoning is that it is so close to good reasoning. For that reason we need to make sure that what we are calling a fallacy really is a fallacy before registering an accusation.

Fourth, when you yourself are caught committing a fallacy, admit the mistake and make the appropriate adjustments in your thinking. Don't try to deny the charge or explain it away by making excuses or by claiming you were misunderstood. Don't be a sore loser.

Finally, avoid the word "fallacy" altogether, if possible. There are subtle ways of informing verbal opponents that they have committed an error in reasoning without having to shout, "Aha! That's a fallacy!" Because names assigned to fallacies vary from list to list and because people are often "turned off" by technical jargon, the wisest course of action would be to find ways of focusing attention on the pattern of faulty reasoning itself. Be imaginative. Find ways of challenging the reasoning processes of others without alienating them or causing them unnecessary embarrassment. After all, our purpose is to assist people in thinking more clearly, not to catch them in a fallacy.

ASSIGNMENTS

A. Recall a recent conversation that you were a part of or a lecture or speech that you heard, in which a speaker made what you think is a logical error in reasoning. Try to reconstruct the context of the error or fallacy and try to determine which of the five criteria the error might have violated. Try to create a name for the pattern of reasoning involved.

B. Read the "Letter to Jim" in the Appendix. It is purely fictional. It was created out of my own experience listening to attacks on the philosophical examination of religion over the many years I have been teaching. The letter is presented strictly as a fun exercise. In it, I have constructed an extended piece of bad reasoning that incorporates every single one of the 60 fallacies studied in this text. Each of them is committed one time and one time only. Each number represents the presence of a named fallacy immediately preceding it. Even though you may not know the name of each fallacy committed by Dad, try in each case to show how it violates at least one of the five criteria of a good argument. You might conceive of this as a kind of "pretest" of your knowledge of fallacious arguments. At the end of the course, more specifically at the end of Chapter IX, you may want to take a "posttest" by taking another look at the "Letter to Jim" and attempting to put proper labels on each of the fallacies.

V

Fallacies That Violate
the Structural Criterion

One who argues for or against a position should use an argument that meets the structural requirements of a well-formed argument, using premises that do not assume the truth of the conclusion, that are compatible with one another, that do not contradict the conclusion, and that are not involved in any faulty deductive inference.

Each of the fallacies discussed in this chapter violates the structural criterion of a good argument, in that it has some structural flaw that prevents its conclusion from following either *necessarily* or *probably* from the premises. Therefore, none of these arguments can do what arguments are supposed to do—provide us with good reasons to accept their conclusions. We will show in each case why no conclusion can or should be drawn from a structurally flawed argument.

The flaw in each case is a formal one, since discovering its flaw does not depend upon any knowledge of the argument's content. If symbols, for example, were substituted for each of the main parts of the argument, we would thereby be made blind to the argument's content. We would be left with only the form or structure of the argument. If by looking solely at that structure it could be determined that it would be inappropriate to draw any conclusion from the argument's premises, the argument would be properly described as committing a "formal fallacy."

There are several different types of these formal fallacies treated in this chapter. The begging-the-question fallacies are flawed in that they assume, in a variety of ways, the truth of the conclusion in their premises. Hence, the premises provide no reason to accept the conclusion. The fallacies of inconsistency are flawed in that they use premises that are incompatible with one another or they draw a conclusion that contradicts one of the premises. All of the fallacies of deductive inference are flawed because they violate well-established rules of deductive logic. We will address only the most common of these rule violations.

BEGGING-THE-QUESTION FALLACIES

An argument can assume the truth of its conclusion in its premises in at least four different ways. For that reason, each of these ways of begging the question has its own name. The arguing-in-a-circle fallacy actually uses the very conclusion that the arguer is trying to establish as one of its premises. One who commits the question-begging language fallacy uses particular language in the discussion of an issue that implicitly assumes the truth of the arguer's position or conclusion about the issue. In the case of the complex-question fallacy, the arguer asks a question in a way that implicitly assumes a particular answer to, or assumes a position on, an unasked question about an issue that is still open. Finally, the question-begging definition fallacy uses a highly questionable definition of a key term in its premises, which has the effect of making the arguer's conclusion "true by definition."

In each of these four ways of begging the question, there is the appearance of evidential support, but the evidence is bogus, since it is actually a form of the conclusion. An argument, by definition, is a claim supported by at least one other claim. If we interpret "other" to mean at least "different," in each of the begging-the-question fallacies, no "other" claim is actually given in support of the conclusion. For that reason, every question-begging argument is structurally flawed, in that it fails to meet the requirements of a well-formed argument.

Arguing in a Circle

DEFINITION *This fallacy consists in either explicitly or implicitly asserting, in the premise of an argument, what is asserted in the conclusion of that argument.*

The arguing-in-a-circle fallacy uses its own conclusion as one of its premises. Instead of offering proof, it simply asserts the conclusion as its "evidence." This fallacy is probably the most common of all the fallacious arguments you encounter. For example, while trying to defend a position on a particular controversial issue, you probably have encountered those who defend an alternative position by just declaring that their position is "true . . . well, simply, because it is true." Such an argument may not always be expressed in such a blatant form, but it is, in actuality, the substance of your opponent's argument, and it begs the very question at issue. But such an argument has a fatal structural flaw.

Moreover, such an argument is a *formally* flawed one, for the mistake can easily be detected in the absence of any knowledge of the specific content of the argument. In standard form, it looks like this:

Since A,

Therefore, A.

Since the argument gives no reason other than its conclusion as a reason for its conclusion, it does not actually function as an argument. Of course, no one is likely to argue in such a nakedly circular way. In real cases, the premise is more likely to be one that simply *assumes* the truth of the conclusion. Consider, for example, the person who argues that God exists because he or she does not want to be sent to hell. Such a person would be concerned about the prospect of being sent to hell only if he or she had already assumed that there is an existing God who would send someone there. But a *premise* that God exists does not support the *conclusion* that God exists.

When the conclusion appears as a premise, it is usually stated in different words or in a different form. The circularity of the argument is therefore not always easy to detect. It is particularly difficult to detect if the questionable premise and the conclusion are widely separated in the argument. Imagine the difficulty of recognizing an instance of circular reasoning that is spread over the whole of an essay, a chapter, or even a book.

The circular argument, it could be said, only pretends to establish a claim. It uses a premise that probably would not be regarded as true unless the conclusion were already regarded as true. Therefore, once you have analyzed the basic structure of a circular argument, you will see that it says nothing more significant than "A is true, because A is true."

Example   One of the simplest and most easily detected forms of circular reasoning uses a single premise that is actually only a restatement of the conclusion in different words. Consider the following argument: "To use textbooks with profane and obscene words in them is immoral, because it is not right for our children to hear vulgar, disrespectful, and ugly words." The form of the argument is clear: "A, because A."

Example
Dylan: This college is very paternalistic in its student policies.
Roman: What reasons do you have for saying that?
Dylan: Because they treat the students like children.

In this particular argument, Dylan may think that he is giving a reason for why the college is paternalistic, but at best he is only explaining what the word "paternalistic" means. But Roman did not ask for a definition of paternalism. He asked Dylan for "reasons" for making the claim. Dylan, however, gave no such reasons; he merely repeated his claim.

Example   "Mr. Goolsby cannot be regarded as a competent music critic because he is biased against all forms of modern, especially atonal, music. And the reason that he doesn't like it is that he simply doesn't have the background and ability to evaluate it properly."

The circularity of this argument can be shown by pointing out its structure:

Since Mr. Goolsby is biased against modern music,

> because he does not have the background and ability to evaluate
> it properly,

Therefore, Mr. Goolsby is an incompetent music critic.

The claim in the subargument of the premise that Mr. Goolsby "does not have the background and ability to evaluate music properly" means the same thing as "is an incompetent music critic." Hence, the question-begging support for the premise fallaciously allows Goolsby's incompetence to be given as a reason for his incompetence.

Attacking the Fallacy   If you are to avoid being misled by those who argue in a circle, it is necessary to keep a very keen eye on the logical structure of arguments. Make sure that no premise is simply an equivalent form of the conclusion or a premise that implicitly assumes the truth of the conclusion. If the argument is an extended one, carelessness in attention or a faulty memory may allow the sameness of premise and conclusion to go undetected.

You may attack circular reasoning directly by calling attention to the fact that the conclusion has already been assumed to be true as a part of the evidence. You will need to carefully identify for your opponent the questionable claim that is doing double duty. This can probably best be done by putting the argument into standard form, which will clearly demonstrate how the premise and the conclusion actually make the same claim.

The fallacious character of arguing in a circle might also be demonstrated by an obvious or absurd instance of it. For instance, if you said, "Reading is fun, because it brings me lots of enjoyment," it should be clear to your opponent that no claim has been established by such an argument. Yet it clearly has the same form, namely "A, because A," as the more subtle argument being attacked.

In many cases, those who argue in a circle will readily agree that they assume the conclusion to be true—because they are genuinely convinced of its truth. Such arguers need to be reminded that in an argument, one's personal beliefs or convictions concerning the truth of a claim cannot be used as evidence for the truth of that claim.

Question-Begging Language

DEFINITION   *This fallacy consists in discussing an issue by means of language that assumes a position on the very question at issue, in such a way as to direct the listener to that same conclusion.*

One who commits the question-begging language fallacy assumes either deliberately or carelessly, but in any case prematurely, that a matter that is at issue has already been settled. By the arguer's careful manipulation of language, the listener is subtly directed to infer a particular conclusion, although no good reasons are presented for doing so. Such slanted or prejudicial language often influences the outcome of an inquiry by generating a response other than what the facts might support. Therefore, a special effort should be made to use only *descriptive* or *neutral* language when there is an important issue to be decided.

Since an argument purports to give reasons to support a conclusion, it cannot smuggle that conclusion into the argument by means of a subtle use of language that assumes a position on the issue in question. Since no supporting evidence is given in such cases, no conclusion can or should be drawn from the "evidence" given.

Example   A plaintiff who testifies in a contract dispute that he or she was "cheated," when the very purpose of the court proceeding is to decide that issue, is using question-begging language. In standard form, the plaintiff's argument would look like this:

Since I was cheated,

Therefore, you should conclude that I was cheated.

A non–question-begging way of testifying in the contractual matter would be to describe what happened and then let the court decide if the plaintiff was "cheated."

Example   Prosecutor to witness: "Would you tell us, Ms. Smeltzer, about the nature of your relationship with the rapist, Mr. Graham?" The prosecutor is using language in his question to Ms. Smeltzer that begs the very question at issue in the courtroom. He is implicitly saying to the jury that "since Mr. Graham is the rapist on trial, the jury should decide that he is guilty of the crime of rape." An alert defense attorney would, of course, object vigorously to the implicit conclusion embedded in the language of the question.

Example   Suppose that you are engaged in a dispute about the moral permissibility of abortion, and the main issue in your dispute is whether the fetus is to be considered a human being. If one of the discussants constantly refers to the fetus as "the baby," he or she has begged the question on the very point at issue. The argument, in effect, says that "since the fetus is a baby human being, the fetus is a human being." This translation of the argument makes it clear why the use of such language in a premise begs the question at issue.

Example   A form of this fallacy with which most of us are quite familiar is one in which an arguer "plants" a proposed answer to a question at issue by the manner in which the question is asked. This variation of the question-begging language fallacy even has its own name. It is called a "leading question." Suppose Professor Scruggs says to a student: "You aren't serious about nominating Professor Reiff as 'Teacher of the Year,' are you?" Professor Scruggs plants the conclusion that she wants the student to come to, which is that Professorr Reiff should not be nominated, but she provides no reason why he should not be nominated, other than the implicit premise that he should not be nominated.

In each of these examples there is the absence of any real evidence in the argument, for the alleged evidence in each case is simply the conclusion in a not-so-good disguise. Since the argument has no premise other than the conclusion restated, it fails to meet the structural requirement of a good argument.

Attacking the Fallacy   Perhaps the best way to confront a person who has committed this fallacy is to point out how his or her very language might prevent the discussion of the issue from being a genuinely open one.

If your opponent will not acknowledge that his or her language may prevent an objective mutual assessment of the merit of the claim, it may be an issue about which he or she cannot be objective. If, for example, your opponent insists on representing another's action with words like "double-cross" or "blackmail," and genuinely believes that he or she is simply being *descriptive*, it may not be possible to get that person to help assess the issue impartially on the basis of the evidence available.

Above all, do not be intimidated by the language of the question-beggar, particularly when he or she introduces a claim by such phrases as "obviously," "any 10-year-old knows," or "any fool knows." This language suggests that the speaker thinks that the issue is not really one that deserves any further discussion or investigation. Such expressions function as defenses against attack, and if you wish not to be the victim of such tricks, you must risk the appearance of being naive, uninformed, or even mentally deficient by announcing, "Well, it's *not* obvious to *me*."

To confront the leading-question tactic, you must find some way to reveal to the questioner that he or she is asking you to grant an assumption that is at least part of the very question at issue. You might point out that you think the position you are being implicitly asked to support requires more evidential support than it now has, or at least that you are not now ready to support the position on the basis of the available evidence. Of course, if the position held by the questioner seems to be a reasonable one or is one you find sufficiently well-supported in other contexts, then it may be that no fallacy has been committed.

Complex Question

DEFINITION   *This fallacy consists in formulating a question in a way that presupposes that a definite answer has already been given to an unasked question about an issue that is still open or that treats a series of questions as if it involved only one question.*

The complex question becomes a question-begging fallacy when the unasked question is about an issue that is not yet settled. Consider the question "What did you do with my watch after you stole it from me?" If the respondent has not admitted to stealing the watch, he or she cannot answer such a question without granting a questionable assumption.

Nearly all questions are complex in the sense that they make assumptions. For example, if I were to ask, "When they are going to announce the Academy Award nominations?" I would be assuming that they *are* going to announce them, but no one is likely to question that assumption; they are certainly not likely to accuse me of begging the question. A question is not fallacious if the questioner has good reason to believe that the respondent would be quite willing to grant the questioner's assumptions. It begs the question only when it is about an issue that is still open.

Another feature of the complex question is that it improperly assumes that the respondent will give the same answer to each question in a series of questions. In this question, "Will you take me home tonight and let me pick up some things from the grocery store on the way?" the questioner has assumed that the answer to each part of this compound question will be the same. Unless the questioner has reason to believe that the same answer will suffice for both questions, he or she has begged the question.

In both types of complex question, there is a structural flaw. The arguer or questioner has assumed a position on a questionable issue and then has used that assumption to support the same questionable position. Look at our "watch" and "take me home tonight" examples after they have been translated into standard form.

Since you stole my watch,
_____

Therefore, you stole my watch.

and

Since all cases of you taking me home will be cases of you also taking me to the grocery store,
_____

Therefore, all cases of you taking me home will be cases of you also taking me to the grocery store.

Such arguments clearly have a structural flaw, in that they do not provide any evidence for the conclusion, which prevents them from being well-formed arguments.

Example   The most common form of this fallacy asks two questions, one of which is explicit and the other implicit. Consider the young man who asks a fellow sophomore, "What fraternity are you going to pledge?" Or the pushy salesclerk who asks, "Will this be cash or credit card?" long before you have decided to buy the merchandise. Or even the worried mother who asks her 30-year-old son, "When are you going to settle down and get married?" In each case, the questioner has assumed a positive answer to an implicit question—namely, that the sophomore has decided to pledge some fraternity, that the customer has decided to buy the merchandise, and that the son has concluded that he will someday get married.

Example   Consider the version of the complex question that treats a series of questions as if it involved only one question: "Are you and Nancy going to the Keller-Trent wedding and to the reception next Saturday, even though you were not invited?"

This innocent-looking question actually involves at least seven different questions. It asks if I am going to the wedding, if I am going to the reception, if my wife Nancy is going to the wedding, if she is going to the reception, if the wedding and reception are to be held next Saturday, if I was invited, and if Nancy was invited. It might be the case that I would answer positively in response to one or more of these questions but negatively in response to one or more of the others. Yet the question as initially posed is asked in such a way that either a simple "yes" or simple "no" is called for. One may, of course, answer "yes" to all seven questions or "no" to all seven questions, but when one considers the possible combinations of all responses that may be given to the seven separate questions embedded in the original, it turns out that there are 128 of them. If there is a possibility that the wedding and reception may not be on the same day, there are 256 questions. Check it out! If the question is not divided, the questionable assumption that is granted to the questioner is that the same answer will be given to each of the questions.

Example   "Why are the children of divorce more emotionally unstable than those children raised in unbroken homes?"

This is a complex question, for the questioner has assumed a position on a questionable claim—namely, that children of divorce are emotionally more unstable than children raised in unbroken homes. That claim must be established before the question calling for an explanation of such a phenomenon can be appropriately asked. Indeed, if the substantive claim can be shown to be false, the call for explanation would be out of order. However, as it was originally asked, the question does not consider the possibility that the substantive claim may be false. Hence, the respondent is "begged" to grant the truth of that assumption.

Attacking the Fallacy   You may attack the complex question in a number of ways. First, refuse to give a straightforward positive or negative response to such a question. If the asker fails to understand your reticence, ask: "Have you stopped cheating on your income tax?" They'll get the idea.

Second, point out the particular questionable assumption in the question and indicate that the issue has not yet been decided. Give assurance, however, that you are prepared to discuss that issue at any time.

Third, insist, if necessary, that the question be appropriately divided so that each of the two or more questions can be answered separately. After all, even the rules of parliamentary procedure give a motion to "divide the question" a priority status.

Question-Begging Definition

DEFINITION *This fallacy consists in using a highly questionable definition as a premise, which has the effect of making the claim at issue "true by definition."*

The fallacy of question-begging definition rests on a confusion between an empirical premise and a definitional premise. A *definitional* premise is simply a claim about what an important term in a discussion means. If it is a proper definition, it should be based on common usage of the term or the thinking of relevant authorities, while a questionable definition would neither conform to ordinary usage nor the thinking of relevant authorities.

An *empirical* premise, however, makes an observational or factual claim. It is a claim about how things *are* in the actual world, and it is subject to correction or confirmation in the light of factual evidence. The truth or acceptability of an empirical claim would be determined by whether it conforms to such things as the experience of our senses, the testimony of relevant authorities, and the results of appropriate experimentation.

One who commits the question-begging definition fallacy substitutes, intentionally or unintentionally, a questionable definitional premise for what is purported in the argument to be an empirical one. Insofar as this questionable definition assumes the truth of the arguer's position on the very question at issue, the argument in which it is embedded is structurally flawed.

There are at least two clues that an arguer has made the question-begging premise switch. First, if the arguer refuses to allow contrary evidence to count against his or her "empirical" premise, there is reason to suspect that the premise is not functioning as an empirical one. A second clue that this deceptive technique is being used could be the presence of such modifying words as "true," "real," or "genuine" before the key term in the discussion of an issue. Even though the arguer may strongly believe that a term *should* be defined in an unconventional way, if the very definition of the term in the premises has the effect of making an empirical claim true by definition, then the fallacy of question-begging definition has been committed.

Example Let us suppose that there is a discussion between Biliana and Kevork about whether any Christians drink alcoholic beverages. If Kevork rejects Biliana's evidence that there are many Christians who *do*, as a matter of fact, drink alcoholic beverages on the grounds that "if they were *real* Christians, they would not drink," it becomes clear that he is not actually addressing the issue as an empirical question. Instead, he is actually *defining* a Christian as one who would not drink. But Kevork's definition neither conforms to ordinary usage nor to the thinking of relevant authorities. Moreover, if he tried to use this highly questionable definition as a premise in an actual argument for the claim that Christians do not drink, it would beg the very question at issue. It would therefore have no place in a well-formed argument.

Example Suppose that Tim maintains the empirical claim that "true love never ends in separation or divorce." When he is presented with examples of true love followed by divorce, he insists that such cases were not genuine cases of true love. His "evidence" that they were not cases of true love is that they ended in divorce. Tim is hereby settling the issue by definition, for his judgment is that any marriage that ends in divorce could not have been a case of true love. Hence, no empirical evidence is allowed to count against his claim. It is when this evidence is presented and rejected that it should become evident to other discussants that the alleged empirical claim is really a definitional one. The argument in standard form should clearly reveal the flaw:

> Since true love is defined as a love that will never end in divorce or separation,
> _____
> Therefore, true love will never end in divorce or separation.

If Tim wishes to define true love as love that would not end in separation or divorce, that is his prerogative, although such a definition is a highly questionable one from the perspective of ordinary language. However, his original claim had the appearance of being a factual assertion, which is an assertion that empirical evidence may either confirm or deny. It was when counterevidence was not allowed to correct the claim that it became clear that the premise was actually a definitional claim.

Example   When a popular politician switched from the Republican party to the Democratic party several years ago, a number of his critics, especially Republicans, claimed that he had obviously not been a "true-blue" Republican or he wouldn't have switched political parties. The only "evidence" the critics could cite for his "non–true-blue" Republicanism was that he switched parties. It was obvious that no evidence would have been allowed to count against the claim. This is, therefore, a case of the fallacy of question-begging definition. The definition of a true-blue Republican is apparently one who would never leave the Republican party. Hence, the only matter that is actually in dispute is whether the definition is an appropriate one; there is no empirical claim at issue.

Attacking the Fallacy   If you suspect that an arguer has employed a question-begging definition in an argument, ask the arguer whether the premise is a definitional or an empirical one. If he or she is puzzled by your question, you might need to explain the difference between them. One way to help test whether the premise in question is really an empirical one is to ask if the arguer can identify any evidence that would count against the claim.

If the claim is discovered to be definitional, it is obviously not subject to falsification by counterevidence, but the question-beggar should be prepared to defend his or her questionable definition against other definitions that seem to be based more securely on common usage or the thinking of relevant authorities. To move the discussion forward, you might suggest one of these more appropriate definitions and ask the arguer on what grounds his or her definition is thought to be a better one.

You might also question the arguer on whether it is likely that the questionable definition would be agreed to by most people who use the term in question and/or whether such a definition is close to any definition in a published dictionary. If necessary, you might together consult a dictionary in order to help settle the issue.

ASSIGNMENTS

A. Begging-the-Question Fallacies   For each of the following arguments, (1) identify the type of begging-the-question illustrated, and (2) explain how the reasoning violates the structural criterion. There are two examples of each fallacy discussed in this section. Arguments marked with an asterisk (*) have sample answers at the end of the text.

1. David says to his nephew Charlie, who is a high school senior, "Where will you be going to college next year, Charlie?"

*2. Sean: The criminal mind simply cannot be rehabilitated. The prisons are wasting time and resources.

Jeannie: That's not true. I know several criminals who have been completely rehabilitated as a result of their prison experiences.

Sean: Well, then, those people must never have had a truly criminal mind.

3. It's supposed to be in the low twenties tonight, so surely we're not going to the football game, are we?

*4. Roy: Why should I do what the Bible says?

Dorothy: Because the Bible is the inspired word of God

Roy: But how do you know that the Bible is actually divinely inspired?

Dorothy: Because it says in the third chapter of II Timothy that "all Scripture is given by inspiration of God."

*5. One of Senator Fisher's constituents asks, "Are you going to vote for the proposed cut in the defense budget—a cut that will surely weaken our military posture around the world?"

6. Celeste: I've thought about this for a long time, and I've come to the conclusion that sane people do not commit suicide.

Chris: What about your friend Shelby, who surprised you and everyone when he committed suicide?

Celeste: Well, he certainly seemed sane, but I guess we didn't know the real story.

7. Professor Taverner: Only the fittest of organisms survive.

Student: How do you know?

Professor Taverner: Well, if they survive, they must be fit.

Student: Yes, but how do you know that it is only the most fit of the organisms that survive?

Professor Taverner: Those creatures who have survived obviously have survived because they were somehow adapted for survival.

*8. Elijah: Don't you have any other houses in our price range to show us?

Real Estate Broker: I've shown you everything in town that is available. Well, there is one other tacky little house that we could look at . . . if you want.

FALLACIES OF INCONSISTENCY

One who attempts to advance an argument that is self-contradictory commits a fallacy of inconsistency. If an argument is self-contradictory, there is an inconsistency or incompatibility among its parts, and the argument is therefore structurally flawed. And it is a very serious flaw, for being caught in a contradiction between premise and conclusion or with contradictory premises destroys the effectiveness of the argument, for no acceptable conclusion can be drawn from the premises.

In most cases, the inconsistency or incompatibility in question is *implicit* rather than *explicit*. Cases in which the inconsistency is explicit are relatively rare, since they would be so easily detectable. The more interesting cases are those that exhibit an implicit inconsistency. Statements are implicitly inconsistent if at least one of them implies or could be legitimately *interpreted* as implying a statement that is inconsistent with another premise or with the conclusion in the same argument.

Incompatible Premises

> DEFINITION   *This fallacy consists in drawing a conclusion from inconsistent or incompatible premises.*

An argument that uses premises that are not compatible with one another cannot function as a good argument. The formal character of its structural flaw can be demonstrated by looking carefully at the argument's form:

Since A,

and not-A,

(No conclusion can be drawn.)

According to the *law of noncontradiction* (not both A and not-A), one of two contradictory premises must be false, and thus no acceptable conclusion can be drawn. A deductive argument that has incompatible or inconsistent premises is one from which *any* conclusion whatsoever can be validly drawn. Hence, it is clear that an argument with such premises must be structurally flawed.

It is, however, sometimes difficult to distinguish between real and apparent incompatible premises. For example, a father who is trying to persuade his child that no one should be trusted is obviously making an exception of himself. If he really were making incompatible claims ("since you should trust no one, and you should trust me,") no rational conclusion could or should be drawn by the child. The incompatible premises are only apparent; the father has simply and carelessly overstated the first premise. If he had said: "Don't trust most people" or "Trust very few people," or "Don't trust anyone except me," he would have had no trouble avoiding the contradiction. However, the claim that "Atheists hate God" has implicit inconsistent premises that are not so easy to reconcile.

Example   "If God is perfectly good, all-powerful, and all-knowing, there would be no evil in the world, and yet there is evil in the world. Therefore either God does not exist, is not all-knowing, is not all-loving, is not all-powerful, or there is no evil in the world." This is a way of stating what philosophers and theologians call the "problem of evil." They assume that if God is all-knowing, he *knows* about the evil, if he is all-loving, he *would want* to prevent it, and if he is all-powerful he *could* prevent it. But evil persists! These claims are clearly incompatible. If they were used as premises in an argument, there would be an implicit contradiction between at least two of them, so no conclusion could or should be drawn. To resolve the problem of contradictory premises, at least one of the five premises would have to be denied or declared false.

Example   A popular ethical theory also exhibits the flaw of incompatible premises. The so-called Divine Command Theory of ethics argues that an act is right because God says it is right. His saying so makes it so. This, they argue, is the case with the Ten Commandments, the rules that they say God gave to his people to live by. If he had given them different rules, those would be the right rules. When questioned whether God could have chosen to tell his followers to rape and pillage, some divine command theorists argue that God would never tell them to do those things, because those acts would be wrong. Such an arguer uses incompatible premises. On the one hand, he or she is arguing that God creates or determines what is right merely by declaring what is right. On the other hand, the arguer is saying that there are certain acts that God would not declare to be right, because they are in fact wrong. Let us look at the structure of this argument:

> (Since we should do what is morally right),
>
> and God determines what is morally right, (A)
>
>> which is illustrated by the Ten Commandments,
>
> and his willing or declaring it to be morally right is what makes it right, (B)
>
> and to those who point out that according to this view God could declare anything to be right, I say that there are some things, like rape, that he would not declare right,
>
>> because they are morally wrong. (Not-B)

(No conclusion can be drawn.)

The arguer cannot have it both ways. If God determines what is right by declaring it so, as the arguer claims in the third premise, then no act can be wrong until He declares it so. Yet the arguer claims in his or her effort at rebuttal in the fourth premise that there are some acts that He would not declare to be right, because they are already wrong. This incompatibility must be resolved before any acceptable conclusion can be drawn.

Example   Each of us has heard a politician ask for our vote on the promise that he or she will maintain or increase all present governmental services and also lower taxes. If we assume no major change in the tax or revenue structure, there is no conclusion to be drawn until the implied conflict in premises is resolved—other than the conclusion that we will not give our vote to someone who attempts to deceive us by deliberately flawed arguments.

Attacking the Fallacy   Since the fallacy of incompatible premises is a formal or structural one, the best way to confront those who commit it is to put their arguments in standard form, convert the premises to symbols, and demonstrate how given the incompatibility of the premises, no conclusion should have been drawn. If the arguer is not familiar with the law of noncontradiction (not both A and not-A), you may have to briefly explain how it is a necessary condition of meaningful intellectual discourse, after which he or she should either abandon the argument altogether or find some way of resolving the incompatibility of the premises.

Another way of attacking the argument with incompatible premises is to ask the arguer what conclusion he or she would draw from the premises. Typically, one who uses contradictory claims actually draws no conclusion, thinking the conclusion is clear. However, it is usually not at all clear what the conclusion is, other than a repetition of one of the claims. If the arguer insists that the premises are not contradictory, he or she is obligated to show why they are not.

Contradiction Between Premise and Conclusion

DEFINITION *This fallacy consists in drawing a conclusion that is incompatible with at least one of the premises.*

An argument that draws a conclusion that contradicts one of the premises cannot be a structurally sound one. The formal flaw can be seen by looking carefully at the form of such an argument:

Since A,

and B,

Therefore, not-A.

The argument draws the conclusion of "not-A," but such a conclusion cannot follow from the premises. According to the law of noncontradiction (not both A and not-A), the conclusion of the argument and the first premise cannot both be true. Therefore, an argument that draws a conclusion that is incompatible with one of the premises is a fallacious one.

Example The classical causal argument for the existence of God seems to be a paradigm case of an argument with a conclusion that contradicts or is incompatible with one of its premises. The argument goes like this:

Since everything has a cause, (A)

and we cannot go back infinitely into the past, (B)

> because if the process of causation never started, we would not be here

and we are here, (C)

Therefore, there must be an uncaused first cause, and that is God. (Not-A)

The conclusion that God was an uncaused first cause clearly contradicts the first premise that everything has a cause. Unless the arguer can find a way of construing the content of the argument in a different way, that conclusion cannot be drawn; and the argument must be declared to be structurally flawed.

Example Another popular philosophical argument commits this same error. In dealing with the so-called mind-body problem, the seventeenth-century French philosopher René Descartes argued that the mind and body are two very different entities that interact with each other. This position is known as dualistic interactionism. If we put the argument into standard form, it looks like this:

> Since the body is physical and occupies space, (A)
>
> and the mind is nonphysical and does not occupy space, (B)
>
> (and personal experience indicates that minds affect bodies, and vice versa), (C)
> _____
>
> Therefore, the mind and body do interact with each other. (Not-B)

Descartes's conclusion is clearly incompatible with the second premise, and his critics were quick to point this out to him. An entity that is nonspatial cannot causally affect that which is spatial. Unless Descartes could find some way of reconciling the second premise and the conclusion, either the second premise or the conclusion must be rejected.

Example   Some arguments in the abortion debate contain a conclusion that contradicts a premise. It is not unusual to hear someone argue that "all human life is sacred, and we have an obligation to preserve it; and since abortion destroys such life, it is wrong, except in cases of rape." By making an exception of rape, the conclusion contradicts the first premise. Since the arguer would probably not want to deny that the child of rape is any less a sacred human life, he or she must either eliminate the exception of rape or alter the inclusive nature of the first premise that says that *all* human life is sacred.

Attacking the Fallacy   Since the fallacy of contradiction between premise and conclusion is a formal or structural one, the best way to confront those who commit it is to put their arguments in standard form, convert the premises to symbols, and demonstrate how the conclusion is clearly contradictory to one of the premises. Unless the arguer shows no respect for the law of noncontradiction, he or she should be convinced by the demonstration and either abandon the argument altogether or at least find some way of satisfactorily resolving the contradiction.

ASSIGNMENTS

B. Fallacies of Inconsistency   For each of the following arguments, (1) identify the type of inconsistency illustrated, and (2) explain how the reasoning violates the structural criterion. There are two examples of each of the fallacies discussed in this section. Arguments marked with an asterisk (*) have sample answers at the end of the text.

*1. I believe that the truth about human knowledge lies in the position of skepticism, which is the view that there is no way that we can know anything to be true, so we may as well give up the search.

*2. Who's to say that I'm wrong and you're right about smoking marijuana? What is right has to be determined by each individual. And I don't see anything unethical about using marijuana. So, you're just wrong.

3. Human life is a precious gift, and no one has the right to take it away. One who murders another human being destroys that gift. That is the reason that I'm in favor of capital punishment for those convicted of murder.

4. Ben: The trouble with you, Ed, is that you just can't think outside the box. You think that if some idea is contradictory, it doesn't make any sense.

Ed: I guess you're right. I do think that noncontradiction is a necessary condition of intelligible human discourse.

Ben: That's just nonsense. That's just your Western mindset coming through. There is no reason to think that contradictory claims cannot be meaningful.

Ed: I agree. A claim would *not* be meaningful, if it were contradictory.

Ben: No, I said it *could* be meaningful, if it were contradictory.

Ed: And I said I agreed. It would *not* be meaningful if it were contradictory.

Ben: What's wrong with you, Ed? Do you not have your hearing aid turned on? You're talking nonsense. I can't make any sense out of what you're saying.

Ed: Exactly!

FALLACIES OF DEDUCTIVE INFERENCE

The fallacies in this section are those that violate one of the well-established rules of conditional and syllogistic reasoning. Two of the fallacies violate rules of conditional reasoning and three of them violate the rules governing categorical syllogisms.

Denying the Antecedent

DEFINITION *This fallacy consists in denying the antecedent of a conditional statement and then inferring the denial of the consequent.*

In a conditional or "if, then" statement, the part of the sentence that comes after the "if" is called the "antecedent," and the part that comes after the "then" is called the "consequent." An example of a *good* conditional argument is called "affirming the antecedent," or *modus tollens*. It has the following form:

Since if A, then B,

and A.

Therefore, B.

If the first two premises are true, we can be assured that the conclusion of this argument is true, for in a well-formed deductive argument, the conclusion follows from the premises with logical necessity. However, an argument that *denies* the antecedent and then denies the consequent does not conform to the structure of a well-formed argument:

Since if A, then B,

and not-A.

Therefore, not-B.

The structure of this argument is a flawed one, since the antecedent is denied in the second premise and one of the rules governing conditional reasoning says that no conclusion follows from a premise that *denies* rather than affirms the antecedent of a conditional proposition.

One who denies the antecedent and draws a conclusion denying the consequent fails to recognize that in addition to A, there are usually *other* causes that could also bring about B, which means that A is not necessary to B's being true. However, by denying A and then concluding that B could not be true, the arguer wrongly assumes that A is the *only* thing that could bring about B. Even though the premises may be true in such an argument, no conclusion follows, for the structure of the argument is fatally flawed. The rule against denying the antecedent is designed to prevent these problems.

Example "If I were a heavy smoker, it would shorten my life. That's why I don't smoke. And I expect to live a long and healthy life." Any number of things could shorten one's life or negatively affect one's health. But this arguer seems to have limited it to the factor of smoking. He or she has treated smoking as if it were the *only* thing that could shorten life. The standard form of the argument exhibits the flaw quite clearly.

Since if I smoke (A), I will have a shortened life (B),

and I will not smoke. (Not-A)

Therefore, my life will not be shortened. (Not-B)

Example "If capital punishment actually deterred people from committing capital crimes, then it would be justified. But as it does not have that deterrent effect, it is not a justifiable practice." There are factors other than deterrence that may be sufficient to justify capital punishment. Hence, the denial of the consequent does not follow from the denial of the antecedent.

Example "Professor Lane told us that we would pass his course if we could correctly identify the fallacy example that he put on the chalkboard. So I guess I failed the course; I couldn't identify it." Professor Lane did not say that the only way to pass the course would be to identify the fallacy; there could be many other ways to do it. But by denying a successful identification and then denying that the course will be passed, the arguer has assumed that identifying the fallacy is the only way to do so.

Attacking the Fallacy An absurd example should clearly demonstrate the structural flaw exhibited in an argument that denies the antecedent:

Since if Jessy is a dog, then Jessy is an animal

and Jessy is not a dog,

Therefore, Jessy is not an animal.

Obviously being a dog is not the only way of being an animal. If Jessy is actually a cat, which qualifies her as an animal, a false and absurd conclusion has been inferred from true premises, which would be impossible if the argument were a well-structured deductive argument. The arguer should see that insofar as his or her argument has the same structure as the Jessy argument, it also is a flawed argument.

Affirming the Consequent

DEFINITION *This fallacy consists in affirming the consequent of a conditional statement and then inferring the affirmation of the antecedent.*

Another example of a well-formed conditional argument is called "denying the consequent," or *modus ponens*. This argument has the following form:

Since if A, then B,

and not-B.

Therefore, not-A.

Just as in the case of denying the antecedent, if the first two premises are true, we can be assured that the conclusion of this argument is also true; for in a well-formed deductive argument, the conclusion follows necessarily from the premises. However, an argument that *affirms* the consequent and then affirms the antecedent does not conform to the structure of a well-formed argument:

Since if A, then B,

and B.

Therefore, A.

By looking solely at its form, we can see that the argument is fallacious, since one of the rules governing the structure of conditional arguments says that no conclusion follows from a premise that *affirms* rather than denies the consequent in a conditional argument. Since the consequent is affirmed in the second premise, the argument violates a well-established rule of conditional reasoning.

One who affirms the consequent and draws a conclusion affirming the antecedent fails to recognize that in addition to A, there are usually *other* conditions that are also sufficient to bring about B. By affirming B and then drawing the conclusion of A, the arguer implicitly asserts that A is the *only* thing that could have caused B. Even though both of the premises may be true in the argument, the conclusion does not follow, for the argument's structure is fatally flawed. The rule against affirming the consequent is designed to prevent these problems.

Example In the criminal courtroom, this fallacy is frequently committed by prosecuting attorneys. "If the defendant were planning on murdering his wife, he would very likely make sure that he had a large insurance policy on her life, and that, ladies and gentlemen of the jury, is exactly what he did. You can draw your own conclusion." This is sometimes called "circumstantial evidence," and along with other evidence may contribute to the prosecutor's *inductive* argument for the defendant's guilt; but in this deductive argument the prosecutor's conclusion does not follow with necessity, because it is not a well-formed deductive argument. It is a classic case of affirming the consequent. The flaw in its form is obvious in the following reconstruction:

Since if a husband is planning on murdering his wife (A), he will
have an insurance policy on her life (B),

And this husband did have a large policy on her life. (B)

Therefore, he murdered his wife (A).

The prosecutor fails to recognize that there are many reasons that could be sufficient for buying an insurance policy on one's wife and wrongly assumes that wanting to murder his wife is the only reason for buying one.

Example "If you do very well on the SAT, you will probably get into a good college. Since you got into Centre College, which is a good school, you must have done well on the SAT." The assumption in this argument is that the *only* way to get into a good school is to get a high score on the SAT, yet there are a number of other conditions that may be sufficient for getting into a good school, such as good grades or athletic prowess.

Example "If I eat red meat after not having eaten any for a long time, I often get ill. Since I woke up sick at my stomach this morning, I assume that there must have been some red meat in that soup we ate at the restaurant last night." Let's look at the form of this argument:

Since if I eat red meat (A), I get sick (B),

and I got sick. (B)

Therefore, I ate red meat. (A)

By affirming the consequent and then affirming the antecedent, the arguer is assuming that the only thing that could cause illness is eating red meat. That is obviously not the case.

Attacking the Fallacy It has been suggested repeatedly that the absurd example method is a good way of exposing fallacious reasoning. To confront the fallacy of affirming the consequent, you might try the following absurd example: "If you have read Professor Damer's book, you should be able to recognize and successfully attack fallacious reasoning, and you are able to do that. Therefore, you must have read Damer's book." Wait a minute! Are there really no other books out there that do anything close to what this book does?

False Conversion

DEFINITION *This fallacy consists in exchanging the subject and predicate terms in a universal affirmative or particular negative categorical statement or in reversing the antecedent and consequent of a conditional statement and then inferring that such converted statements retain their original truth value.*

An argument whose premise is a conditional statement (If A, then B) and whose conclusion reverses the antecedent and the consequent of that conditional statement (If B, then A) is one in which the conclusion does not follow from the premise. Its form is such that it violates a rule of deductive logic. It is true that if a light comes on when the switch is flipped, the bulb is a good one, but it does not follow that if the bulb is a good one, then the light will come on when the switch is flipped. There are a number of other conditions that have to be in place for the light to come on.

Understanding why an argument whose premise is a categorical statement and whose conclusion reverses the subject and predicate terms is a flawed argument will require some knowledge of the nature of categorical statements. A categorical statement consists of a subject and predicate and asserts that either *all* or *some* of the class of things referred to by the subject term are either included in or excluded from the class of things referred to by the predicate term. There are four types of such statements: every categorical statement is either an A, E, I, or O type of proposition. An A statement is a universal affirmative statement, as in "All college students are intelligent," and an E statement is a universal negative statement, as in "No college students are rude." The sign of a universal statement is the word *all* or *no* (or their equivalents). An I statement is a particular affirmative statement, as in "Some professors are helpful," and an O statement is a particular negative statement, as in "Some professors are *not* helpful." The sign of a particular proposition is the word *some*, which means at least *one* and fewer than *all*.

The fallacy of false conversion takes place only when the subject and predicate is exchanged in either an A or an O statement. It is not false conversion when the subject and predicate is exchanged in either an E or an I statement. The difference has to do with the notion of distribution. A term is distributed if the statement in which it occurs says something about *every* member of the class of things that is designated by that term. A term is *not* distributed if the statement in which it occurs does *not* make a claim about every member of the class of things that is designated by that term.

The facts of distribution are as follows: Universal statements have distributed subjects and negative statements have distributed predicates. Another way of stating this is that the subject term of a universal statement (A or E) is always distributed, and the predicate term of a negative statement (E or O) is always distributed; all other terms are undistributed. If we apply this rule to all four types of statements, in an A statement, only the subject term is distributed; in an E statement, both terms are distributed; in an I statement, neither term is distributed; and in an O statement, the predicate term is distributed.

The reason that universal affirmative (A) statements and particular negative (O) statements cannot be converted is that there is an *uneven* distribution of the two terms in each of those statements; in the A statement only the subject is distributed and in the O statement only the predicate is distributed. In contrast, the reason that universal negative (E) statements and particular affirmative (I) statements *can* be converted is that there is an *even* distribution of the two terms in each statement, since both terms in E statements are distributed and neither term in I statements is distributed.

For example, the A statement "All chemists are scientists" cannot be converted to "All scientists are chemists." Because of the *uneven* distribution of terms in an A statement, the first statement is true while the converse is false. A claim is being made about all chemists, but no claim is being made about all scientists. In contrast, the E statement "No atheists are priests" *can* be converted to "No priests are atheists." Because of the *even* distribution of terms, both the first *and* the converted statement are true. A claim is being made about all atheists (they are all excluded from the class of priests) and a claim is also being made about all priests (they are all excluded from the class of atheists). Similarly, the I statement "Some professors are easy graders" can be converted to "Some easy graders are professors." Because of the *even* distribution of terms in an I statement, both claims are true, since no claim is being made about all professors and no claim is being made about all easy graders. In contrast, the O statement "Some scientists are not biologists" cannot be converted to "Some biologists are not scientists." Because of the *uneven* distribution of terms in an O statement, the first statement is true, while the converse is false. In the original O statement, no claim is being made about all scientists, but a claim *is* being made about all biologists. That claim is (and this is tricky) that the particular scientists referred to in the subject term of the statement that "Some scientists are not biologists" are excluded from the entire class of biologists. If that explanation is difficult to follow, just remember the facts about distribution and the rule that statements with uneven distribution cannot be converted.

Example From the claim that religious people are those who rely on a being outside themselves, it could not be inferred that people who rely on a being outside themselves are religious. One could show this to be a false conversion by reciting the facts of distribution and the rule about uneven distribution or one could show that the converse of the A statement is false by pointing out a counterexample to the converted claim, namely that a child could rely on a being outside himself or herself, such as a parent, and not be religious at all.

Example "If it is true that all heroin addicts started by smoking marijuana, it cannot be inferred that the converse is true—that is, that all who started out as marijuana smokers are or will become heroin addicts." The converted statement not only violates a well-established rule of deductive logic, it is also a very different empirical claim whose truth must be independently supported by the evidence.

Example "If one is a Christian, then he or she loves and cares for other people. Therefore, if you love and care for other people, you must be a Christian, whether you call yourself one or not." According to the rule of deduction governing conversion, one cannot reverse the antecedent and the consequent of a conditional statement and retain its same truth value. It is also the case that there are many persons who love and care for other people who are thoroughly engaged in non-Christian religious traditions.

Attacking the Fallacy An absurd example should convince your opponent that conversions of A and O statement are logically illegitimate. From "all chemists are scientists" no opponent is likely to want to conclude that "all scientists are chemists." Neither is he or she likely to want to conclude from "some scientists are not chemists" that "some chemists are not scientists." To attack the false conversion of a conditional statement, you might try the following absurd example to demonstrate its faulty character: "If someone is the President of the United States, that person is at least 35 years old and a natural-born citizen; yet obviously if one is at least 35 years old and a natural-born citizen, one is not necessarily the President of the United States."

Undistributed Middle Term

DEFINITION *This fallacy of syllogistic reasoning consists in inferring a conclusion from two premises, neither of which distributes the middle term.*

A properly formed categorical syllogism is constituted by three statements, two of which are premises and one of which is a conclusion. It also has three and only three terms, each of which appears two and only two times in the argument. One of the terms, the *middle term*, appears in both the premises but not in the conclusion. The other two terms are called "end terms." One end term appears in one premise and the other end term appears in the other premise. They each appear as either the subject or predicate of the conclusion. The following is an example of a well-formed syllogism:

Since all professors are competent, (A)

and no competent people are underpaid, (E)

_____

Therefore, no professors are underpaid. (E)

The middle term of this syllogism is *competent,* and the end terms are *professors* and *underpaid*. The first premise is an A statement and the second premise and the conclusion are both E statements. Since this is a structurally sound argument, we can assume that if the premises are true, the conclusion is necessarily true.

To understand why this argument is structurally sound, it will be necessary to understand at least two rules that govern correctly formed or valid syllogisms. *First, the middle term must be distributed at least once. Second, an end term that is distributed in the conclusion must also be distributed in one of the premises.* There are other rules for the well-formed syllogism, but a syllogism that violates one or more of these other rules usually violates one of the rules just stated; and the violation of a single rule is sufficient for declaring an argument structurally flawed.

If we apply these two rules to the "professors" argument, we will discover that it violates neither of the stated rules. The middle term *competent* is distributed at least once. It is not distributed in the first premise, since it is the predicate of an A statement, but it *is* distributed in the second premise, because it is the subject of an E statement. Therefore, the first rule is satisfied. The end terms *professors* and *underpaid* are both distributed in the conclusion, but they are also both distributed in the premises. Therefore, the second rule is also satisfied. Because the argument satisfies both rules, we can conclude that it has no structural flaws.

The fallacy of the undistributed middle term is committed when an arguer derives a conclusion in a syllogistic argument in which the middle term is distributed in neither of its appearances in the premises. If the middle term makes no claim about all the members of the class designated by the term, there is no basis for determining whether any member of that class is to be included in the generalization expressed by the end terms in the conclusion. Look at the following argument in which the middle term is not distributed:

Since all professors are underpaid,

and all competent people are underpaid,

_____

Therefore, all professors are competent people.

Unless some claim is made about every member of the class of underpaid people, and no such claim is made in this argument, since the middle term is distributed in neither premise, there is nothing that connects the classes represented by the end terms in the conclusion together. Thus, no conclusion can or should be drawn, since we have no way of knowing from the argument whether any member of the class of competent people is in the class of professors, or vice versa.

However, when the middle term is distributed, that problem is solved: "All professors are underpaid (A). All underpaid people are competent people (A). Therefore, all professors are competent people (A)." In this argument's second premise, the middle term is distributed in accordance with the rules, that is, a claim is made about all members of the class of underpaid people, which properly connects the class of professors and competent people. Hence, the conclusion must be true if the premises are true, because it follows necessarily from the premises of this structurally sound argument.

Example "Since some philosophers are poor discussion leaders (I), and some of our professors here are philosophers (I), we know that at least some of our professors are not very good at leading discussions (I)." The middle term *philosophers* is the subject of an I statement in the first premise, which means that it is not distributed and is the predicate of an I statement in the second premise, which means that it is not distributed there either. Since *philosophers* is undistributed, we have no way of knowing whether the professors referred to in the subject of the conclusion are included in the class of poor discussion leaders. In other words, there is nothing in the argument to connect the class of professors with the class of poor discussion leaders. An argument that *would* make that connection would be one in which the *some* philosophers in the first premise is changed to *all* philosophers. Such a change would have the effect of distributing the middle term.

Example Some arguers, intentionally or unintentionally, use the undistributed middle term fallacy to try to bring about a positive view toward a particular political perspective or action: "Democrats care about helping the least advantaged in the society (A). Jesus always cared about helping the least advantaged, too (A). Jesus, no doubt, would have been one of us (A)." Such a conclusion could not be drawn, since the argument is structurally flawed. A middle term that appears in the predicate position of two A statements is not distributed.

Example The arguer can also use the fallacy to try to bring about a negative view toward a particular political perspective or action: "Supporters of the Klan are against gun control (A). Republicans are also against gun control (A). So some Republicans must be supporters of the Klan (I)." That conclusion could not be drawn from this argument. In fact, no claim could be drawn, since it is a structurally flawed argument. As in the last example, the middle term is not distributed.

Attacking the Fallacy Many of the arguers you confront will be unacquainted with either the notion of distribution or the rules of a valid syllogism. However, unless you are acquainted with these matters, you can never be certain that a fallacy has been committed. The absurd example method is, to be sure, a very effective method of demonstrating the fallaciousness of an argument, but an understanding of the mechanics of syllogistic reasoning would surely facilitate a wiser and more confident use of that method. You would then be in a better position to confront your opponent with an example of a syllogism that has true premises and an obviously false conclusion but that follows the same pattern of flawed reasoning exhibited in his or her argument. If the fallacy is that of an undistributed middle term, try this one: "Professors read books. Children read books. Therefore, professors are children."

Illicit Distribution of an End Term

DEFINITION *This fallacy of syllogistic reasoning consists in drawing a conclusion that includes a distributed end term that is not distributed in one of the premises.*

One of the rules governing syllogistic reasoning says that if a term in the conclusion makes a claim about the whole of its class, the "evidence" or premises that support that claim must also make a claim about every member of that class. *Illicit distribution of an end term*, then, is, in effect, a case of making an unsupported claim, for on the basis of what is true of some members of a class, a claim is made about what is true of all members of the class. Since this move violates a well-established rule of deductive reasoning, the argument that contains it must be recognized as a structurally flawed one.

Example "Those who ignore the relevant facts in a situation are likely to come to a false judgment (A), and since no jury in a criminal trial ignores the relevant facts (E), no jury in a criminal trial is likely to come to a false judgment (E)." The fallacy in this one is not at all easy to detect, but a close examination will reveal that one of the end terms, *those who come to a false judgment*, is distributed in the conclusion but not in the premises. The problematic end term appears in the first premise as the predicate of an A statement. But since it is not distributed, no statement is made there about every member of the class of those who come to a false judgment, so no claim about every member of that class can be made in the conclusion. There are surely reasons other than ignoring the facts that could cause a jury to come to a false judgment.

Example "Everything that is morally right is just (A), but some actions that bring about the greatest good for the greatest number are not just (O). Therefore, we would have to conclude that some morally right actions are not actions that would bring about the greatest good for the greatest number of people (O)." The end term, *actions that would bring about the greatest good for the greatest number of people*, is distributed in the conclusion but not distributed in the second premise, because it is the subject of an O statement. In the conclusion, a claim is made about all the members of the class of *actions that would bring about the greatest good for the greatest number of people*, but in the premise a claim is made only about some of the members of that class.

Example "Newly constructed homes are very expensive (A). Nevertheless, new homes are very energy efficient (A). So, an energy-efficient home is going to be expensive (A)." Not necessarily. The end term *energy-efficient homes* makes a claim about all energy-efficient homes in the conclusion but not in the second premise, where it is the predicate term of an A statement. Since the argument is structurally flawed, it cannot be concluded that an energy-efficient home is an expensive one.

Attacking the Fallacy You may attack the fallacy of illicit distribution of an end term by simply citing the rule about distribution. Or you could simply point out, as we have done, that a conclusion has been drawn about all members of a class of things that is based on a premise that makes a claim only about *some* members of that class. In any case, you can always use an example of an argument with true premises and an obviously false conclusion that uses the same pattern of reasoning that is found in the flawed argument. The following argument has the same form as the first example in this section about criminal juries: "Since all fathers have children (A), and no mothers are fathers (E). Therefore, no mothers have children (E)." You might have to use this silly argument if your opponent does want to hear about the technicalities of distribution and the rules of the valid syllogism.

ASSIGNMENTS

C. Fallacies of Deductive Inference   For each of the following arguments, (1) identify the type of fallacy of deductive inference illustrated, and (2) explain how the reasoning violates the structural criterion. There are two examples of each of the fallacies discussed in this section. Arguments marked with an asterisk (*) have sample answers at the end of the text.

1. If Picasso's "Guernica" has artistic merit, then it will be appreciated by most people, and it is. Hence, I think we can conclude that it has artistic merit.

2. We know that the earth is spherically shaped, because spheres always cast curved shadows and we have found that the earth casts a curved shadow on the moon during a lunar eclipse.

3. Since none of our better teachers are tenured, and our tenured faculty members are all very politically conservative, we at least know that none of our better teachers are conservative.

*4. People who obey the law will stay out of trouble with the police. Therefore, it could be concluded that those who have managed to stay out of trouble with the police are those who don't go around breaking the law.

5. If Congress had strong, vigorous leadership, it would be able to override the President's veto on this strip-mining bill. However, because the Congressional leadership has not exhibited any strength whatsoever, Congress will not be able to override the President's veto.

*6. Since most morally justified acts are nonviolent and most acts of civil disobedience are nonviolent, there are at least some acts of civil disobedience that are morally justified.

*7. Sherry: If my mother saw me go into this X-rated movie, I'd really be embarrassed.

   Sarah: Well, obviously your mother is *not* going to see you. You told me that she was out of town for the weekend, so there's no way you're going to be embarrassed by going to this movie.

8. If a person is given a proper upbringing by one's parents, he or she will treat others with respect. So if a person treats others with respect, we must conclude that he or she has indeed been given a proper upbringing.

*9. Esther told me that if she failed Philosophy 101, she would drop out of school. As she has left school, I assume that she failed the course.

*10. Those who are really interested in acquiring the ability to reason correctly will be serious about the study of logic. Those who are serious about studying logic will read this book. Therefore, the people who read this book are people who are genuinely interesting in learning about the proper way to reason.

D. For each of the following arguments (1) identify, from among all the fallacies studied in this chapter, the fallacy illustrated, and (2) explain how the reasoning violates the structural criterion. There are two examples of each fallacy discussed in this chapter.

1. You're not going to vote for a man who would give an interview to a magazine like *Playboy*, are you?

2. Yes, Mr. Brokaw, if I had used the money contributed to my special campaign fund for personal purposes, it *would* have been immoral, but I do not use a penny of it for personal purposes. Therefore there was nothing immoral about having such a fund.

    3. A server to a restaurant patron: "What may I bring you for dessert?"

    4. Since Presidents have the right to use executive privilege as a reason for withholding information, and no Cabinet Officer is the President, no Cabinet Officer can use executive privilege as a reason for withholding information from the special prosecutor.

    5. If he planned on shooting him, he would have to have a gun, and he did own a gun, so he must have killed him.

    6. Since all professors have advanced degrees in a particular field, my advanced degree in biology qualifies me to teach in your biology department.

    7. I think that lying to other people destroys trust and poisons healthy relationships. I've seen it happen over and over again with parents who do not deal honestly with their children when the children are growing up. That's why it is important never to lie to your children—except, of course, for things like Santa Claus and stuff. And sometimes children are just too young to understand the truth, so for their own good, you fudge the truth a little.

    8. Legal measures that would put some controls on corporate monopolies are clearly in the public interest, because the good of the community would be decidedly improved if we could find some legal way of preventing the total control of the production and distribution of a particular service or product by a single corporation.

    9. Beckie: As an American, I can do anything I want. Freedom is what our ancestors fought and died for. Nobody can tell me what to do and what not to do.

    Megan: But there are laws, Beckie. Don't you have to obey the speed limit and not take money that doesn't belong to you?

    Beckie: Well, of course, you have to obey the laws, but the government still can't tell me what to do.

    10. All 18-year-olds are eligible to vote. Of course, some people who are eligible to vote do not exercise their right. Hence, there must be some 18-year-olds who do not exercise their rights.

    11. Dawn: If a man really loves a woman, he wouldn't let her work outside the home.

    Eleanor: But doesn't your daughter teach school? And her husband surely loves her.

    Dawn: Oh, he acts like he loves her, but I'm not so sure about that. If he really loved her, he would insist on being the sole provider.

    12. I just discovered on the Internet last week that if a cat licks antifreeze, it is deadly. I left my cat out last night and I found her dead in the garage this morning. Somehow, she must have got into the antifreeze from my car. Perhaps the radiator was so hot when I came home last night, it spilled over or something.

    13. Client to stockbroker: When are you going to pay me back that $5,000 I gave you that you lost in the stock market?"

    14. Since some unhappy people commit suicide, and some rich people kill themselves, then it must be the case that for some people having lots of money doesn't bring happiness.

    15. Barry: I've been a Baptist all my life, and I believe that the Bible is literally true.

Tim: But there are a number of contradictions in the Bible, such as the two very different creation accounts in Genesis, and there are discrepancies in a number of other stories and events recorded in the Bible.

Barry: Just because there are differences in the accounts of the events doesn't mean that it isn't literally true.

16. If most well-adjusted people do not commit suicide, we can conclude that most people who commit suicide are not well-adjusted.

17. **Professor Withers:** Unless someone wishes to add anything further to the discussion of this absurd issue, I suggest that we move on to the next topic.

18. Deanna must not be home; she said that if the light was on when we came by, we could be assured that she had arrived home and the light is not on.

19. I think that capital punishment for murderers and rapists is quite justified; there are a number of good reasons for putting to death people who commit such crimes.

20. First-time parents experience a lot of anxiety. But they have a right to be anxious. It is a big responsibility to care for a child. But it *does* help to know that those who experience anxiety have good reasons for it.

21. Something cannot be created out of nothing. At least we are not aware of any such phenomenon. In other words, whatever exists must be created out of something else. But we know that before the universe existed, there was nothing. Therefore, God must have created it.

22. **Professor Letson:** All philosophical questions are solvable.

Keiko: But what about the problem of beauty? We haven't solved that problem.

Professor Letson: That's not a philosophical problem.

Keiko: Why is it not a philosophical question?

Professor Letson: Because philosophical questions are solvable and that one isn't.

E. Submit a found or created argument (different from the one submitted for Assignment A in Chapter III but follow the same procedure). Point out any named fallacies that violate the structural criterion. Then construct, with the help of the guidelines for "Making Arguments Stronger" in Chapter III, a stronger argument with the same conclusion.

F. Following the model used in the text, use a 3×5 card to submit an *original* example (found or created) of each of the fallacies that violate the structural criterion.

G. Create your own strategies or suggestions for attacking each of the fallacies that violate the structural criterion.

VI
Fallacies That Violate
the Relevance Criterion

One who presents an argument for or against a position should attempt to set forth only reasons that are directly related to the merit of the position at issue.

The patterns of faulty reasoning discussed in this chapter are fallacies that violate the relevance criterion of a good argument, in that they employ premises that are logically irrelevant to the truth or merit of their conclusions. A premise is relevant if its acceptance provides some reason to believe, counts in favor of, or has some bearing on the truth or merit of the conclusion. A premise is irrelevant if its acceptance has no bearing on, provides no evidence for, or has no connection to the truth or merit of the conclusion.

Arguments with irrelevant premises are often called *non sequiturs*, which means that the conclusion does not follow from the premises. They are also sometimes called *argumentative leaps*, which suggests that since no connection is seen between the premises and the conclusion, a huge leap would be required to move from one to the other.

The fallacies treated in this chapter display irrelevance in a variety of ways. For example, some faulty arguments make an appeal to public opinion or to inappropriate authorities, while others employ reasons that appeal to us on a purely emotional level. These fallacies are divided into two basic categories: (1) fallacies of irrelevance and (2) irrelevant emotional appeals.

FALLACIES OF IRRELEVANCE

The fallacies of irrelevance are those that use premises that are based on irrelevant considerations. One way to do this is to try to make a case for a particular position by quoting an authority who is not really an authority about the matter in question or to try to defend a view by pointing out that the view is held by large numbers of people. Another irrelevant approach is to evaluate a thing in terms of its earlier context, ignoring changes that may have altered its character. Some arguers use premises to try to justify their position that sound plausible but are not the real reasons supporting their conclusions, because they wish to conceal the real reasons for their ideas or actions. Finally, some arguers set forth reasons to try to lead us to a point of view, but then draw a conclusion other than the one that the reasons actually support—or they do the opposite; they make a claim and then produce reasons other than the reasons that would support the claim in question. In all of these cases, the premises are irrelevant to the conclusion.

Irrelevant Authority

DEFINITION   *This fallacy consists in attempting to support a claim by appealing to the judgment of one who is not an authority in the field, the judgment of an unidentified authority, or the judgment of an authority who is likely to be biased.*

An authority in a particular field is one who has access to the knowledge that he or she claims to have, is qualified by training or ability to draw appropriate inferences from that knowledge, and is free from any prejudices or conflicts of interest that would prevent him or her from formulating sound judgments or communicating them honestly.

There is nothing inappropriate about appealing to the judgment of qualified authorities in a field of knowledge as a means of supporting some particular claim related to that field. When the "authority" on whose judgment the argument rests fails to meet the stated criteria, however, the argument should be regarded as fallacious.

The fallacious appeal to authority occurs most frequently in the form of a transfer of an authority's competence in one field to another field in which the authority is *not* competent. An entertainer or athlete, for example, is appealed to as an authority on automobile mufflers or weed-killers; a biologist is called on to support some religious claim; or a politician is treated as an expert on marriage and the family. Indeed, the judgment of a famous and highly respected person is likely to be indiscriminately invoked on almost any subject.

An unidentified authority is questionable because there is no way for us to determine whether the unnamed authority is in fact a qualified one. If we do not know who the authority is, we are not in a position to know whether his or her testimony should count in favor of the claim being defended.

Another type of improper authority is a biased one. Some people may be qualified in a particular field by training, ability, and position, yet they are so vitally "interested" in or affected by the issue at stake that there would be good reason to treat their testimony with suspicion.

If an arguer uses an unqualified, unidentified, or biased authority to support a particular thesis, then he or she has used a premise that is irrelevant to the conclusion. The testimony of an unqualified or biased authority has no bearing on the truth or falsity of the conclusion. The testimony of an unidentified authority may have some bearing on the truth of the conclusion, but because it is unidentified, there is no way to know whether it does so. It must therefore be treated as if it is coming from an irrelevant or questionable authority. When there is contradictory testimony from what appear to be equally qualified and unbiased authorities, the proper response would be to accept the testimony of neither authority, unless you have some independent evidence for accepting the testimony of one and not the other.

Example "It's not true that the government is innocent of any wrongdoing with regard to pollution. I read the other day that government agencies are responsible for more than 50 percent of the country's water pollution." This example of the fallacy of irrelevant authority could be reconstructed in the following way:

> Since some unidentified source says that the government is responsible for 50% of the water pollution in this country,
>
> and water pollution is wrong,
> _____
>
> Therefore, the government wrongfully pollutes the country's water supply.

Although it may be true that the U.S. government is in some sense responsible for much of our water pollution, there is no reason to believe such a claim, because the source of the claim is as yet unidentified. It should be clear that it is not the arguer's honesty that is being questioned. The first premise is irrelevant because we are not in a position to evaluate the qualifications of the source. Hence, the premise cannot count for or against the truth of the conclusion.

Example "I think that we should adopt this new curricular proposal. After all, it has been unanimously endorsed by the college's governing board. The people who are entrusted with running the college should know what they're talking about when it comes to deciding the best curriculum for the school."

In virtually every college or university the governing board turns over the management of the curricular to the faculty, who are the experts on such matters. While members of governing boards may be relevant authorities about fiscal or organizational matters, they are not relevant authorities on curricular matters. Their "endorsement" is primarily a ceremonial or perfunctory action. To use the board as a reason for adopting the curricular is to use an irrelevant authority, which is a violation of the relevance criterion of a good argument.

Example "Senator, if you think that the FBI has been engaging in unauthorized or illegal activities, why don't we ask the director and his staff to testify at this hearing so that we can get to the bottom of this matter? Who is in a better position to testify about FBI operations than the director and his division heads?"

The appeal to authority here would be proper in most inquiries concerning FBI operations; yet such testimony might be questionable if the inquiry were intended to evaluate claims of wrongdoing within the Bureau that might even involve its director.

Attacking the Fallacy If an argument in support of a claim invokes an unidentified authority, a first step in attacking the argument may be to ask for the authority to be identified. If the arguer is able to do this, then you would be in a position to evaluate that authority by the standard criteria. If the arguer is not able to identify the authority, and especially if the claim at issue is a serious one, you should regard the testimony as having no bearing on the claim.

In determining whether an authority is a biased one, you should be careful not to disqualify a source too quickly by claiming that he or she is prejudiced. Unfortunately, it is all too common a practice to find or to fabricate some reason why the judgment of almost any authority might be biased. Such a charge should be registered against an authority who is otherwise qualified only when the possibility of bias is clear and might impede the discovery of the truth. If you suspect that an authority may have a conflict of interest, you might point out the presence of that possible conflict, without in any way accusing the authority of either bias or dishonesty. That will at least get the issue out on the table, so that it can be directly addressed.

Big name endorsements are a big business but, unfortunately, a fallacy-ridden business. If an argument uses an authority in one field to support a claim in another, you might use an absurd example like this: "That would be like using Michael Jordan, the former Chicago Bulls superstar, to support a claim about Chevrolet trucks." That should convince the arguer about the inappropriateness of his or her own move. If the response is "That's different!" ask him or her to explain just where the difference lies.

Finally, do not be intimidated when great names are used in support of various claims. Shakespeare, Socrates, Jesus, Mark Twain, Abraham Lincoln, Will Rogers, Billy Graham, John Kennedy, and many other famous and well-respected people were or are experts, if at all, in very limited ranges of subject matter, and they are not at all qualified to speak authoritatively in most other areas of human concern.

Appeal to Common Opinion

DEFINITION   *This fallacy consists in urging the acceptance of a position simply on the grounds that a large number of people accept it or in urging the rejection of a position on the grounds that very few people accept it.*

Two other names sometimes given to this fallacy are *bandwagon fallacy* and *consensus gentium*. The bandwagon notion suggests that an idea or action must be true or good because everyone is accepting it or jumping on it as if it were a wagon full of musicians in a circus parade. *Consensus gentium* is literally translated "consent of the people." If a claim or idea is accepted by a majority, we are often led to believe that it is true or worthy of our belief also. However, the truth or merit of an idea is in no way dependent on the number of people who support it.

Nevertheless, we commonly infer that a film is a good one if there are long lines of people waiting to see it, or we infer that a restaurant serves good food if there are a great number of cars outside it. Remember, however, that crowds are not usually noted for sound judgments and that a number of other factors could account for the long lines and the large number of cars.

An argument that uses the number of people that accept or reject an idea as a premise for determining its merit uses an irrelevant premise. An argument that employs such a premise as its principal and perhaps only support cannot qualify as a good one, because the criteria of a good argument require that the premises have a bearing on the truth or falsity of the argument's conclusion.

Example   "If tanning beds were really unsafe, then millions of Americans would not be using them every week. Neither can the sun be all that harmful to your skin. Virtually everyone I know goes to the beach every year for one primary purpose—

the sun. Do you know anyone who goes to the beach and then sits inside the hotel or beach house?"

What large numbers of beachgoers and tanning salon users think is the truth is irrelevant to what is actually the case. Neither should anything be inferred about the issue from what large numbers of tan-seekers actually do. Consider the argument as it is expressed in standard form:

> Since millions of Americans use tanning beds every week and go to beaches every year to enjoy the sun's tanning rays,
>
> and what large numbers of people do must not be harmful,
> _____
>
> Therefore, the use of tanning beds and sunbathing on the beach are activities that are not harmful to the skin.

Once the argument is in standard form, it is difficult to believe that anyone would think that the conclusion follows from the premises presented. This, of course, is one of the benefits of reconstruction. The mere sight of the argument in standard form often reveals the flaw.

Example   "Marijuana can't be all wrong. According to a recent Gallup survey published in yesterday's *Wall Street Journal*, more than 60 percent of the adult American population sees nothing wrong with it."

The benefits or dangers of smoking marijuana cannot be ascertained by taking a poll. Polls may indicate what people are thinking, doing, or anticipate doing, but very little regarding the truth or merit of an idea, claim, or action can be inferred from such surveys.

Example   "I'm going to buy Eminem's new album. It's been at the top of the charts for more than a month. It must be a good one."

What large numbers of people do or believe tells us nothing more than what large numbers of people do or believe. It tells nothing about the quality of the thing in question.

Attacking the Fallacy   Since this fallacy is so tempting to commit, we perhaps should remind ourselves daily to infer nothing about anything on the basis of what large groups or even the majority of people believe. The weight of public opinion is simply not relevant to the matter of whether a claim is true.

You might also remind the arguer that public opinion is quite fickle. To illustrate your point, find some reliable poll that shows a shift in public support from one candidate or side of an issue to another, and ask the arguer if the truth of a claim or the rightness of an action shifts with each shift in the polls. Although it is unlikely that anyone would answer "yes" to such a question, you should be prepared to point out that such thinking could lead to the absurd conclusion that a claim is both true and false, depending on when the people are surveyed.

If your opponent is still unconvinced, you could remind him or her about beliefs from both science and history that were at one time held to be true by large numbers of people, yet turned out to be false. Or you could cite examples of claims that at one time most people believed to be false but that turned out to be true. Probably the best strategy would be to use examples from your opponent's own experience. You might refer, for example, to a claim that the arguer had recently and correctly assessed as false, even in the face of its being believed to be true by large numbers of people.

Genetic Fallacy

DEFINITION *This fallacy consists in evaluating a thing in terms of its earlier context and then carrying over that evaluation to the thing in the present, while ignoring relevant changes that may have altered its character in the interim.*

The genetic fallacy occurs when one attempts to reduce the significance of an idea, person, practice, or institution merely to an account of its origin or genesis, thereby overlooking the development, regression, or difference to be found in it in the present situation. One who commits this fallacy typically transfers the positive or negative esteem that he or she has for the thing in its original context or earlier forms to the thing in its present form.

The genetic fallacy thus exhibits a pattern of reasoning that fails to meet the relevance criterion of a good argument—that the premises must have a bearing on the truth or falsity of the claim in question. Since the origin of a thing rarely has any relevance to its present merit, an argument that uses such a premise as a basis for accepting or rejecting a claim about the thing in question should be regarded as a flawed one.

Example "You're not going to wear a wedding ring, are you? Don't you know that the wedding ring originally symbolized the ankle chains worn by women to prevent them from running away from their husbands? I would not have thought you would be a party to such a sexist practice."

There may be reasons why people may not wish to wear wedding rings, but it would be logically inappropriate for a couple to reject the notion of exchanging wedding rings on the sole grounds of its alleged sexist origins. The argument in standard form might look like this:

Since wedding rings were originally symbols of ankle chains placed upon women by their husbands,

(and the symbol means the same thing now as it did then),

and such actions would constitute a sexist practice,

Therefore, one who follows this practice now is engaging in a sexist practice.

Since the second premise is clearly false or unacceptable, the first premise must be declared as irrelevant. This is so because how things were in their origins is not relevant to how they should be assessed in the present, if those things have changed and are no longer like their origin. Since one premise of the argument is false and another now seen as irrelevant, the conclusion does not follow from the remaining premise.

Example The genetic fallacy is sometimes committed by religious leaders and others who forbid certain practices on the basis of their supposed origins. For example, some religious groups have argued that "a good Christian" should not dance, because dancing was originally used in pagan mystery cults as a way of worshiping pagan gods. Even if there were good reasons to argue against some forms of dance, the alleged genesis of the dance is not one of them.

Example   "I wouldn't vote for Derek Kestner for anything. You see, I grew up with him. We went to grade school together. He was just one big 'goof-off.' You couldn't depend on him for anything. I shudder to think of his being governor of any state in which I lived."

The arguer here is assuming that Kestner is the same kind of person now that he was when he was in grade school. The speaker overlooks the possibility that he may have matured or changed into quite a different person than he was then.

Attacking the Fallacy   Getting an arguer to disregard the origin or original context of an idea or thing is not easy. Strong emotional responses connected to those origins are particularly difficult to dismiss. Consider, for example, how difficult it is to evaluate objectively the attractiveness of a mate's suit or dress that was selected by a former lover. Where a thing comes from tends to have a rather potent effect on the way we evaluate it. Nevertheless, it is important to try to dismiss such factors in our deliberations about their worth. When an opponent uses such considerations, it would be appropriate to ask what there is about the thing itself that he or she finds either objectionable or worthwhile.

To demonstrate the appropriateness of separating the worth of a thing from how it started, consider an emotional issue such as one's love for a mate. Ask the arguer if he or she would feel any differently about his or her mate if it were just discovered that their first meeting or "date" was part of an elaborate practical joke or, even worse, a case of mistaken identity. Such an undesirable beginning surely would be regarded as irrelevant to the assessment of the present worth of the relationship. If the arguer can make that kind of separation in this case, he or she should be able to do it with regard to other matters.

If you need an absurd example to convince another of the irrelevance of origins, try this: "You say that Jacob is a great chef, but I remember how as a kid, he used to make pies out of mud. I'm not about to eat any food prepared by him. There's no telling what might be in it." No person would consider Jacob's mud pie past as relevant to the present, but the form of the argument is no different from many other arguments that some persons unfortunately seem to find convincing.

Rationalization

> **DEFINITION**   *This fallacy consists in using plausible-sounding but usually fake reasons to justify a particular position that is held on other, less respectable grounds.*

Rationalization is properly described as a violation of the relevance criterion of a good argument, because the argument's fake premises are not relevant to the conclusion. The stated premises have little or no relationship to the conclusion, because they are not the real reasons for the conclusion drawn. Because of embarrassment, fear, or some other unknown cause, the real reasons are unstated or concealed.

The general character of rationalization has to do with defending an action or belief rather than with trying to determine whether it has merit. Rationalization, then, is a kind of dishonest substitute for good reasoning. In good arguments, the belief or conclusion follows from the evidence. In rationalization, the "evidence" comes after the belief has already been determined. The rationalizer is simply using premises that make his or her questionable position or action appear to be rationally respectable.

Some instances of this fallacy could be construed as also violating the acceptability criterion of a good argument. Since the premises are simply "made up" for the purpose of defending an action or propping up a belief arrived at on other grounds, they are not likely to be true or acceptable ones, which is another reason why they do not support the conclusion.

Example   Miguel, a senior philosophy major at a small college, says to Professor Stone, "I didn't do well on the Law School Admissions Test. You see, I just don't do very well on tests. Tests just don't show my real ability. Besides, the day before I took the LSAT, I had some really bad news from home. I'll do better next time."

Miguel is probably rationalizing. He is trying to give plausible-sounding reasons for his weak performance on the LSAT, but the reasons sound hollow. They cannot bear the weight that he places on them. He wishes not only to cover his embarrassment but also to offset the effect of his poor LSAT score on Professor Stone's image of him. Miguel's argument in standard form looks like this:

> Since I do not perform well on tests,
>
> and tests do not demonstrate my real grasp of the test material,
>
> and I received disturbing news the day before the test,
>
> _____
>
> Therefore, I cannot be expected to perform well on the Law School Admissions Test.

If Miguel is a senior philosophy major, he has probably taken many tests and performed decently on them, or he would never have made it to the senior level. If for some reason he really does not do well on tests, that fact would probably already be known to Professor Stone and he would not need to be reminded of it.

An experienced professor would also probably discount the "I had bad news from home" reason for a poor performance and see it for what it probably is—a backup argument in case the "I do not do well on tests" reason does not work. Indeed, the dragging in of the backup argument is a very good clue to the fact that a rationalization is in progress. If this analysis seems harsh or insensitive, it must be remembered that when dealing with what appears to be a rationalization, some such analysis must be done in order to get beyond the fake reasons and to try to address the real reasons for the poor performance. The real reason may be that some parts of the LSAT are simply very difficult and in order to do better on those parts the next time around, Miguel would need to focus on developing the skills required for those parts of the test. However, as long as he insists on giving fake reasons for the poor performance, not only does it not adequately help others to understand the results, it might even prevent him from improving on them.

Example   After losing a boyfriend to another young woman, Sofia says, "Well, I was going to dump him anyway. It was really getting boring having him around. I should have left him long ago; I just felt sorry for him."

Sofia is trying to deal with the fact that the relationship with her boyfriend is over. To make that break more personally palatable, she finds fake reasons to justify it to herself and to anyone who cares to listen.

Example "I suppose I really should have gone to my cousin's wedding, but we have never really been close. And I only met the bride one time. She probably wouldn't even remember me. Besides, I really didn't know what to buy them for a wedding gift. From what I hear, they have everything a couple would need. Anyway, there were so many people there, they surely did not miss me."

This bit of rationalization is familiar to most of us. The real reasons for not going to the wedding were probably less admirable. This person perhaps didn't want to spend the money for the gift, didn't want to get dressed up, or simply preferred to watch a ballgame on television. The stated reasons, then, probably had little or no relevance to or connection with the decision made.

Attacking the Fallacy Let your rationalizing opponent know that you have reason to believe that you have not heard the real argument. You may ask for the arguer to give you the real reasons for the action or belief, but since the rationalizer is probably engaging in a bit of face-saving behavior—the very reason for the rationalization—it is not likely that you will get a straight story. The rationalizer has a vested interest to protect, and revealing the actual reasons would jeopardize that interest. Therefore, you will probably have to concentrate your attack on the *stated* argument, as we did with Miguel's argument about the LSAT.

You might also ask if the arguer would still hold to the belief or defend the action if the stated premises turned out to be false or irrelevant. If the arguer answers "yes," he or she is admitting that the premises are not relevant to the conclusion drawn and the argument is therefore a faulty one. If the arguer answers "no," you might try to find some way of demonstrating that the premises are indeed false or irrelevant in order to call what you think is the rationalizer's bluff. If the attack is successful, the best result would be for the arguer to either abandon the belief or alter the action.

Since rationalization could be justifiably construed as an act of deliberate dishonesty, the rationalizer perhaps deserves to suffer moral embarrassment at being caught giving fake and therefore irrelevant reasons for holding a belief or engaging in a particular action. However, since our main purpose is to get at the truth, we ought to focus all our efforts on finding the *real* reasons rather than on exposing the arguer's dishonesty. If we could discover the reasons, we would then be in a position to evaluate the real argument in terms of the standard criteria.

Drawing the Wrong Conclusion

DEFINITION   *This fallacy consists in drawing a conclusion other than the one supported by the evidence presented in the argument.*

The fallacy of drawing the wrong conclusion is often referred to as the fallacy of missing the point, as in "missing the point of the evidence." The argument in its conclusion misses the main thrust of the evidence provided. Even though this is one of the fallacies of irrelevance, it is not just a typical case of an arguer using an irrelevant premise or two. This is an argument in which a well-developed evidential case for a particular conclusion is presented, at the end of which the arguer simply draws the wrong conclusion from his or her own premises. The target of the argument is poised to receive the conclusion to which the evidence seems to be leading and is startled when the arguer draws a very different one. Even though the conclusion purports to follow from the evidence, the evidence presented actually supports some other, although perhaps related, conclusion. However, the evidence has little or no bearing on the truth or merit of the stated conclusion. For that reason, the argument violates the relevance criterion of a good argument.

In some cases, reasoning in a way that draws the wrong conclusion or misses the point of the evidence may be deliberate. An example is the prosecutor who is allegedly supporting the claim that a defendant is guilty of rape, but who presents "evidence" that supports another conclusion—namely, that the rape was a heinous crime. The prosecutor hopes, of course, that the jury will infer the stated conclusion ("the defendant is guilty of this rape") rather than the unstated one ("the rape was a heinous crime"), which is the one actually supported by the evidence presented. But the jury should not do so. If it does draw the "guilty" conclusion, it too will be drawing the wrong conclusion from the evidence.

In some cases, drawing the wrong conclusion occurs because of carelessness in the formation of the argument. However, in most cases the wrong conclusion is drawn because of the subtle, perhaps even unconscious, prejudices of the arguer. The arguer may want the conclusion to be true so much that he or she draws that conclusion, even though it is not the conclusion supported by the evidence presented. For example, if the arguer is concerned about society's unfair treatment of women, all the evidence of sexist behavior in society might be brought forth in support of a plea for a particular piece of equal rights legislation. But although that evidence may support a claim that ours is a sexist culture, it would not necessarily support the claim that a particular piece of legislation should be enacted.

This fallacy is one of the clearest expressions of the violation of the relevance criterion. Since the criteria of a good argument require that premises have a bearing on the truth or merit of the conclusion, and since the premises in this kind of argument have little or no relevance to the truth of the conclusion, such an argument cannot be a good one. Given the evidence presented, the arguer should have drawn a different conclusion.

Example   At the time of the Supreme Court decision concerning the Texas sodomy case, President George W. Bush held a press conference and was asked about the court action. He indicated what appeared to be support for the position of the court, that consenting adult citizens, whether heterosexual or homosexual, have a right to privacy with regard to their sexual behavior. When asked about gay or lesbian marriage, however, he said that he believed in the sanctity of marriage, and therefore he believed that marriage should be between a man and a woman. If the President's remarks can be construed as an argument, it would look like this in standard form:

Since I believe in the sanctity of marriage,

(And that means that marriage is a very important social institution),

(And as President, I support useful and important social institutions),

---

Therefore, I believe that marriage should be between a man and a woman.

In the President's argument, the move to the conclusion is a jarring argumentative leap. No reason is given to show the connection between the "sanctity" of marriage and the conclusion that it should take place only between a man and a woman. If the Principle of Charity suggests that the listener should construe the meaning of "sanctity" as "holy" or "sacred," rather than "an important social institution," it is still not clear, without further evidence, what the connection is between the claim about the "sacredness" of marriage and the President's conclusion that it should be between a man and a woman. Most of us, of course, are not so naive as to be unaware that he was walking a tightrope with his constituency on this issue. Nevertheless, the President clearly seems to have drawn the wrong conclusion.

Example "The present method of evaluating public school teachers, which, at best, is an occasional perfunctory check by an administrator, is quite inadequate. If a teacher turns out to be a poor one, there is presently no effective way of getting rid of him or her. Therefore, teachers should be hired for a 'term of service,' after which they will reenter the job market, seeking jobs through the usual screening processes."

There may be good reasons for hiring teachers for terms of service, but that conclusion does not follow from the evidence presented. A more relevant conclusion might be that some method of systematic evaluation should be instituted that would provide a defensible basis for discharging incompetent teachers.

Example "Reporters keep the public informed, and we all know that a well-informed public is necessary to bring about any semblance of justice. Besides, reporters keep public officials and others 'honest' by digging out the facts behind their claims and exposing them when they don't tell the truth or when they engage in questionable practices. Therefore, I think that the courts are grossly unfair to newspaper reporters when they force them to go to prison just because they won't reveal the sources of their information."

The weight of evidence in this argument supports the view that newspaper reporters perform a very useful and important service for their readers; it does not support the claim that the courts have been unfair to reporters. That particular conclusion is the wrong conclusion to draw from the evidence presented.

Attacking the Fallacy In responding to this fallacy, it might be helpful to point out what conclusion the evidence *does* support, in order to encourage the arguer to change his or her conclusion to the right one. Since the arguer is not likely to agree that his or her conclusion was the wrong one to draw from the evidence, be prepared to be patient in helping him or her to line up the right evidence with the right conclusion. If the arguer is not interested in the "right" conclusion—that is, the one to which you are led by the evidence—and insists on focusing on the original conclusion, you should make clear that that conclusion requires some very different evidence.

Using the Wrong Reasons

DEFINITION *This fallacy consists in attempting to support a claim with reasons other than the reasons appropriate to the claim.*

This fallacy may best be described as the reverse of the fallacy of drawing the wrong conclusion. The difference between the fallacy of drawing the wrong conclusion and the fallacy of using the wrong reasons is found by looking at where the emphasis lies in the context of the argument. If the arguer, in a rush to get to the favored conclusion, simply misses the point of his or her own evidence, the fallacy of drawing the wrong conclusion has been committed. But if the arguer is attempting to defend a particular conclusion, for which relevant evidence may be available, but uses some other evidence instead, he or she has committed the fallacy of using the wrong reasons. In the case of using the wrong reasons, the conclusion is usually uttered *before* the premises, while in the case of drawing the wrong conclusion, the conclusion is usually drawn *after* the presentation of the premises.

Why would arguers give the wrong reasons for their conclusions? In some instances, it could simply be a case of carelessness. Because the arguer is already convinced of the truth of the conclusion, almost any evidence that sounds related is taken as being supportive. It is also often the case that the arguer started with the conclusion and then was simply unable to find the right or relevant evidence to support it.

This fallacy is commonly committed in the arena of political debate—particularly when one is arguing *against* something. For example, one often hears arguments against a policy or program on the grounds that it does not or would not achieve certain goals. But when these are goals that the program or policy was never designed or expected to achieve, the reasons given for the negative evaluation of the policy are the wrong reasons. The arguer has arbitrarily assigned goals and functions to a program and then criticized it for not achieving those goals.

Almost any program, policy, or piece of legislation has limitations that its designers quite readily recognize. Moreover, few programs, when implemented, are such that their most ideal consequences can be or are expected to be fulfilled. Therefore, when these results are not achieved, that is not a sufficient justification for abandoning the program. This is especially true if the program may accomplish some other goal or perform some other important function that might not otherwise be brought about. There may be some good or relevant reasons for abandoning a particular program, but those reasons must be relevant to the realistic and/or expected goals and functions of the program. Otherwise, the judgment against it uses the wrong reasons.

Example "Certain population groups should not be targeted by tobacco advertising. Tobacco has been shown to cause cancer, it is an expensive habit, and it is offensive to family members, associates, and others who have to put up with the smoker's smoke." When put into standard form, the argument looks like this:

Since tobacco has been shown to cause cancer,

and tobacco is expensive,

and secondhand smoke is offensive to others,

Therefore, specific population groups should not be targeted by tobacco advertising.

When put into standard form, the argument looks like a case of drawing the wrong conclusion, but it must be remembered that in the original argument the arguer started with the conclusion and was clearly attempting to support that conclusion—with the wrong reasons. The reasons given may all be true and good reasons not to smoke; however, they have very little to do with the main issue here. Very different reasons would be required to bring someone to the conclusion that specific population groups should not be targeted by tobacco advertisers.

Example The following is a summary of a typical conversation between many a college philosophy major and his or her critics.

> **Lynn:** Do you really think that philosophy will ever solve all of our problems?
> **Owen:** No, probably not.
> **Lynn:** Then why are you wasting your time studying it?

What the critic fails to recognize is that no philosopher would ever claim that philosophy can solve all human problems. The philosopher simply claims that philosophical inquiry can be very effective in helping us to solve many of our problems. There would be no justification for abandoning it simply because it is not effective in helping us to solve all of them. Lynn has used the wrong reasons for her conclusion that a major in philosophy is a waste of time.

Example Many critics of gun-control legislation have argued that, because gun-control laws will not prevent criminals from using guns in the course of committing crimes, there is no good reason to pass such legislation. But those critics are using the wrong reasons to come to their conclusion against gun-control legislation.

The proponents of gun-control legislation recognize that it will probably have only a limited effect on the control of crime. They know that the serious criminal will not be significantly affected by the restricted sale and registration of guns. Since the legislation is proposed with full awareness of this limitation, it would not be fair or relevant for a critic to argue against it on those grounds. The legislation, however, could serve other very important functions, such as making guns less readily available as a means for settling domestic quarrels. Moreover, gun-control might have the effect of reducing the number of accidental killings. Hence, in spite of its limitations, proponents think that there are very good reasons for passing legislation that would control gun use. An argument *against* gun control that used relevant reasons would be one that showed that the stated functions of the legislation could not be accomplished by enacting it or that some other more important principle was in conflict with the proposal.

Attacking the Fallacy The situation in which many of us encounter the kind of faulty reasoning that uses the wrong reasons is one in which we may tend to agree with the conclusion of an arguer, but not for the reasons given in his or her argument. One way to be helpful to the arguer in such a situation is to say something like this: "I find that you have an interesting idea, and it might even be a defensible one, but not for the reasons you give." You might even suggest some reasons that seem more relevant and more supportive of the claim at issue.

One way to prevent a critic from inappropriately assigning irrelevant goals and functions to proposed programs and policies as a basis for a negative evaluation is to make every effort to specify up front the limited goals of the program or policy. It might even be helpful to remind your listener of your awareness of such limitations as often as possible. The critic may thereby be prevented from taking a "cheap shot" at the program. If the critic persists, make it clear that he or she is attacking a misrepresentation of the claim—that is, a claim that no one is making.

ASSIGNMENTS

A. Fallacies of Relevance For each of the following arguments, (1) identify the type of fallacy of irelevance illustrated, and (2) explain how the reasoning violates the relevance criterion. There are two examples of each fallacy discussed in this section. Arguments marked with an asterisk (*) have sample answers at the end of the text.

*1. I think we should hire Karen Cox as the new third-grade teacher. She lives here in the community, she has children in school here, she loves to work with children, and she has been active in the PTA.

*2. A pregnant bride should not wear white! A white wedding dress symbolizes purity. And you, Debra, hardly qualify!

*3. Your honor, Dr. Chamberlain is a respected psychiatrist and has been a friend of the defendant's family for many years. She is in a unique position to be able to testify as to the state of the defendant's mental health at the time of the crime.

*4. Yes, I subscribe to *Playboy*, but I do it for the great articles in there. There was a great piece last month taking a new look at Bill Clinton's presidency.

*5. Many people without Ph.D.'s are much better teachers than people with Ph.D.'s. Getting a Ph.D. doesn't make one a better teacher. Therefore, I don't think we should hire a person with a Ph.D. to fill this position in our chemistry department.

*6. I don't see why you don't want to take your husband's name when you get married. The vast majority of Americans obviously think it should be done that way. It's hard to believe that that many people could be wrong!

7. I wasn't invited, but I wouldn't have gone anyway. I just don't care to spend my time with such snobs. Besides, I've already been skiing twice this winter.

8. Grades don't really give us much information about a student. If a prospective employer or graduate school were to find from a transcript that a student got a B– in a particular course, very little could be inferred about the particular character or quality of his or her work in that course. Hence, I think that we ought to go to a simple pass-fail system.

9. The voters of Massachusetts overwhelmingly defeated a proposed gun-control law in the state, which proves that gun control is not a good idea.

10. No, I don't want my boy to join the Boy Scouts. Did you know that the Boy Scouts were organized as a paramilitary organization? They even trained the young boys in accordance with a military scouting manual. The word *Scouts* in Boy Scouts literally refers to military scouts. None of my children is going to join such an organization with my blessing.

11. Henry: I've gone off my diet. It just wasn't working.

Richard: But I thought it was working really well. Haven't you already lost about 20 pounds?

Henry: Sure, I've lost weight, but my social life hasn't improved one bit!

12. Joy: Did you know that interference from in-laws is the number one cause of divorce in this country?

Teresa: Really? How do you know?

Joy: I heard it on *Oprah* yesterday.

IRRELEVANT EMOTIONAL APPEALS

A number of arguers deliberately bypass the reasoning process altogether and attempt to persuade others by means of emotional techniques. In addition to violating the relevance criterion of a good argument, any success that this approach enjoys is probably short-lived. A person who is convinced on emotional grounds alone is less likely to sustain that belief or the acceptance of the idea over the long haul. The most common of these appeals, which are discussed in this section, are appeals to the traditional way of doing things, appeals that threaten or force another into accepting a view, appeals that target the self-interest of the victim, and finally, a variety of appeals that attempt to manipulate a person's strong natural feelings, attitudes, and prejudices as a means of gaining acceptance for an idea or action.

Appeal to Force or Threat

DEFINITION   *This fallacy consists in attempting to persuade others of a position by threatening them with some undesirable state of affairs instead of presenting evidence for one's view.*

There is nothing wrong, of course, with pointing out the consequences of a particular course of action. In fact, if certain consequences are a natural outcome of an action, calling attention to them might be very much appreciated. In some such cases, being aware of the consequences of an action might even cause one to alter one's course. However, if an arguer tries to force another to accept the truth of a claim or the rightness of an action by threatening some undesirable action, then the arguer is guilty of using an irrelevant appeal, which is a clear violation of the relevance criterion of a good argument.

One particular form of this fallacy is called *authoritarianism*. Authoritarianism consists in appealing to someone as an authority, not because of that person's skill, knowledge, or expertise in a field but because of his or her power or influence over the one to whom the argument is directed. In such a case, a threat-laden demand for submission to that authority takes the place of relevant evidence in behalf of the truth of a belief or the rightness of an action.

In most cases, the appeal to force is used to lead another not to a particular belief but to a course of action. Suppose that a lobbyist for the American Association of Retired Persons (AARP) asks a congresswoman to vote for a particular piece of legislation, as he reminds her that the AARP represents 10,000 voters in her Florida district. Unfortunately, the implicit threat is not relevant to the rightness of the action sought. Even though such an appeal to force may bring about the desired action, it is not because a good argument was presented. His argument could not qualify as a good one, because the threatening premise has no bearing on the merit of the conclusion.

Example   Many of us are aware of cases of sexual harassment in which a graduate school supervisor may demand sexual favors from a graduate student over whom he or she has control in return for continuation in the Ph.D. program. In such cases, the supervisor has not persuaded the victim of the rightness of the action—only that cooperation may be necessary to maintain one's present status. Hence, the threat may be effective, even though the argument is a bad one. To see clearly how bad it is, let us convert the argument into standard form:

Since I want you to have sex with me,

(and I have virtual absolute control over your future professional life),

(and you do not want anything to jeopardize your professional life),

(and I will jeopardize it if you don't have sex with me),

Therefore, you will have sex with me.

Such an argument would not convince anyone of the rightness of the action sought, but it has probably brought about compliance with the request more often than one might think. In other words, it is a potent device to achieve results, but it is not a good argument, because the implicit threatening premise along with the other implicit premises that are employed in such arguments are irrelevant ones.

Example   The following exchange is another example of authoritarian thinking.

Student: Professor Boltwood, why do we have to type our homework?

Professor Boltwood: Because that is what I require.

The student is asking why the class members are required to type their homework assignments, but Professor Boltwood responds in an authoritarian fashion. He simply appeals to his power over the students to force their compliance. His argument is fallacious, for it implicitly issues a threat instead of giving relevant reasons for typing the homework.

Example   A local businesswoman reminds the editor of a local newspaper that she spends a lot of advertising dollars in the paper and would prefer that the story concerning her recent arrest for drunk driving not appear in it. This is clearly an attempt at intimidation. She gives no reasons why it should not appear there, other than the implied threat that the newspaper will experience a loss of revenue if it does. A threat is not a relevant reason for doing or not doing something. It may work, but it shouldn't, for it has no bearing on the issue at stake.

Attacking the Fallacy   It is sometimes difficult to withstand the pressure of a threat, particularly when it comes, as it usually does, from someone with the power to place you in a very vulnerable situation. Indeed, your ability or inclination to reject such irrelevant appeals may depend on your own sense of personal, economic, and professional security. Nevertheless, one who is guilty of appealing to force or threat should at least be exposed. One way of doing this might be to say to such a person, "I know what you're going to do to me if I don't accept your position, but are there any good reasons for believing your position to be true or right?"

Appeal to Tradition

DEFINITION   *This fallacy consists in attempting to persuade others of a point of view by appealing to their feelings of reverence or respect for some tradition instead of to evidence, especially when there is some more important principle or issue at risk.*

The comfortable or warm feelings that we may have for a particular traditional way of doing things may be one reason we revere it, but such feelings are not a reason for regarding the tradition as the best way of doing things, especially when a more important principle may be at stake. Good feelings cannot be an appropriate substitute for evidence.

Emotional attachments to the past are common and pleasant experiences for almost all of us. It is also true that many traditions perform social functions of great importance. Insofar as they embody the distilled wisdom of earlier generations, they relieve us of the burden of having to invent our own solutions to the problems created by social interaction.

But there is also a dark and negative side to many traditions. Even though most traditions might originally have had good reasons behind them, those reasons may no longer be relevant considerations. Powerful traditions can perpetuate earlier injustices and stifle creative approaches to life or to better ways of doing things. Indeed, the English philosopher John Stuart Mill claimed that "the despotism of custom is everywhere the standing hindrance to human advancement."

To point out that a particular practice has the status of a tradition sheds no light on whether it is a wise or foolish one. When there is no more important principle at stake, the appeal to tradition is neither a fallacy nor a matter that should concern us. But if holding to a tradition threatens to prevent a solution that enlightened reflection supports, then any positive aspects it may embody must be weighed against the damage that it may inflict. If a tradition has serious negative or harmful features connected with it, then the fact that it is a tradition should be a minor consideration in its support—good feelings aside.

An argument that attempts to persuade by an appeal to tradition when other important considerations are at issue is using an irrelevant premise, which is a violation of the relevance criterion of a good argument. The rightness of an action or the truth of a claim in such a context is not supported by the fact that it is part of a tradition.

Example   "I just don't understand why you and Daniel didn't have your baby circumcised. You can't just abandon a long tradition like that, Denise. Boys have always been circumcised in our culture. When Jimmy is a little older and realizes that he is out of step with the rest of the male world, whatever reason you may have had for not having him circumcised is not really going to matter." Let us see how this argument looks in standard form:

Since boys in our culture have always been circumcised,

and an uncircumcised boy will sooner or later feel self-conscious about his body,

(and we ought to follow tradition, unless it conflicts with something more important),

and there is nothing more important than following the tradition of circumcision,

---

Therefore, parents should have their boys circumcised.

In this argument, the reason given for circumcising non-Jewish boys is that it is a tradition. However, the appeal to tradition is irrelevant in this case, because there are several larger issues at stake that should take precedence over a concern for the comfortableness of a tradition. First, the original religious basis of circumcision is no longer a relevant consideration for non-Jewish parents. Second, attempts to defend the practice on the grounds of health are no longer generally supported by health professionals. The comfortableness of tradition would therefore not appear to be strong enough to override the financial costs and the extreme pain connected to the practice of parents' altering the bodies of their male children.

Example   "But, John, our family has always been Southern Baptist. Your grandfather was a Southern Baptist minister, and you have two uncles who are Southern Baptist ministers. Your mother's family has also always been Southern Baptist. I just don't understand how you could even think of joining the Methodist church."

John's father has pointed out several facts to John in order to impress on him the family tradition. However, the more important ecclesiastical or theological considerations that are at stake in this situation are given no attention at all; only feelings of reverence for a family tradition are considered.

Example   "When I was in public school, we had prayer every day at the beginning of the school session. It was a very meaningful thing for me. I just don't see why my children can't have the same kind of experience."

No counterargument is offered here that considers the more important principle at stake, addressed by the Supreme Court argument that required prayer in public schools constitutes an "establishment of religion"; the only appeal is to the comfortableness of a tradition.

Example   "Virginia Military Institute should never have allowed women to enroll. Ever since Stonewall Jackson, VMI has been an all-male school. My father graduated from there and went on to fight and die in Korea. He would turn over in his grave if he knew that women are now allowed to go to VMI."

Several issues greater than tradition are at stake here. First, VMI. is a tax-supported public college. Second, the school has always discriminated against women in its admissions policy. Third, the courts have said that the school cannot do that. In other words, these political, moral, and judicial considerations clearly take precedence over the feelings of reverence for a tradition—no matter how deeply they are felt.

Attacking the Fallacy   Assure your verbal opponent that there is nothing intrinsically wrong with doing things in a traditional way. In fact, you might even admit that you, too, often feel more comfortable with traditional ways of doing things. When nothing else is at stake, following family or cultural traditions should probably be encouraged. However, you should also point out that if a more important principle is in conflict with that tradition, then there is a good reason for changing a traditional way of acting or discontinuing a particular practice. In such cases, a reverence for the past is not a relevant consideration in the process of determining what to do in the present.

Appeal to Self-Interest

DEFINITION   *This fallacy consists in urging an opponent to accept or reject a particular position by appealing solely to his or her personal circumstances or self-interest, when there is some more important issue at stake.*

An argument that appeals to the personal circumstances or self-interest of another when there may be more important issues at stake is using a premise that is not relevant to the merit of the question at issue. What is usually regarded as a more important issue is one that significantly affects other people and/or one that might have a greater impact on society both now and in the future. Satisfaction of personal self-interest is not a relevant consideration when addressing those issues.

Almost all of our daily decisions and actions are legitimately motivated by a consideration of what would be advantageous to our personal life and welfare and the welfare of our family and friends. When it does not cloud or take precedence over considerations directly related to a larger issue, consideration of the effect of an action or policy on one's personal life may be quite appropriate. But when larger issues are at stake, an argument that appeals solely to personal circumstances would be a violation of the relevance criterion of a good argument. The effect that a proposed public policy might have on one's personal life has no bearing on whether it is a good idea. For example, the fact that Senator Blaney happens to own a second home in Washington, D.C., should not be a consideration in whether or not he votes for a tax bill that disallows the taking of interest on a second home mortgage as a tax deduction. If the Senator thinks that passing such a bill would have good effects on the economy and/or the general welfare, he should lend his support to it.

It is ironic that some of the same people who appeal to us with arguments based on personal circumstance or motives in order to get us to do something that they want us to do, regard it as morally questionable if we accept or reject some *other* proposal solely on the basis of self-interest. It would seem, therefore, that even those who use such appeals are probably aware, in their more reflective moments, that personal circumstances or interests should not be considered relevant when dealing with the merit of broader issues.

Example "I really don't see how you can oppose the administration's bill to cut income and capital gains taxes. After all, you're in a tax bracket that will benefit considerably from the cut, and if you sell any of that real estate and those stocks you own, you're going to realize a lot more from the sale if the capital gains tax is lowered." Look at this argument in standard form:

Since the administration's tax bill cuts income and capital gains taxes,

and you will benefit from the bill,

because you have a high income and potential capital gains looming,

Therefore, you should support the bill.

While it may indeed be to the advantage of the target of this argument to have lower taxes, there may be a more important issue at stake here. Lowering income and capital gains taxes could have the effect of curtailing other important government programs, increasing the national debt, or creating other more serious economic problems for the country. While the potential personal benefits may be tempting, they are not relevant in judging the merit of public policy proposals.

Example   "Nancy, I would have thought that you would be actively supporting an affirmative action program here at the university. Because you're a woman, you
of all people should see the merit of using every means available to hire more women to
work in areas that have traditionally been dominated by men."

The special circumstance that Nancy is a woman is not a relevant or sufficient
reason for her to support such a program. Whatever reasons might be given for actively
supporting affirmative action, being a woman should not be one of them.

Example   One faculty member, who supports the foreign language requirement, appeals to the personal interests of another to get him to vote against a proposal
to drop the requirement: "Don't you realize, Professor Griffin, that if the faculty votes to
drop the foreign language requirement, very few of our students will be likely to take a
foreign language? Don't you agree that without the requirement it will be difficult to get
a decent enrollment in your German classes? The requirement helps you to pick up majors and minors. No one comes to college planning to major or minor in German."

The question of whether a foreign language should be required of all students
should be determined on the basis of factors relevant to the requirement. The fact that it
might provide majors, minors, and larger classes for Professor Griffin is not a relevant
consideration.

Attacking the Fallacy   If someone appeals to you on a personal level or on the
level of self-interest, you can head the debate in a more positive direction if you ask for
an alternative argument that makes no reference to what may be of personal benefit to
you. Let it be known that you are concerned about the truth or rightness of the position
at issue, not whether it will benefit you personally. If a good argument for the idea can
be formulated, accept its conclusion without embarrassment, even if it *does* benefit you
personally.

Playing to the Gallery

DEFINITION   *This fallacy consists in attempting to persuade others to accept a position by
exploiting their strong emotions instead of presenting evidence for the position.*

The "gallery" to which this appeal is made refers to the undiscriminating public, which is easily swayed through manipulation of their strong feelings and prejudices.
In the absence of a rational argument for a view, this appeal invites an unthinking acceptance of an idea or action on the basis of passion rather than evidence. Some of the
emotions or feelings exploited in this way are feelings of compassion, vanity, loyalty,
shame, and negative attitudes toward others. The arguer's choice of which sentiments
to exploit is, of course, determined by his or her purpose and the constituency of the audience or gallery. Attitudes that are frequently exploited are those that are negative toward such things as labor unions, big government, right-wing conservatives, religious
fundamentalists, taxes, gays and lesbians, lawyers, doctors, feminists, tax-and-spend
liberals, big corporations, and the "other" political party.

There are several types of emotional manipulation that are so common that
they even have their own names. *Appeal to pity* is probably the most common form of
emotional manipulation. It consists in attempting to persuade others of a position by

appealing to their sympathy instead of to relevant evidence, *especially when some more important principle or issue is at stake.* Since the introduction of pity into a discussion can never settle a question of fact, the pitiable consequences of a claim's being true have no bearing on the truth or merit of the claim. The possibility that someone may be disappointed or suffer some kind of mental anguish because of your failure to give a desired response to a claim or proposal is usually not a relevant consideration in the determination of the merit of the claim or of the proposed action.

Nevertheless, there may be some situations in which the potential hurt to others is a relevant consideration in adopting or rejecting a course of action. Many such calls to compassion are in fact moral arguments that appeal implicitly to moral principles. In such cases, the description of the pitiful situation may simply be a device used to call attention to a relevant moral consideration. However, an appeal to pity in a context in which no relevant and defensible moral premise is lurking about exploits our vague feelings of generosity or concern for others, while usually neglecting (or at least obscuring) a more relevant principle or issue at stake. In such a situation, the appeal to pity would be a fallacious one.

A second common type of emotional manipulation is the *use of flattery*. This fallacy consists in attempting to persuade others of one's view by engaging in excessive praise of them, instead of presenting evidence for the position in question. For example, you have probably heard a speaker say something like this: "Because you are a mature audience of highly educated professionals, I'm sure that you can clearly see the merit of my proposal." High praise, of course, is not fallacious by itself. It only becomes fallacious when it is used as a substitute for evidence.

A third common type of emotional manipulation is that of *assigning guilt by association,* which consists in attempting to manipulate an opponent into accepting one's view by pointing out that the opposing view is held by those with negative esteem or by persons or groups that the opponent does not like or usually disagrees with, instead of presenting evidence for one's position. This device encourages one to accept the arguer's position in order to avoid any guilt by association with one's personal or ideological enemies. But there is no reason why we should be intimidated into believing or doing something in order to avoid being identified with someone we don't like, since it would be absurd to assume that we will always agree with those whom we like and disagree with those whom we do not like. Whether we like or dislike a person who holds a view that we are contemplating could not possibly affect the truth or falsity of that view or the rightness or wrongness of an action.

Playing to the gallery violates the relevance criterion of a good argument, which requires that premises must be relevant to or count in favor of the truth of the conclusion. It should be clear that premises that are constituted by devices that do no more than manipulate our emotional feelings and attitudes would have no bearing on the merit of a conclusion.

Example   "I can see that you are a person who understands the stock market and how it works, so I won't bore you with how our brokerage firm handles its transactions. You wouldn't have come to us if you had not already done your research and discovered what kind of a firm we are. What can I do for you today?" The use of flattery in this argument, especially when it is translated into standard form, gives it an intimidating tone:

Since you are obviously intelligent and resourceful,

and would not do anything without being thoroughly informed,

and you have come to this brokerage firm,

Therefore, you need no additional information before placing your stock trades with us.

The reconstruction clearly shows that the stockbroker's argument has given the client no reasons that are relevant to the merit of using the brokerage firm for stock trades. But it would take a very self-confident person to say, "Wait just a minute. What is your commission rate?" or " Do I have to make a minimum number of trades a quarter?"

Example "Brad, I really think that you ought to take Nicole to the spring dance next Friday. She hasn't had a date all year. In fact, she has never been invited to go to any dance. Have you ever thought what it might be like to sit alone in your room every time there is a campus dance, while all your friends are doing what you'd like to be doing?" If there is any doubt about whether this appeal to pity is a fallacious one, look at the argument in standard form:

Since Nicole is sad and lonely,

> because she hasn't had a date all year, nor has she been invited
> to a dance before,

(and no one has asked her to the spring dance),

(and she would like to go to that dance),

(and Brad is available and not taking any other person yet),

Therefore, Brad should take Nicole to the spring dance.

If this is a moral argument—and the conclusion's "should" suggests that it could be—it is not clear what the implicit moral premise is. Could it be that "one is obligated to do what would help relieve sadness and the loneliness of another person, if one is in a position to do so"? Such a broadly stated moral premise could lead to some rather strange moral judgments, such as "one should spend one's weekends, if possible, visiting sad and lonely professors." In any case, there seems to be a *more* relevant principle at stake here. If the very purpose of dating is to spend enjoyable time with someone to whom one is attracted, the relevant question is whether he should let any feelings of pity he may have for Nicole play a significant role in deciding whether to invite her to the dance. Moreover, if Nicole shares the view held by most of us about the purpose of dating, she may not want to be the object of Brad's pity. A nonfallacious argument for inviting Nicole to the dance would be one that provides evidence that spending an evening with her would be an enjoyable experience. If he took her simply because he felt sorry for her, the reason for doing so would be an irrelevant one.

Example "The fact that you witnessed the gang rape doesn't matter, Gloria. When your own brother-in-law is one of those accused, you just don't get up on the witness stand and spill your guts. It is quite possible that you could help send a member of your own family to prison for 20 years." Look at what this appeal to family loyalty is asking Gloria to do:

> Since the accused rapist is your brother-in-law,
>
> and you know he is guilty,
>
> because you witnessed it,
>
> and you have the option of lying or telling the truth in your court testimony,
>
> and telling the truth may send your relative to prison for 20 years,
>
> (And considerations of family loyalty demand that you should lie),
>
> _____
>
> Therefore, you should lie about what you saw.

The appeal to Gloria's feelings of loyalty is an irrelevant appeal in this context, but the family member is trying to manipulate Gloria's natural feelings for her family. If Gloria fails to recognize that the implicit premise is irrelevant, she could very well contribute to a miscarriage of justice, which is a more important principle than family loyalty.

Example   The following argument, recently overheard in a conversation between a man and a woman, is a clear example of an attempt to manipulate another to feel shame. The woman was apparently angry that the man had not opened her car door for her. She said, "Any decent man would have opened the door for a lady!" No evidence is given for why the man should feel *ashamed* or *indecent* for not opening the car door, other than the fact that she is a woman.

Example   "How could you vote for Senator Cohen? He's been endorsed by every gay and lesbian organization in the country. How could you tell anybody whom you voted for?" If the person being questioned is homophobic, this strategy of trying to assign some kind of guilt by association just might work—but it shouldn't.

Attacking the Fallacy   While playing to the gallery is most effective when it is directed to the uninformed or the uncritical, even some of the most reflective people can be aroused by a skillful manipulation of their emotional sensitivities. It therefore behooves all of us to make a special effort not to allow such appeals to intrude on the process of making a reasoned judgment about an issue. One who allows oneself to be overcome by the force of such an emotional appeal is no less guilty of fallacious reasoning than the one who formulates the appeal. More important, we should not let speakers who attempt to exploit our feelings and attitudes think that they have offered relevant reasons in support of a claim.

In response to the use of flattery, there is no need to insult someone who gives you a compliment, but the flattery should not be allowed to affect in any way your evaluation of the merit of a view or the rightness of an action. Even if you are convinced that the praise was designed to manipulate a particular response, you could still thank the arguer for his or her remarks and then proceed to ask the questions appropriate to a careful evaluation of the claim.

In cases involving appeals to pity, it might be wise in some situations to acknowledge your aroused feelings openly, yet to state specifically that you are not going to allow them to interfere with the process of coming to a defensible judgment. Point out that accepting a proposal primarily because of those feelings may mean sacrificing what may be a more important principle.

There are two ways you could respond to an arguer who insists that there must be something wrong with you if you think like the "enemy" or the unliked. First, you could forthrightly assert that it makes no difference to you who holds the view in question, if they do it for the right reasons. Second, you might point out that a consistent application of the arguer's claim would reduce it to absurdity. Surely the arguer would not want to say that the merit of an idea or action should be controlled by the whims or behaviors of our rivals. If that were true, we would have to change our views every time they changed theirs.

Finally, since arguments with irrelevant premises can sometimes be significantly improved by the substitution of relevant premises, ask the arguer to try to so modify the argument. If he or she is unable to do so without appealing to the sentiments in question, take the initiative in the discussion and try to engage the arguer in a serious examination of the merit of the claim at issue by indicating some relevant considerations that should be addressed.

ASSIGNMENTS

B. Irrelevant Emotional Appeals   For each of the following arguments, (1) identify the type of irrelevant emotional appeal illustrated, and (2) explain how the reasoning violates the relevance criterion. There are two examples of each fallacy discussed in this section. Arguments marked with an asterisk (*) have sample answers at the end of the text.

*1. Rachel, I just can't vote for him, even though I agree with what you say about the two candidates. It's just that we have always been Democrats. I'm not sure that I could live with myself if I voted for a Republican.

*2. What's wrong with you taking my name when we get married, Dawn? It would really be embarrassing to me if we got married and you refused to take my name. In fact, I don't think I would want to be part of a relationship in which you would show me that kind of disrespect.

*3. I just don't understand why you are opposing federal aid to parochial schools. We Catholics know how badly our schools are in need of financial resources. If this bill for financial assistance to parochial schools doesn't pass the Congress, it will probably mean that many of our schools will have to close their doors.

*4. A timeshare broker: "You mean that after we flew you down here to Florida at no cost to you, put you up in a Gold Crown resort for three days with all meals provided, and took you to Disney World, you're not going to buy one of our timeshares?"

5. Tal, you can't be serious about going to Annapolis! Our family has always been army—your brother, your father, your uncles, and even your grandfather. All of them, as you well know, went to West Point.

6. Professor Beamer, are you sure you want to openly oppose this new curricular proposal? You know that both the president and the dean are pushing it pretty hard—and you don't have tenure yet!

7. If the faculty and staff of this college are not willing to endorse my reelection to Congress, it may be a long time before you get that new off-ramp that you've been wanting—one that leads directly from the interstate to your campus.

8. I think that we ought to give the Teacher of the Year award to Professor Raley. Ever since his wife died last year, he just hasn't been the same. I think that this award would really lift his spirits. He always seems so sad. I think this year has really been hard for him. And he's not really that bad a teacher.

C. For each of the following arguments (1) identify, from among all the fallacies studied in this chapter, the fallacy illustrated, and (2) explain how the reasoning violates the relevance criterion. There are two examples of each of the fallacies discussed in this chapter.

1. I can't believe that you are having both your Mom and your Dad walk you down the aisle at your wedding. No one in our family or anyone I know has ever had her Mom walk her down the aisle. People expect certain things to happen at weddings. You should simply do it the way we've always done it, Beverly.

2. Coach, I sure hope my son gets some quality playing time this season. I sure wouldn't want to reconsider my $50,000 pledge for the new stadium project.

3. Lou, I would have thought that, as a coach, you would *favor* a new NCAA rule lowering the academic eligibility requirement for first-year athletes. That would allow you to have a much larger pool of recruits, and being a nonscholarship school, we need all the help we can get.

4. **Barbara-lyn:** I've been going to Weight Watchers religiously twice a week for over a year.
   Tom: Why did you choose Weight Watchers? Aren't there lots of different weight loss programs?
   Barbara-lyn: Well, Weight Watchers says that their program is the only way to lose weight safely and effectively.

5. I would never go to Emory & Henry College. It used to be an all-male school. There is no way that we women would be given the same rights and privileges as men.

6. The Surgeon General has said that AIDS cannot be transmitted by swimming in a pool with an infected person. But almost *nobody* believes that is true.

7. I was going to let Matt win the match anyway. I haven't been feeling well lately, and I was tired of playing in the hot sun. Besides, I hadn't eaten anything since breakfast.

8. No matter how hard I study, I still don't do well on tests. I always seem to study the wrong stuff. I guess I should just not study at all and take the test blind.

9. I am a strong supporter of capital punishment. The present method of trying to rehabilitate criminals isn't working. Released convicts and parolees always seem to find their way back into prison.

10. Officer, I know that you were only doing your job when you stopped me. In fact, if we had more officers like you the streets would be much safer. But I have learned my lesson—thanks to you. Do you think we can let this go without a ticket?

11. I don't see how the administration could possibly be serious in telling us to change our pledging program. The pledging activities we engage in have been used for more than 50 years to test the mettle of the pledges. My father went through those same

tests 30 years ago. You can't put restrictions on a rich history like that. There's no way we could change the program.

12. Son, both your mother and I want you to go to Washington & Lee University. If you want us to pay for your education, I think you'd better apply there. Okay?

13. I oppose a zoning variance that allows the opening of a new restaurant in town. It would almost certainly take away some of the customers from our restaurant and cut into our profits.

14. You know, Mindy, that any sweetener that has aspartame in it is really bad for you. I heard the other day that it even breaks down DNA particles.

15. My mother told me about the hazing by the sororities when she was in school here. I would never join a sorority because I do not want to participate in such degrading practices. I don't think hazing is right.

16. I know there are some people who oppose capital punishment, but there is no way that you can say capital punishment is morally wrong. After all, more than 80 percent of the American people approve of it.

17. The reason that I failed all my classes this term is that my teachers don't like me. It's probably because I often disagree with them in class. I also compared my tests with those of several other students, and they all got a higher grade than I did for basically the same answers I gave. Besides, my parents were having marital problems this term.

18. Vitamins are an important supplement to our daily diets. They help make up for what we miss in our food, so I think you should take at least 500 milligrams of Vitamin C every day.

19. We need to build a new swimming pool for the community, because swimming is one of the most effective exercises for cardiovascular improvement, it doesn't require any special equipment, and it can be used as a lifelong form of regular exercise.

20. Senator Baker: I think it's time we developed some kind of national health care plan.

Senator Bradford: You must be losing it, Bob. That's socialized medicine—the very thing that Ted Kennedy, Hillary Clinton, and the other liberals have been trying to shove down our throats for years.

D. Submit an argument (different from the one submitted for the assignment in Chapter III, but follow the same procedure). Point out any named fallacies that violate the structural criterion or the relevance criterion. Then construct the strongest possible argument in support of an alternative position on the issue.

E. Following the model used in the text, use a 3 × 5 card to submit an *original* example (found or created) of each of the fallacies that violate the relevance criterion.

F. Create your own strategies or suggestions for attacking each of the fallacies that violate the relevance criterion.

VII
Fallacies That Violate
the Acceptability Criterion

One who presents an argument for or against a position should attempt to use reasons that are likely to be acceptable by a rationally mature person and that meet standard criteria of acceptability.

Each of the fallacies discussed in this chapter employs a premise that fails to meet the conditions of the acceptability criterion. An acceptable premise is a premise that a reasonable person ought to find acceptable. To give assistance in the task of determining the acceptability of particular premises, we earlier suggested seven conditions of acceptability and five conditions of unacceptability. If each of the premises of an argument conforms to at least one of the conditions of acceptability and if none conforms to a condition of unacceptability, they should be regarded as acceptable.

The fallacies treated in this chapter that violate the criterion of acceptability are divided into two groups: (1) fallacies of linguistic confusion and (2) unwarranted assumption fallacies.

FALLACIES OF LINGUISTIC CONFUSION

Words, regardless of how carefully they are chosen, are always a potential source of misunderstanding. A change in context can cause a subtle change in the meaning of a word or even a whole sentence. If careful attention is not given to this phenomenon, our arguments may be ineffective, be misunderstood, or cause others to draw unwarranted conclusions. Therefore, anyone who is interested in good reasoning must attend to the problem of the imprecision of our language.

The fallacies in this section suffer from some confusion in the meaning of a key word or phrase used in the premise of an argument. According to the conditions of unacceptability, a premise that is linguistically confusing cannot be an acceptable premise, and since the criteria of a good argument require that an argument have acceptable premises, an argument whose language is confusing is a flawed one. Some of the most common linguistic flaws that cause arguments to go wrong involve shifting the meaning of a word or phrase and using it in two different senses in the same argument, using a word that can be interpreted in two or more different ways without making clear which meaning is intended, and placing a misleading emphasis on a word or phrase. Other linguistic confusion results from a *listener* placing emphasis on a speaker's word or phrase and then drawing a contrasting claim, from manipulating language in such a way that a conclusion is suggested while not asserted, and from drawing an inappropriate inference from or defending a particular view based on an obviously vague expression. Finally, significant confusion is found in cases in which one carefully manipulates the language to make an important distinction between two things when there is no real difference between them.

Equivocation

DEFINITION *This fallacy consists in directing another person toward an unwarranted conclusion by making a word or phrase employed in two different senses in an argument appear to have the same meaning throughout.*

In a good argument, the words or phrases employed must retain the same meanings throughout the argument, unless a shift in meaning is understood or specified. One who equivocates has either intentionally or carelessly allowed a key word to shift in meaning in midargument. A shift of this kind is particularly difficult to detect in long arguments in which the transition in meaning can be more easily concealed.

One who uses a word or phrase that functions in one part of an argument in a very different way from how it functions in another part may cause an opponent to draw an unwarranted conclusion, because it looks like support is being given to the claim at issue, simply because the words have the same *appearance*. Because the key terms lack a uniformity of meaning, the logical connection that was assumed to exist between the premises has been severed; but such a connection is *required* if the premises are to support the conclusion. Such confusion renders the premises unacceptable, and no conclusion can logically be inferred from them.

Example "Gambling should be legalized because it is something we can't avoid. It is an integral part of human experience; people gamble every time they get in their cars or decide to get married."

The first use of "gambling" in this argument for legalized gambling refers to games of chance and/or the use of gaming devices, whereas the second refers to the risk feature of life itself. Because there is no uniformity of meaning in the key word, nothing follows from the premises. Here is the argument in standard form:

Since people gamble every day,

and gambling is an integral part of human life,

and such gambling is unavoidable,

Therefore, gambling should be legalized.

This argument almost seems convincing. After all, if gambling really is unavoidable, it should certainly be legal. But that conclusion does not follow if the meaning of the word shifts in midargument. And it does.

Example   "I think that the government has no choice but to support welfare programs. The Constitution is very clear on this issue. It says that the government has the responsibility to do those things that promote the general welfare."

In its first use, the key word "welfare" refers to specific government programs that directly help people who have difficulty making it on their own. The reference to welfare in the Constitution has to do with the government's overall responsibility to provide for the well-being of all citizens. Because the meaning of this key word shifts, the conclusion of the argument is unwarranted or does not follow.

Example   "My college adviser suggested to me that I should take logic because logic, he said, teaches one how to argue. But I think that people argue too much as it is. Therefore, I do not intend to take any course in logic, and I am of the opinion that perhaps logic shouldn't be taught at all. It will only contribute to increasing the tension that already exists in the world."

The first use of the word "argue" refers to the process of carefully supporting claims with evidence and sound reasoning. The second use of the word refers to a bitter controversy or to a kind of disagreeable haranguing between individuals. This shift in the meaning of the word could lead one to the unwarranted conclusion that a course in logic teaches one how to be disagreeable.

Attacking the Fallacy   If you have reason to believe that you are being confronted with an argument involving equivocation, there are at least three ways of dealing with it. One way would be to identify the problematic word or phrase and point out to the arguer the two different ways the word functions in the argument in question. If there is some dispute about whether the arguer has equivocated, you might ask for precise definitions of the suspected words or phrases. If the definitions are different, then the charge will be proved.

A second way is to translate the word in one of its instances into words that clearly express what you think is the exact meaning of the term and then use the same translation in its other instances. If the argument then makes no sense, it at least loses its appearance of being a good argument.

A third way to demonstrate the fallacious nature of reasoning that involves equivocation is to use the absurd example method. Construct a simple argument with true premises, but one in which the meaning of the key word shifts in meaning from one of the premises to the other. For example:

Since only man is rational,

and no woman is a man,

_____

Therefore, no woman is rational.

The equivocation on the word "man" leads to a conclusion that is obviously absurd. The arguer should be able to understand from such an example how the confusion created by equivocation fails to support the intended conclusion and/or directs one to an unwarranted one.

Ambiguity

DEFINITION   *This fallacy consists in directing another person toward an unwarranted conclusion by presenting a claim or argument that uses a word, phrase, or grammatical construction that can be interpreted in two or more distinctly different ways, without making clear which meaning is intended.*

If one does not know which of two or more meanings to assign to an argument's premise, then it is an unacceptable one, because it makes a claim whose meaning is unclear or not known. Hence, no appropriate conclusion can be drawn, because the truth or falsity of a conclusion depends on the acceptability of the premises.

This fallacy can be committed in two ways. First, an arguer may use a word or phrase with two or more meanings in one of the premises of an argument. This kind of ambiguity is sometimes referred to as *semantic ambiguity,* as it stems from confusion about a word or phrase. Since a majority of the words in our language have more than one meaning, there is obviously nothing fallacious about using a word with more than one meaning. The fallacy is committed only when the context does not make clear which of the several possible meanings of the word or phrase is intended. This lack of clarity may render the listener unable to draw any conclusion at all or perhaps cause him or her to interpret the word in an unintended way and thus arrive at a false or inappropriate conclusion. Semantic ambiguity can be remedied by clarifying the meaning of the particular ambiguous word or phrase.

Second, an arguer may present a claim that can be legitimately interpreted in two or more distinctly different ways because of its syntactical construction. This *syntactical ambiguity* differs from semantic ambiguity in that it can be remedied by a grammatical reconstruction of the sentence. Some of the most typical grammatical errors that render a claim syntactically ambiguous are *unclear pronoun reference* ("Fred never argues with his father when he is drunk"); *elliptical construction,* in which words are omitted but supposedly understood ("Celeste loves teaching more than her husband"); *unclear modifier* ("I have to take my makeup test in an hour"); careless use of *only* ("Schiano's Restaurant will accept take-out orders only on Saturday"); and careless use of *all* ("All of the fish Doug caught weigh at least 6 pounds"). Such ambiguous constructions are often referred to by grammarians as *amphiboles.*

A genuine case of either semantic or syntactical ambiguity makes it impossible to find a claim acceptable or to draw any conclusion, if the ambiguous premise is the only support presented for it.

Example   Several years ago a faculty colleague and I were leaving the campus after a late afternoon meeting. Our homes were within walking distance of the campus, but because it was raining, I said to him, "How about a ride home?" He said "okay" and we walked toward the parking lot. I later discovered that he had accepted what he thought was an offer of a ride home, while I thought he had agreed to my request for a ride home. As we stood in the rain in an empty parking lot looking for a car—but not the same car—we learned an important lesson about ambiguity. If this exchange had been put into the standard form of an argument, my question "How about a ride home?" could have been interpreted by my colleague as the first premise of the following argument:

Since Ed has *offered* me a ride home,

(and he couldn't *offer* me a ride if his car were not available),

---

Therefore, his car will be in the parking lot.

Or the question could have been interpreted as the first premise of a very different argument:

Since Ed has *asked* me for a ride home,

(and he would not *ask* me for a ride if his car were available),

---

Therefore, his car will not be in the parking lot.

The unwarranted conclusions and embarrassment to which we were led by the syntactical ambiguity of my question could have been avoided if I had been more careful in formulating it. But my colleague was just as guilty of ambiguity. In the absence of clarification about the ambiguous first premise, he should have drawn no conclusion about what to expect to find in the parking lot, although he unthinkingly chose to draw the conclusion that he wanted to be true—the first formulation.

Example   A student says to her adviser: "Last term I took Logic and Introduction to Philosophy. I hope I have more exciting courses this term." Should the adviser help her sign up for additional philosophy or philosophy-type courses or should the adviser help her find courses that are very different from philosophy courses? Without an understanding of the intended meaning of the student's syntactically ambiguous statement, the adviser would have no idea what conclusion to draw.

Example   A recent announcement on our college bulletin board was semantically ambiguous. It simply read: "Personal Security for Women Has Been Canceled for the Rest of the Semester." Given the fact that our campus security chief had just resigned, it was not clear whether one should conclude that there would perhaps no longer be any security provided at women's residence halls or that maybe a scheduled class focused on personal safety for women would not be meeting for the remainder of the semester. Without further clarification, we should draw neither conclusion.

Example   Consider the semantic ambiguity involved in this familiar scene with two people driving in city traffic.

Laura: You'll have to tell me how to get there.
Eleanor: Okay. Turn right here. [Laura turns right.] Hey, I didn't mean
for you to turn right! Couldn't you see that I was pointing left?

In this case, of course, Eleanor meant for Laura to turn left *immediately*, but as Laura did not happen to see Eleanor's leftward pointing, her verbal directions were surely ambiguous and Laura should have sought clarification before doing anything. In standard form, the argument might look like this:

Since Eleanor knows how to get to the destination
and Laura is willing to follow those directions
and Eleanor says to turn right here,

Therefore, Laura should turn right here.

The problem is that the ambiguous meaning of "right here" makes it inappropriate to draw any conclusion, because it is not known which of the two meanings of "right here" is intended.

   Attacking the Fallacy   As in the case of the fallacy of equivocation, you should identify the word, phrase, or problematic syntactical construction and, if possible, ask the speaker for the intended meaning. Make it clear why you are asking for a clarification. Don't be deterred by the accusation that you are being "picky," for it is not being "picky" to ask for help in understanding something that you do not understand, and you obviously cannot assess the worth of an arguer's claim or argument if you do not understand it.

   If the arguer is not immediately available to provide clarification, use your own knowledge of the arguer's larger perspective as a clue to the possible intended meaning. If you are unable to ask your opponent for clarification and you have no knowledge of any larger perspective, perhaps you should draw no conclusion at all. If you must do so, you might hypothesize about the intended meaning and draw a very tentative conclusion based on that speculation. If the conclusion is consciously tentative, it can be more easily changed with additional information or clarification.

   Finally, be careful not to falsely accuse an opponent of ambiguity when none is present. The fallacy of ambiguity has not been committed if the context makes clear the proper interpretation of the word or sentence. One who interprets a word, phrase, or sentence in an unjustified way because of his or her deliberate disregard of or careless attention to the context commits an error that might be called "false ambiguity." For example:

> **Buck:** How can they afford to do that?
> **Lila:** Do what?
> **Buck:** Give pizzas away!
> **Lila:** What do you mean?
> **Buck:** Belah's Pizza! It says right here in the ad, "Belah's Pizzas Delivered Free!"

Buck has no right to make such an interpretation of the advertisement. The grammar of the ad is perfectly clear: "free" refers only to the *delivery* of the pizzas.

   If someone draws an improper conclusion from your statement when its context makes the meaning clear and then attempts to place the blame on you, don't be intimidated. Shift the responsibility back to your opponent as quickly as possible by showing how the context of your statement does not support such an interpretation.

Misleading Accent

DEFINITION   *This fallacy consists in directing another person toward an unwarranted conclusion by placing improper or unusual emphasis on a word, phrase, or particular aspect of an issue or claim. It is sometimes committed by taking portions of another's statement out of its original context in a way that conveys a meaning not intended.*

   The fallacy of misleading accent is found not only in advertisements and headlines but also in other very common forms of human discourse. A headline may cause the reader to infer a conclusion other than the one supported in the article that follows. An advertisement for a product may address the quality but not the exorbitant cost of a product or may focus on the advantages of a service but fail to mention an important downside of that service. A news article may tell us what one party in a court dispute said about the case but not what the other party said about the same aspect of the case. In all these cases, the writer or speaker places an accent on a selected feature of an issue that may cause another to come to an unwarranted conclusion about it.

One of the most common ways of engaging in the practice of improper accent is to lift words or statements out of their larger whole, thereby omitting important contextual meanings of, or qualifications to, their claims. For example, suppose that Professor Daigle tells Sela's roommate that Sela has to have her term paper in by today or he won't accept it. It would be a gross case of misleading accent if the roommate reported to Sela that Professor Daigle called and said that he wouldn't accept her paper.

The acceptability criterion of a good argument requires that an argument's premises be acceptable. A premise that emphasizes (or fails to emphasize) certain words or phrases in a way that creates confusion or conveys misleading information that may cause another person to arrive at a false or unwarranted conclusion is an unacceptable premise. Hence, an argument that employs such a confusing premise cannot be a good one.

Example   In the midst of the Clinton impeachment frenzy, a network newscast reported that it was disclosed that day that the Clinton 1996 campaign had accepted more than ten million dollars in improperly reported campaign contributions. A day later another network reported that the Clinton campaign had accepted ten million dollars in improperly reported campaign funds *and* that the Dole campaign had accepted more than seventeen million dollars of such contributions. The first report was either a case of incompetent reporting or a clear case of misleading accent. If we put the argument into standard form, it might look like this:

> Since the Clinton campaign committee accepted more than ten million dollars in improperly reported campaign contributions,
>
> and such action is against the law,
>
> ——————————————————————————————
>
> (Therefore, Clinton's campaign committee should be prosecuted.)

Based on knowledge of the "partial story," one might possibly draw this conclusion, but once we know the "full story," our judgment would no doubt be different. In view of the fact that both campaigns violated the law, other conclusions might perhaps be more appropriate. One *could* conclude that "both campaign committees should be prosecuted," but it is more likely that one would conclude that "it is time that both parties get serious about campaign finance reform" or at least that "campaign contributions should be more carefully monitored."

Example   If a father were speaking of the problems of raising his three children and said of his oldest daughter, "*She* won't listen to me" (with a hard emphasis on "she"), you might conclude that the other two children *do* listen to him. If that is not the case, the father might be justifiably accused of directing his hearers to a false conclusion by putting the stress on "she."

Example   Suppose the following headline were printed in your local newspaper: "Jerry Falwell Favors Homosexuals." This headline might lead one to infer something about Falwell's sexual interests or his support for gay rights, whereas the article might simply be reporting an interview in which Falwell said that he saw no reason why *repentant* homosexuals should not be ordained into the ministry.

The actual words of the headline or title may form a true statement, yet the statement may be misleading in that it suggests some additional claim because of an unusual stress. Such headlines or titles often lead to understandings that are put into proper perspective only by the articles to which they are attached. This is commonly the case with supermarket tabloids.

Example

Karen: If Ben doesn't stop harassing me, I'm going to report him to my supervisor.

Mark (speaking to Ben later): Karen was talking to me today about your harassing her, and she said that she was going to report you to her supervisor.

In this example, Mark's conveying of the message from Karen leaves out the important part of Karen's statement. If the entire message had been delivered, Ben would probably conclude that ceasing the harassment would cause Karen to withdraw her threat to report him. But without the important "if" statement, Ben would probably draw a very different conclusion—that Karen will report him no matter what he does.

Attacking the Fallacy   In most cases, one can confront the fallacy of misleading accent much as one does the fallacy of ambiguity. Point out the part of the argument or claim that you suspect of being inappropriately accented and ask, where possible, for a clarification or an explanation of the larger context.

You can also guard against being led astray by a case of misleading accent by taking some precautionary measures. Always read or ask for the larger context of any statement you suspect of being accented. You might preclude the possibility of being misled by questionable headlines or titles by determining, if possible, to read the articles to which they are attached. At least you should be very cautious about drawing any inference based on a headline or title alone.

In general, it is always wise to follow the rule "When uncertain, ask." Don't be embarrassed to ask about something you don't understand or suspect of being improperly accented. It is better to be a skeptic, or even run the risk of appearing naive or uninformed, than to come to a false conclusion.

Illicit Contrast

DEFINITION   *This fallacy consists in a listener's directly inferring from another's claim some related but unstated* contrasting *claim by improperly placing unusual emphasis on a word or phrase in the speaker's or writer's statement.*

This fallacy is one in which the listener, rather than the speaker, does some improper accenting. It is also very similar to false ambiguity, in which a listener or reader interprets a claim in a way that is not justified by the context. In the case of illicit contrast, one is claiming that the *speaker* accented some particular part of a claim, which led to the inference drawn, even though there is no evidence that any such emphasis was introduced by the speaker. Indeed, it is the listener who has introduced the misleading emphasis. He or she has inappropriately added something to the meaning of the speaker's claim. The listener has taken the speaker's claim that "X is true of Y" and extended it to also mean that "X is *not* true of some *contrast* of Y." For example, if the speaker claims that logic teachers are very smart, the listener would be inappropriately extending the meaning of that claim if he or she infers that the speaker is also saying that professors in other fields are *not* smart. In this case it is the listener who has employed an unacceptable premise, and an argument with such a premise is a flawed one.

Example If a young woman, after an unhappy love affair, claimed that men are insensitive brutes, it would be fallacious to infer from her statement that she was implicitly contrasting males to females, saying that females are *not* insensitive people. The young woman was probably not trying to characterize the differences between men and women; she was probably just responding emotionally to her own hurt feelings. Moreover, even if she were making the claim that all men are insensitive, nothing should be inferred about her thinking regarding the sensitivity of women.

Example If a Catholic cardinal were dealing with a situation in which a young priest had been discovered to be relating sexually to a married woman, he might caution all the priests in his diocese that "it is improper for priests to relate sexually to married women." It would be fallacious, since it would be unjustified by the context, to assume that the cardinal is suggesting that it is *not* improper for priests to relate sexually to *unmarried* women.

Example The following conversation between my two daughters and me took place many years ago, and one of my daughters would prefer that the conversation not be included in this text:

Dad: Isn't that Diana's dress you have on, Cynthia?
Cynthia: It's mine now. Diana gave it to me. It's too little for her.
Dad: Well, it looks very nice on you.
Diana: (speaking from across the room) Then you don't think it looked nice on me?

In standard form, Diana's argument looks something like this:

Since Dad said that my former dress looked good on *Cynthia*,

and he did not say that it looked good on me,

(and he could have done so),

Therefore, he must not think that it looked good on me.

In this short domestic exchange, Diana committed the fallacy of illicit contrast, because she falsely accused me of accenting the word "you" when I said, "It looks nice on you." The fact was, however, that I did *not* stress the word "you"; I was simply describing how the dress looked on Cynthia. I was making no implicit comment on how it looked or might have looked on someone else.

Attacking the Fallacy Because your opponent is implicitly and falsely claiming that you have accented some particular part of a claim that led him or her to the questionable contrasting claim, you should insist that the burden of proof is on your accuser to demonstrate that the context or your voice inflection encouraged such an interpretation. You, of course, have a peculiar advantage, because you can almost always point out that the contrasting claim was not specifically uttered. But your opponent has already acknowledged that you did not actually utter the claim in question; the issue is whether you implicitly made the claim and whether you are prepared to defend it.

People should be responsible for only those claims that they have made. If you think you have been mistakenly heard making a claim that you have not made, you might express your willingness to examine the unstated contrasting claim in question, while making it quite clear that your original statement had in no way implied that claim. Unless you wish to reserve judgment about the merit of the claim, you could even deny it outright—in addition to denying that you implicitly made it. Denying that you made the claim and denying the claim itself are two different issues, and that point should be made clear to your accuser.

Argument by Innuendo

DEFINITION   *This fallacy consists in directing another person toward a particular, usually derogatory, conclusion by a skillful choice of words that implicitly suggests but does not assert that conclusion.*

The force of this fallacy lies in the impression created that some veiled claim is true, although no evidence is presented to support such a view. This method of arguing is commonly used to attack a person, group, or idea when there is little or no evidence to justify a straightforward claim or accusation. The power of suggestion is used in this way to compensate for the lack of evidence. Because the questionable claim is not explicitly made, one who uses an argument by innuendo would probably refuse to accept responsibility for it or for any other inference that others might draw from it.

Nevertheless, the speaker wants the target of the argument to draw the implicit or suggested conclusion, even though it does not merit acceptance. The suggested claim is not only confused with the asserted claim, but the suggested claim is one for which no evidence is, or is likely to be, given. Hence, it cannot be part of a good argument.

Example   The power of innuendo usually depends on the tone of the speaker.

Ginger: Are Allison and Eddie still going steady?

Luci: Well, according to *Eddie*, they are.

The straightforward claim is that Eddie believes that he and Allison are going steady. The tone of the response might suggest that Eddie is unaware that Allison thinks differently about their relationship or even that Allison is dating other men—a fact unknown to Eddie. Even though it is difficult to make explicit the tone and implicit suggestions of an argument by innuendo, the standard form of this argument might look like this:

Since Eddie believes that he and Allison are going steady,

(and Eddie is unaware that Allison knows and/or perhaps acts otherwise),

---

(Therefore, Eddie and Allison are not actually going steady.)

The implicit conclusion here is based on the implicit second premise. However, the second premise in the reformulation is just one possible interpretation based on Luci's arrangement of words. Because the meaning of her words is confusing at best, the target of the argument by innuendo should not draw the conclusion that the arguer wants. A confusing and unsupported claim cannot be an acceptable premise of a good argument.

Example   Sometimes the addition of a single word or phrase in an utterance can lead to a false or unjustified conclusion, even though the words together do not express anything that is not true. Suppose that a Dean of Students at a college is asked by an employer if a prospective employee had ever been in any kind of disciplinary difficulty while attending that college. The Dean might look at the records and say, "No"; or she might say, "No, we were never able to convict him of any violations of college rules." The latter response, unfortunately, would probably have a negative effect on the prospective employee's chances for employment, even though it might express a true proposition.

Suppose that the prospective employee were still a student at the college in question and the Dean said in response to the same question, "No, not yet!" The addition of the last two words transforms a straightforward negative answer into one filled with innuendo. Moreover, the conclusion that the employer might draw from such a response is one for which the Dean would probably not wish to accept responsibility.

Example   Suppose that you heard the following statement uttered by one of the candidates in a hard-fought gubernatorial race: "If you knew that one of the candidates in this race was receiving money from illegal sources, would that affect your voting decision? Look into the matter and see where the campaign funds of my opponent are coming from. The facts might surprise you." The speaker has allegedly made no serious claim against his opponent that requires any kind of defense, but the power of suggestion has done its work.

Example   A student says, "I often see Professor Winterling, but never with his *wife*." The particular way in which this last phrase is added to the claim, especially with the emphasis put upon the word "wife," would probably suggest that Professor Winterling spends a great amount of time with someone other than his wife or that he never spends time with his wife in public. The sentence itself, without stress on any particular word, may express a true proposition—namely, that the student has not seen Professor Winterling with his wife. However, because of the arrangement of the words in the sentence and the stress on the word "wife," a listener may be led, perhaps falsely, to infer one or both of the other two interpretations of the statement.

Attacking the Fallacy   Although an arguer usually will not wish to take responsibility for an unspoken claim, you should perhaps spell out the conclusion to which you have been led and ask the arguer to justify it. In no case should you accept an implicit claim without being satisfied on evidential grounds, because an implicit assertion requires the same justification as does an explicit one. If the speaker is not inclined to defend the claim in question, suggest that he or she specifically deny the implicit claim and take definite steps to counterbalance the effect it has had.

Misuse of a Vague Expression

DEFINITION *This fallacy consists in attempting to establish a position by means of a vague expression or in drawing an unjustified conclusion as a result of assigning a very precise meaning to another's word or phrase that is quite imprecise in its meaning or range of application.*

There is nothing wrong with using vague language. Almost all of us use vague expressions as a part of our linguistic style. Indeed, they usually function quite well for us when nothing important is at stake. The fallacy occurs when vague expressions are misused.

Vague terms may be misused in two ways. First, a vague expression is misused when it is a key word in a premise used to establish a position. According to the conditions of premise unacceptability, a premise that is not understood cannot be accepted as providing support for some other claim, and a premise cannot be understood if the key term in it is quite imprecise in its meaning. Neither can such a premise be refuted. If we do not know the range of application of a vague term, we cannot know at what point counterevidence may do some damage to the claim in which it appears. For example, if we wish to argue against an employee's claim that she is overworked, we must know precisely what it means to be *over*worked before we can know whether the counterevidence we might have weakens or refutes the claim.

The second way in which a vague expression may be misused is to infer a very specific conclusion from another's vague expression. Since we are not likely to know the intended meaning of another's vague language, any specificity that we may give to it would have to be arbitrary—and any inference from it would be equally arbitrary.

A claim with a key term whose meaning is vague or unclear cannot be used as support for any other claim; neither is it one from which any more specific claim can be inferred. If such a claim appears in an argument's premise, the premise is rendered unacceptable, which is a violation of the acceptability criterion of a good argument.

Example During a public-school textbook controversy many years ago in southwest Virginia, some critics claimed that the use of a particular series of textbooks constituted a violation of a state law that requires public schools to engage in "moral education." They claimed, for example, that to read stories that use profane language or have characters involved in immoral acts taught students to be immoral—the very opposite of what the state had mandated the schools to do. The argument in standard form is as follows:

Since the state constitution mandates that public schools pursue "moral education" as part of their goal,

and requiring students to read literature that uses questionable language or includes descriptions of immoral behavior is a violation of that mandate,

because it is "*im*moral education" or teaches immorality,

Therefore, public school students should not be assigned reading in such books.

In this case, a very questionable interpretation has been given to the vague term "moral education." The precision given to the term by the critics would outlaw almost all literature. Even the Bible could not be read, for it is full of stories of people doing immoral acts. This is not to say that the term can be easily defined or given a precision on which all would agree, but the critics' assigned meaning seems at best arbitrary and is therefore a misuse of a vague expression.

Example At a faculty meeting several years ago, the president of our small college told us that our student enrollment figure was moving us toward a financially dangerous low point and that perhaps we should show a little more concern for some of our weaker students, some of whom were dropping out of school because of failing grades. In response to the president's remarks, one faculty member indignantly exclaimed that he would quit before he would let the president force him to give a passing grade to a student who did not deserve it.

The faculty member in this case gave his own specificity to the president's vague request to "show a little more concern for some of our weaker students." Of course, if previous experience gave the faculty member reason to believe that "show a little more concern" was a euphemism for "don't fail any students," then his interpretation would have been justified. In this instance, however, it was not.

Example A Supreme Court ruling regarding pornography included the view that what is "pornographic" should be determined in accordance with "community standards." However, a prosecutor who tried to establish a case against a distributor of pornographic materials on the grounds that he or she had acted in violation of "community standards" would have to assign a very precise meaning to that very vague criterion—a precision to which it does not lend itself.

Legal concepts are often expressed in vague language, and those who apply them to particular situations sometimes cannot avoid assigning more specificity of meaning to those words. In doing so, however, one must not assign a meaning in a particular context that is more precise than the original language could possibly support. For example, if one assumes that the specific meaning of the Supreme Court's notion of "community standards" can be reduced to a formula like "whatever presently offends more than 50 percent of the people in the community" and then uses that highly questionable assigned meaning of a term to draw a conclusion about the illegality of an act, then one might reasonably be charged with misusing a vague expression.

It would be just as fallacious, of course, to argue a case by means of an untranslated notion of "community standards." For example, it would be a misuse of vague language to argue that "since this act involving pornographic materials was not in accordance with 'community standards,' then this act should be regarded as against the law." It would appear, then, that perhaps no effective use of the term "community standards" could be applied to a situation without misusing a vague expression.

Attacking the Fallacy In most cases, vague expressions can be attacked in the same way that ambiguous expressions can—that is, you can insist on further clarification or stipulation of meaning. If a word's range of application is indeterminate, ask for a more precise meaning of the expression. You would then have to determine if the precision given to the term is appropriate to the present context of the discussion. Such a procedure is particularly important if the issue is a significant one and it is desirable to continue the debate. If nothing of significance is at stake, you can, of course, simply ignore the imprecision.

If you wish to avoid committing the fallacy yourself, refrain from using imprecise language as much as possible when dealing with important or controversial issues. Find new words to replace those that may have become hopelessly vague, or at least specify the meaning of any words that may have become too vague in ordinary usage to convey your intended meaning clearly.

If you do not give specificity to your words, there are other people who will be quite happy to do so. Vague language, by its very nature, invites others to impose precise meaning on it. For example, if someone were to say to you, "If you were really concerned about the pollution problem, as you say, you would help us pick up highway trash this Saturday," he or she would be giving an unduly precise meaning to your expression of concern. Since there is no legitimate basis for drawing such a specific conclusion, you should not be intimidated by this manipulative tactic. Your words do not necessarily mean what somebody else says they do.

When an opponent attempts to support a particular claim with a key statement that contains a vague word, challenge the acceptability of the premise on the grounds that you cannot assess the evidential value of the support as long as the meaning of the vague term remains unspecified. You may disagree with your opponent about the particular meaning that he or she may assign to it, but you are at least in a better position to evaluate the argument. Indeed, part of your evaluation might very well center on the appropriateness of the assigned meaning.

Distinction Without a Difference

DEFINITION   *This fallacy consists in attempting to defend an action or position as different from some other one, with which it might be confused, by means of a careful distinction of language, when the action or position defended is no different in substance from the one from which it is linguistically distinguished.*

Probably the most common occasion of this fallacy is one in which an arguer wishes to diminish the possible embarrassment he or she feels in holding what is probably an untenable position or in engaging in what is probably questionable behavior. One is free, of course, to stipulate the meaning of any term he or she uses, but if the new meaning functions in the same way that the original meaning functions, no difference is made by the attempted distinction. Moreover, since the fallacy is usually committed in response to some form of challenge to another's position, the alleged distinction, because it constitutes no real difference in meaning, does not blunt the force of the challenge.

An argument that rests on a fundamental confusion about the meaning of a key claim cannot be a good one, for a confusing premise cannot qualify as an acceptable one. In the case of the fallacy of distinction without a difference, there is reason to believe that the claims are substantively the same. Hence, a premise asserting that they are distinguishable claims would be a questionable and therefore unacceptable premise.

Example   "I'm not saying anything against feminism; I just happen to sincerely believe that the male should be the head of the household." Let us put this argument into standard form:

Since I believe that the male should be the head of the house,

(and there is no contradiction between holding the feminist view and the view that the man should be the head of the house),

Therefore, I have no serious disagreement with feminism.

This is an example of what is probably an attempt to hide one's opposition to the feminist or antisexist movement. The first premise and the conclusion are contradictory, although the arguer claims that they are not. But saying that they are not contradictory does not make them not contradictory. The arguer attempts to make a distinction without a difference. Such a claim is confusing at best and false at worst. It at least represents a misunderstanding of the feminist perspective. Since a confusing claim is an unacceptable one, the conclusion does not follow.

Example Suppose the question is whether a particular person is a good driver. It is generally agreed that the ordinary "good driver" obeys the rules of the roads, keeps his or her mind on the task of driving, and is courteous to other drivers. Suppose that the individual in question is easily distracted by events taking place along the road and frequently turns and talks to other people in the car, thus failing to see and respond appropriately to important road signs. The response to the accusation that he is not a very good driver might be, "I'm not really a bad driver; I just don't pay much attention to the road." The accused person has made a distinction that exhibits no real difference. Hence, the force of the accusation against the driver has not been blunted.

Example "We must judge this issue by what the Bible says, not by what we think it says or by what some scholar or theologian thinks it says."
The radio preacher who made this claim apparently thought he was making an important distinction, but it is no distinction at all. If the Bible requires interpretation, and it does, then all persons are interpreters. The Bible or any other text doesn't say anything until it is interpreted by someone—either by a scholar, by a theologian, by an ordinary reader, or by the radio preacher. Therefore, there is no intelligible distinction to be drawn between what the Bible says and what someone says it says. In this particular case, the preacher apparently thought he was telling us what the Bible said, but as a matter of fact, he was merely telling us what *he* thought it said.

Attacking the Fallacy Because many people are unaware that their attempted distinctions are not true differences, the first step that you might take is to try to point out to them the futility of their efforts. If your verbal opponent takes issue with your assessment, which is likely, you might ask for an explanation of just how the alleged distinction differs in meaning. If you are unconvinced by this explanation, you may be inclined to offer a lesson in semantics. But as that would probably not be fully appreciated, why not settle for the absurd example method? Consider the following example: "I wasn't copying; I was just looking at her paper to jog my memory." Such an example should clearly illustrate how very different words can function in very similar ways.

ASSIGNMENTS

A. Fallacies of Linguistic Confusion For each of the following arguments, (1) identify the type of linguistic confusion illustrated, and (2) explain how the reasoning violates the acceptability criterion. There are two examples of each fallacy discussed in this section. Arguments marked with an asterisk (*) have sample answers at the end of the text.

   1. Patti to Nancy: "Your husband seems to have to work late at the office a lot. Does his new female assistant usually have to work also?"

   *2. Just as you can know that the wind exists because you can feel it, even though you cannot see it, God exists, because even though you cannot see Him, you can feel His presence.

   3. A new play in town was reviewed by the local newspaper's drama critic as being "a great success, considering the lack of facilities and the poor quality of actors with whom the director had to work." The play was then publicized as "a great success."

   *4. I didn't lie to you; I merely stretched the truth a bit.

   *5. Dave: I sure feel good today.
   Dan: I didn't realize that you had not been feeling good.

   6. Paul: In the college handbook concerning cafeteria regulations, it says, "Appropriate dress is expected at all times."
   Nancy: That's terrible. Why should I have to wear a coat and tie just to eat in the cafeteria?

   7. Laura: Sofia is starting her cooking class next week.
   John: I'd like to sign up for it. Is she a good teacher?

   *8. Anita: Is Valerie helping with the charity show this year?
   Lisa: Well, she comes to our meetings!

   9. According to our judicial system, a person is innocent until proven guilty. Hence, the investigation of William Smith, the president's security adviser, was simply an effort by the media and the Senate to damage the reputation of an innocent man.

   *10. A headline in a country newspaper reads, TWO DOCTORS FOR 50,000 PATIENTS. The article to which it is attached explains that there are only two veterinarians for the estimated 50,000 animals in the county.

   11. I didn't betray your confidence. I just thought your parents should know what you told me.

   12. Shandra: No, I don't think I should go out tonight. I take my studies very seriously, and I just have to get some work done tonight.
   Depaki: What makes you think that I don't take my studies seriously?

   *13. I don't know anything about Ron Diss, except that he's a liberal, so I didn't vote for him. I didn't want to add another voice to the ranks of the critics of the military in the Congress.

   *14. Roman: When I asked Dad to help me with my calculus homework today, he said that he couldn't.
   Sela: That's strange! He was a great help to *me* when I was taking calculus.

UNWARRANTED ASSUMPTION FALLACIES

   The patterns of argument discussed in this section are fallacious because they employ highly questionable, although sometimes popular, assumptions. Typically, these assumptions are implicit or unstated but nevertheless crucial to the force of the argument. Because these implicit yet unacceptable assumptions are used to support premises in arguments, the premises built on them are likewise unacceptable, for one of the conditions of unacceptability states that a premise is unacceptable if it "is based on a usually unstated but highly questionable assumption." Hence, such premises cannot serve as premises of good arguments, for they violate the acceptability criterion of a good argument.

Consider the argument that the college baseball team will have a better win-loss record next season, because the college has hired a new baseball coach. The single premise of the argument is clearly based on the unstated, unwarranted assumption that "new is better." But the assumption behind this "fallacy of novelty" is contradicted by the evidence. Every idea, law, policy, or action requires a defense that is independent of its novel character. Indeed, a pattern of reasoning that assumes that whatever is new is better would result in the absurd consequence that every proposed alternative to the present way of doing things would automatically deserve our acceptance.

The assumption concerning novelty and many other unwarranted assumptions are a part of our conventional wisdom, because they have a ring of truth. They may even be true in some contexts. The problem is that in *other contexts* or under *other circumstances,* they are clearly false. Some of the most common of these assumptions that will be treated in this section include the assumption that small differences on a continuum between extremes have a negligible effect, that what is true of the parts is true of the whole, and that what is true of the whole is true of the parts. Other common assumptions are that alternatives are usually limited to two and that one of them is true; that what is the case, ought to be the case; that what we *want* to be the case, *will* be the case (and vice versa); and that rules or principles have no exceptions or that a rule can be refuted by a single exception. Finally, it is generally assumed that the middle position between extremes is the best position, because it is the middle position, and that things that are alike in one or more respects are alike in some other respect. No argument should be allowed to proceed under the conviction that any one of these common assumptions is always true.

An argument that rests on an unwarranted or unacceptable assumption may have its faulty character blatantly exposed by spelling out the beguiling assumption as part of a reconstructed argument. Articulating the assumption in this way is by itself sometimes sufficient to convince even the arguer of its unacceptability. Once the unacceptable premise is recognized as being crucial to the force of the argument of which it is a part, then the argument too should be seen as a faulty one.

Fallacy of the Continuum

DEFINITION   *This fallacy consists in assuming that small movements or differences on a continuum between a thing and its contrary have a negligible effect and that to make definite distinctions between points on that line is impossible or at least arbitrary.*

The assumption involved in this fallacy is a very common one, and it is not always easy to persuade others of its dubious character. It is often expressed in the common claim that "it's only a matter of degree." This "only a matter of degree" kind of thinking can sometimes have the consequence of driving us to the absurd conclusion that contraries, as long as they are connected by intermediate small differences, are really very much the same. It fails to recognize the importance or necessity of sometimes making what might appear to be arbitrary distinctions or cutoff points.

A more graphic name for this fallacy might be the *camel's back fallacy*, as in "One more straw won't break the camel's back." Anyone who has played the child's game "The Last Straw" knows that one more straw *can* break the camel's back. The game rules specify that each player be given a handful of very lightweight wooden "straws." Then each player in turn places a single straw in a basket on the camel's back. The player who places the straw that breaks the camel's back—that is, causes it to collapse—loses the game. There *is* a straw that makes the difference between the camel's back's breaking and not breaking. Similarly, a distinction can often be made on a continuum between one category and its contrary, even though clear distinctions between these categories are sometimes very difficult to draw. Vague words particularly lend themselves to this difficulty. At what point, for example, does a warm evening become a cool one or a girl become a woman? There is a difference between a warm evening and a cool evening, just as there is a difference between a girl and a woman. To make distinctions may in some cases seem somewhat arbitrary, but it is appropriate in some contexts that distinctions be made. At any rate, it would be fallacious to assume in one's thinking that such distinctions could not be made.

The ancient name of this fallacy is the *fallacy of the beard*. Such a name probably originated in the context of an ancient debate about "How many hairs would one have to have in order to have a beard?" We would probably be reluctant—because it would appear arbitrary—to specify a certain number of hairs, but obviously there is a difference between having a beard and not having a beard. For practical purposes, then, some cutoff point has to be established.

This fallacy may be committed not only when dealing with conceptual issues, such as the questions of when death occurs or when the fetus becomes a human being, but also when dealing with questions of behavior. For example, it is often argued that if one is justified in taking a small step in a particular direction, such as drinking one more beer, additional steps seem to be justified as well. There seems to be no good reason to stop at any particular point—as long as the steps are small ones. Nevertheless, to avoid the fallacy of the continuum, we must develop criteria for imposing appropriate stopping points.

The implicit premise used in the fallacy of the continuum—namely, that small differences are unimportant or that contraries connected by intermediate small changes are not significantly different—is an indefensible or unwarranted assumption. For that reason, the premise is an unacceptable one and cannot be used as part of a good argument.

Example   More than a few people have been convinced that a slightly larger monthly payment isn't going to make very much difference.

> **Customer:** I just can't afford that much for a new computer right now.
> **Salesclerk:** Why don't you just put it on your MasterCard?
> **Customer:** But the monthly payment on my account is already $215 a month.
> **Salesclerk:** But if you buy the computer now, you can have it during the whole school year, which is when you really need it. Besides, it will only add about 50 bucks to your minimum payment.

Let us put this argument into standard form:

> Since putting the computer on your credit card will raise your monthly payment from $215 to about $265,
>
> (and small movements or differences on a line between a thing and its contrary have a negligible effect),
>
> ---
>
> Therefore, you can afford to buy the computer.

Such reasoning, if it leads one to a purchase, need occur only a few times before the customer might be in serious financial difficulty with credit card limits and/or monthly payments.

Example   Arguments using the assumption involved in the fallacy of the continuum are very persuasive. Indeed, even students who have carefully studied the fallacy have been heard to argue in the following manner: "Professor Gaia added five points to every student's final numerical average. It seems to me that if she added five points, she could have gone on and added six points. Then I would have passed the course. After all, there is very little difference between five points and six points. Yet that one point made the difference between passing and failing the course. Clint had a 60 average after the five-point addition, and I had a 59. He passed and I didn't; but does he really know that much more about psychology than I do?"

It is probably the case that the student with the 59 average did not know much less psychology than the student with the 60 average, but for practical purposes some cutoff point has to be established somewhere in order to avoid making extremes—for example, knowing and not knowing psychology—indistinguishable.

Example   What person on a diet or trying to cut down on smoking has not been deceived by the argument that one little doughnut or one more cigarette surely can't make any real difference?

Attacking the Fallacy   The kind of reasoning exhibited in the fallacy of the continuum can be easily reduced to absurdity by the following strategy: Ask the person who has committed this fallacy for the definition of some vague term such as "rich person." Try to get him or her to be very specific about the amount of assets in dollars that a person would have to have in order to qualify as rich. Call that amount X. Then subtract a small amount, for example, a hundred dollars, from that number and ask if a person having X minus a hundred dollars would still be rich. Your opponent will no doubt say "yes." Repeat the question again and again, subtracting another hundred dollars or more each time. Your opponent will probably continue to say "yes" every time, until it becomes clear where the questioning is going to lead—namely, that he or she will soon be assenting to the claim that a person having X minus X dollars is rich, which is an absurd claim. The arguer should be able to recognize from this example that it is the assumption that small differences are unimportant that renders him or her vulnerable to such manipulation. The arguer should also be able to see that the same kind of thinking is exhibited in his or her own argument and could lead to a similarly absurd conclusion.

It would be naive to deny that making distinctions is sometimes very difficult, but distinctions can and sometimes must be made. For example, there must be a difference between failing and passing a course and between staying on a diet and not staying on a diet. Moreover, since hot and cold are discernible distinctions, it is not likely that your opponent will claim that a hot day is not much different from a cold day, even though they are extreme points separated on a continuum by a large number of small intermediate differences.

Fallacy of Composition

DEFINITION *This fallacy consists in assuming that what is true of the parts of some whole is therefore true of the whole.*

The implicit premise used in the fallacy of composition—namely, that what is true of the parts of a whole is therefore true of the whole—is an indefensible or unwarranted assumption. Although that assumption may be true in some cases, it does not merit our acceptance as a general claim. Moreover, any premise that explicitly or implicitly employs such an unwarranted assumption cannot be an acceptable one.

This fallacy is committed principally in those cases in which a "whole," because of the particular relationship of its parts, may take on different characteristics from those of its individual parts. For example, the fact that each of the players on a football team is an excellent player would not be a sufficient reason to infer that the football team is an excellent one. The gathering together of players with excellent individual skills might produce a team that is *not* so excellent if, for whatever reason, the skills are not effectively meshed into team play. One cannot attribute to a whole those characteristics that are attributed to each of its parts, simply because it is a whole made up of those parts. Such an assumption ignores or fails to understand that the way the parts relate, interact, or affect each other often changes the character of the whole.

This fallacy should not be confused with the fallacy of inferring something about a whole class of things on the basis of one or a few instances of that thing. That fallacy has to do with insufficient evidence. The fallacy of composition is using the unwarranted assumption that we can infer something about a characteristic of some whole based on a characteristic of each of its parts.

Some cases of the fallacy of composition are so obviously flawed that we have probably never heard them uttered, such as: "Look at it this way, Larry. I love spending time with you, and Barbara is my best friend and I love spending time with her, so I'm sure that if the three of us took a vacation together, I would love it. It would be great." Neither are we likely to hear anyone, other than perhaps a small child, express this argument: "I love the taste of orange juice and I love raisin bran, so I think that if I put orange juice on my raisin bran rather than milk, it would taste great." Some instances of this fallacy, however, are not so easy to detect.

Example   I have sometimes heard comments like the following: "Professor Patel and Professor Warden are going to team-teach a course next spring in the philosophy of science. They are two of our best teachers, so it ought to be a really good course." The standard form of this argument is as follows:

Since Professors Patel and Warden are going to team-teach a course,

and they are among our best teachers,

(and what is true of the parts is true of the whole),

Therefore, the course ought to be very well taught.

If Professors Patel and Warden are good teachers in the sense in which that term is ordinarily used in an academic context, it could very likely be the case that the team-taught course would be a poor one. Many "good" teachers are good by virtue of their total and singular control of the classroom. A team-taught course usually does not allow for such control. There could also be other reasons, of course, why the professors might not work well together.

Example   "Our college concert choir auditions brought in several hundred people to try out for the choir this fall. That process yielded 30 excellent singers. We should have a really excellent choir this year." This claim made by the choir director, who should know better, falsely assumes that excellent parts will make an excellent whole. There are a number of factors that could prevent the choir from being an excellent one. For example, there may be distinct differences in the voice qualities of very good singers that might not blend well with the voice qualities of other good singers, and as a result, the choir sound might turn out to be quite mediocre.

Example   Who has not heard this fallacy committed in the most casual comments? "Dan is a fine young man, and Rebecca is a fine young woman. They'll make a fine couple."

The whole called "marriage" is more than a sum of its parts. Hence, the parts, by virtue of their relationship in the marital whole, might create something very much lacking in "fineness."

Attacking the Fallacy   It is important to recognize that wholes are not always different in character from their parts. For example, if every cup of punch taken from the punch bowl is sour, it would be entirely warranted to draw the conclusion that all the punch in the punch bowl is sour. In this case, there is nothing about a cup of this punch that, when it was mixed with all the other cups of punch, would change the taste or character of the whole bowl of punch.

In some cases, then, evidence for a claim about a whole is provided by facts about the parts. For an "attack" strategy, then, you might say to your opponent that you understand why he or she might have drawn a conclusion about a characteristic of the whole based on a characteristic of the parts, for in some cases the parts do provide that evidence. At the same time, you might use an example to illustrate how such an understandable assumption can lead to absurd conclusions in other cases. Consider this example: If it is the case that Diana has a very pretty blouse, a pretty skirt, and pretty shoes, they will not necessarily make a beautiful outfit together. The clash of patterns or colors could render the outfit quite garish. The unwarranted assumption, you should point out, lies in assuming that a characteristic automatically passes over to a whole from the parts.

Fallacy of Division

> **DEFINITION**   *This fallacy consists in assuming that what is true of some whole is therefore true of each of the parts of that whole.*

The fallacy of division is the opposite of the fallacy of composition. Rather than assuming that a characteristic of the parts is therefore a characteristic of the whole, it makes the unwarranted assumption that a characteristic of the whole is therefore a characteristic of each of the parts. However, as we have seen, a whole often represents something quite different from its parts.

Another way of committing the fallacy of division is to infer something about a particular member of a class on the basis of a *generalization* about the whole class. In this case, the characteristic of the whole should not be applied to the parts because the characteristic of the whole is only a statistical generalization based on the characteristics of *most* of the parts. Such a characteristic of the class is attributable to many of its parts, but because it is impossible to know to which members of the class the generalization may apply, it would be fallacious to assume, without additional evidence, that the characteristic accurately describes any particular member of the class.

The implicit premise in the fallacy of division involves an unwarranted assumption and is therefore an unacceptable one. It is simply not the case that what is true of some whole is always true of each of its parts. Neither can one infer that what has been generalized to be true about a class of things is true of every member, or any particular member, of that class.

Example Suppose that a high school senior rejected the idea of attending the University of Virginia on the grounds that he or she preferred small, intimate classes. To think in this way would be to commit the fallacy of division, because the student could not properly infer that a large university would have only large classes. Such an argument in standard form would look like this:

> Since I do not want to attend a college with large classes,
>
> and the University of Virginia is a large college,
>
> (and what is true of the whole is true of each of the parts),
>
> ---
>
> Therefore, I will not attend the University of Virginia.

The unacceptable third premise is an implicit unwarranted assumption and therefore violates the acceptability criterion of a good argument. Moreover, even if it were statistically true that large universities have large classes, the student could not reasonably infer that all classes or any particular class in a large university would be large.

Example It may be true that John has a handsome face; yet it may not be true that any particular part of his face—for example, his nose or his mouth—is handsome apart from the rest of his face. In this case, a characteristic of the whole is not necessarily a characteristic of the parts.

Example Although normal human beings are conscious entities, we should not infer from such a characteristic of the whole, as some have done, that individual cells or parts of that whole are conscious entities.

Attacking the Fallacy The attack on the fallacy of division is similar to the attack on the fallacy of composition. Say to your opponent that you understand why he or she might have drawn a conclusion about a characteristic of the parts based on a characteristic of the whole, because in some cases evidence for a claim about the parts is provided by facts about the whole. Then you might demonstrate how such an understandable assumption could lead to absurd conclusions in some cases. For example, you might point out how absurd it would be to assume that a particular state is diversified in terms of its climate simply because it is a part of the United States, which is so diversified.

To make the case against drawing conclusions about members of a class based on a generalization about the whole, you might try this example: If it is statistically the case that Maytag washing machines do not break down during their first three years of use, it would be absurd to exclude the possibility that your particular Maytag machine might break down during its first three years.

False Alternatives

DEFINITION *This fallacy consists in restricting too severely the number of proposed alternatives and in assuming that one of the suggested alternatives must be true.*

Because a reduction in the number of alternatives often means that only two extreme alternatives are considered, this fallacy is sometimes referred to as the *black-and-white fallacy*. The fallacy of false alternatives, however, is not just thinking in extremes; it is an oversimplification of a problem situation by a failure to entertain or at least recognize all its plausible alternative solutions.

Thinking in extremes, of course, requires much less mental effort than looking diligently for all possible solutions to a problem. However, with a minimum of imaginative effort it is possible to demonstrate that the assumption that all plausible solutions to a problem can be reduced to a small number, usually two, is false or unwarranted. The phony "either-or" premise is therefore an unacceptable one and cannot be part of a good argument.

The fallacy of false alternatives often derives from the failure to differentiate properly between contradictories (negatives) and contraries (opposites). Contradictories exclude any gradations between their extremes. There is no middle ground between a term and its negative—for example, between hot and not hot. Contraries, on the other hand, allow a number of gradations between their extremes. There is plenty of middle ground between a term and its *opposite*—for example, between hot and cold.

A common way to commit the fallacy of false alternatives is to treat contraries as if they were contradictories. In the case of contradictories (a term and its negative), one of the two extremes must be true and the other false. It is either hot or it is not hot. In the case of contraries (a term and its opposite), it is possible for both extremes to be false. It could be neither hot nor cold. To assume that it must be either hot or cold would be to treat contraries as if they were contradictories and thereby commit the fallacy of false alternatives—that is, to assume too few alternatives and to assume that one of the alternatives must be true.

Example Suppose that Professor Saliba claims that abortion is either morally right or morally wrong, and goes on to say that very few people, if any, would argue that abortion is something that we *should* do, so abortion must be wrong. Since Professor Saliba is defining "morally right" as morally obligatory and "morally wrong" as morally prohibited, he has committed the fallacy of false alternatives, because there is at least one other morally relevant alternative—to treat abortion as morally permissible. The terms right and wrong, then, should be treated as contraries or opposites. Professor

Saliba's treatment of them as contradictories resulted in his unwarranted either-or. The unwarranted assumption embedded in this argument is clearly revealed when we convert the argument to standard form:

> Since abortion is either morally obligatory or morally prohibited,
>
> (and these are the only moral alternatives, so one of them must be true),
>
> and no one would argue that it is morally obligatory to abort a fetus,
>
> ---
>
> Therefore, abortion is morally prohibited.

This conclusion would not follow but for the unwarranted second premise, which precludes the option of the moral permissibility of abortion.

Example   A case of treating contraries as if they were contradictories is also seen in one of the well-known sayings of Jesus: "If you are not for me, you must be against me." A similar instance may be found in the claim that if one is not a theist, then one must be an atheist. Neither claim seems to allow for the alternative of neutrality (or agnosticism).

Example   One would clearly commit the fallacy of false alternatives by assuming that a particular political candidate was running on the Democratic ticket simply because she was not running on the Republican ticket. There are a number of alternative tickets on which one might run, or one could be running on no ticket at all.

Attacking the Fallacy   Genuine "either-or" situations are very rare. If you are presented with one, it probably would be a good idea to treat it with a bit of skepticism—unless, of course, the either-or is a set of contradictories. In almost all other cases, more than two alternatives are available, although those additional alternatives may have been ignored by the arguer.

As a means of attacking an argument based on limited alternatives, ask the arguer if the alternatives presented exhaust all the plausible options? If the arguer is unable or unwilling to come up with any additional alternatives, point out a number of them yourself, and challenge the arguer to show why they do not qualify as plausible solutions. Once all the plausible alternatives have been considered, then the question becomes that of determining which of the plausible alternatives is best supported by the evidence or by good reasons.

Is-Ought Fallacy

DEFINITION   *This fallacy consists in assuming that because something is now the practice, it ought to be the practice. Conversely, it consists in assuming that because something is not now the practice, it ought not to be the practice.*

The is-ought fallacy is permeated by moral or value overtones. The "way things are" is regarded as ideal or "as it should be" simply because "things" are as they are. No reasons are given in support of the appropriateness of a thing's being the way it is. It is simply assumed that if it is, it must be right, and if it isn't, that must be right also; the possibility of changing it is not seriously entertained.

This fallacy should not be confused with the appeal to tradition. In the case of the irrelevant appeal to tradition, it is argued that the status quo should be maintained out of reverence for the past, but in the case of the is-ought fallacy, it is argued that the status quo should be maintained simply because it is the status quo. It is assumed that if it is the status quo, then that fact alone is sufficient reason for its appropriateness.

The is-ought fallacy should also not be confused with the irrelevant appeal to common opinion. The appeal to common opinion is usually used in an attempt to establish the *truth* of a claim; that is, an opinion or judgment is erroneously assumed to be true, simply because it is held by a large number of people. The is-ought fallacy, however, is used to establish the rightness or appropriateness of a particular kind of *behavior* or *practice,* simply because it is presently engaged in by a large number of people. Although the distinction is sometimes very subtle, the appeal to common opinion is a faulty method of establishing the *truth of a claim,* whereas the is-ought fallacy is a faulty method of establishing the *rightness of a practice.*

A premise that embodies an unwarranted assumption is not an acceptable one, and the is-ought fallacy embodies the unwarranted assumption that because a thing is now the practice, it ought to be the practice. But the fact that a particular practice is current says nothing about its defensibility. To support a judgment about its rightness, other evidence would be required.

Example   "Schoolteachers and professors should not seek to engage in collective bargaining. After all, very few teachers are presently involved in such tactics. There is simply very little interest in that sort of thing in our profession." Consider this argument as it appears in standard form:

> Since teachers and professors do not now engage in collective bargaining,
>
> (and whatever is now the practice should continue to be the practice),
>
> ---
>
> Therefore, teachers and professors should not engage in trade union collective bargaining.

The unwarranted assumption expressed in the second premise is now exposed. That assumption, of course, should play no role in determining the merit of the conclusion, because a premise based on an unwarranted assumption is not an acceptable premise. The fact that very few teachers may now be members of labor unions is not a sufficient reason for concluding that such involvement is not a good idea.

Example   "Smoking marijuana is illegal, son! If there were nothing wrong with it, it wouldn't be illegal. Don't you understand?"

The fact that the sale and possession of marijuana are illegal constitutes no reason for the propriety of that status. In other words, there is no logical justification for claiming that because it is illegal, it ought to be illegal.

Example

Professor Taylor: Students should be allowed to be more involved in the decision-making processes at this school.

> **Professor Smith:** The fact is that a college is just not very democratic. So let's not tamper with the institutional structure. Let's concentrate on some other important things that need our attention.

Professor Smith does not even entertain the possibility of introducing more democracy into the institutional structure, simply because that is not the "way things are."

Attacking the Fallacy A good argument always requires evidence or good reasons to support its conclusion. If no evidence or reason is given other than the status quo, you should point out that fact and insist that some specific evidence or reasons be provided. If the arguer is able to provide such support, you can then evaluate that evidence to determine whether the conclusion merits acceptance.

As an illustration, you might point out that although some people are being discriminated against because of their gender, that fact is not an acceptable reason for continuing the practice of sex discrimination. If an arguer has other reasons for the view that people should be treated differently on account of their gender, then those reasons should be presented for proper evaluation.

In some cases, you may need to resort to the absurd example method. You should have no trouble finding good examples, but consider this one: "Since the majority of drivers break the speed limit, drivers *should* break the speed limit." The faulty character of this argument should be transparent to even the most committed users of the is-ought.

Wishful Thinking

DEFINITION *This fallacy consists in assuming that because one wants something to be true, it is or will be true. Conversely, it consists in assuming that because one does not want something to be true, then it is not or will not be true.*

All of us spend a lot of our time wishing that things were a particular way. This way of thinking becomes fallacious when one treats a wish as if it were a premise in an argument. Such a premise unwarrantedly assumes that wanting something to be so will make it so.

The fallacy of wishful thinking is sometimes difficult to distinguish from rationalization. Both the rationalizer and the wishful thinker want a claim to be true, but while the rationalizer attempts to establish that claim by means of a phony argument, the wishful thinker tries to establish it directly from his or her strong desires.

This implicit premise in a wishful thinking argument is the unwarranted assumption that our feelings or emotions about a particular claim have some bearing on the truth or merit of that claim. Indeed, many of our strong religious and other ideological beliefs seem to be built on no more of a foundation than our intense wish that those beliefs be true. Some writers have even suggested that wishful thinking could be called the *fallacy of belief* or even the *fallacy of faith*. "If you have faith," we are sometimes told, then it will be true. We are even told that something can be true "for you" if you believe it to be so. Although it is possible that wanting something to be true may give you the motivation to try to help bring it into being, believing does not make *anything* so.

Since there is no reason to believe that our wishes affect the truth of claims, the implicit premise used in wishful thinking is an indefensible one, and an argument that uses such an unacceptable premise cannot be a good one.

Example   An argument for life after death put forth by a British theologian goes like this: "There must be a life after death, because almost all people desire it. It is a part of the very nature of human beings to desire it. If there were no life after death, then why would all humans desire it?" The standard form of this argument might look like this:

> Since all persons desire life after death,
>
> (and whatever one wishes to be true is or will be true),
>
> _____
>
> Therefore, there is life after death.

Even if the claim about the universality of the desire for an afterlife is true, it is quite conceivable that a universal desire could go totally unsatisfied. Consider, if you will, the desire of most people to have more money than they have. Wanting something to be the case, even if it is universally desired, does not make it so.

Example   "My husband has been missing for more than ten years, but I know he's still alive. He just couldn't be dead." It may be true that he is still alive, but her wishing him to be alive has no bearing on whether it is true.

Example   "There is a perfect marriage partner out there for everyone in this world. That is what everyone wants—a perfect marriage. If you look hard enough for it and then work hard enough at it, you'll have a perfect marriage."

Sometimes wishing that something will happen can have some effect on whether it does, but only in those cases in which we are directly and dynamically related to the situation. Even then, we rarely have total control over it, especially something as complex as marriage.

Attacking the Fallacy   One method of attacking the fallacy of wishful thinking would be to offer strong evidence for a claim that is contrary to the claim at issue and to ask your opponent to evaluate that evidence. The serious believer will presumably want to find some way to counteract the force of that evidence, and in order to do so will have to abandon his or her exclusive reliance on a wish premise.

Another strategy would be to set forth a denial of the wishful thinker's belief and then cite as your only "evidence" your wish or belief that your claim is true—the same "evidence" that your opponent cites for his or her view. Since your conclusions are contradictory, at least one of you must be wrong, because contradictory claims cannot both be true. Determining who is wrong may require, if all goes well, a cooperative evaluation of other, independent evidence.

Finally, you might try an absurd example. Ask your opponent if his or her wish-based thinking is any different from a woman's believing that she is not pregnant, simply because she does not *want* to be pregnant.

Misuse of a Principle

DEFINITION   *This fallacy consists in misapplying a principle or rule in a particular instance by assuming that it has no exceptions. Conversely, it consists in attempting to refute a principle or rule by means of an exceptional case.*

One who commits this fallacy overlooks the fact that there are usually exceptions to almost any principle or rule, which can cause the arguer to misuse it in two ways. One way is to make the unwarranted assumption that a principle or rule can be applied in every case, no matter what the circumstances, and then to apply it to a situation for which it was not intended. The arguer simply fails to take into account reasonable exceptions to the principle's range of application.

The second way of misusing a principle is to falsely assume that unusual or exceptional cases will falsify or refute it. Unusual circumstances do not usually negatively affect the general truth or merit of a principle or rule. As a matter of fact, just the opposite is probably the case, which makes sense of that strange-sounding phrase sometimes directed to those who think they have refuted a principle by pointing out exceptions to it: "The exception proves the rule."

Because this fallacy involves the problem of dealing with unusual or accidental circumstances, it is sometimes referred to as the *fallacy of accident*. Regardless of what it is called, it is an argument that uses an unacceptable premise. The implicit premise that a general rule has no exceptions or that an unusual case can refute a general principle represents an inaccurate understanding of the nature of rules, principles, or generalizations.

Example   Suppose that Monica plans to operate a used-car business on her property in a residential area of town, and she argues that zoning restrictions do not apply, because it is her property and she can do anything she wants with it. In standard form, her argument looks like this:

> Since I want to operate a used-car business on my residential property,
>
> (and the relevant principle is that I can do whatever I want with my own property and that principle has no exceptions),
> _____
> Therefore, I should be able to operate my used-car business on my own property.

A principle to which most of us would subscribe is that people are generally entitled to use their own property in whatever way they wish. But it would be a misapplication of this principle to claim that no restrictions should or could be imposed on the use of one's property. The second premise in the argument that claims that the principle has no exceptions is an unwarranted assumption and is therefore an unacceptable premise.

Example   If the rule with regard to X-rated movies shown at a drive-in theater is that "no one under 18 will be allowed into the theater," it would be a misapplication of this rule for an attendant to refuse to allow a couple to bring their infant child with them. The rule was not intended to be applied in such cases.

Example   The opposite form of this fallacy might be shown by an argument that attempts to refute the principle that "lying is wrong" by pointing out that a psychological counselor surely would be justified in lying, if necessary, to keep from betraying a confidence. This exception to the principle against lying would not allow the arguer to draw the conclusion that lying is not wrong. It should simply be the occasion to recognize the fact that moral principles often come into conflict and that a choice must be made between them, usually in terms of which principle has the greater worth or priority in the context.

Attacking the Fallacy   One way of pointing out the fallacious character of a particular misapplication of a principle is to examine very carefully the purpose of the principle or rule and then to discuss how exceptions would be in order when that purpose is not being violated or when it is superseded by some more important, conflicting principle. Then try to show in the particular case that either the exception is not inconsistent with the purpose of the principle or that there is a more important principle at stake. In other words, an attempt should be made to show that the unusual case in question really is an exception to the principle by virtue of its special or unusual circumstances.

Another line of attack might be to find some general principle with which your opponent would agree, and then find an exception to that principle with which he or she would also agree. If the arguer recognizes legitimate exceptions in your illustration, he or she should be willing to acknowledge possible exceptions to the principle being misused. For example, your opponent would probably agree that parents have the responsibility to raise their children in whatever way they think best, but he or she would probably also agree that parents do not have the right to use physical torture as part of their method.

Fallacy of the Mean

DEFINITION   *This fallacy consists in assuming that the moderate or middle view between two extremes must be the best or right one, simply because it is the middle view.*

Another name for this bit of faulty thinking is the *fallacy of moderation*. It is often assumed—indeed it is a part of our conventional wisdom—that a position on an issue that is somewhere in the middle is always the best, simply because it is in the middle. In many situations, a moderate view may in fact be the best or most justifiable position to take, but it is not the best simply because it is a moderate position. In many cases, the so-called extreme or radical solution to a problem is the most defensible one. The fact that a particular position is a moderate one has nothing to do with its worth.

Although it is *not* a fallacy to compromise in order to settle a dispute, it *is* a fallacy to assume, apart from evidence, that a compromise solution is the best one. It might well be the case that the position of one of the parties involved in the dispute or conflict has no legitimacy whatsoever.

The implicit premise that the moderate or middle position is best is a highly questionable assumption that is not warranted by any evidence. It therefore is an unacceptable premise whose use would violate the acceptability criterion of a good argument.

Example   Suppose that Greg is looking for a used refrigerator for his apartment and he finds one that seems to be the right size at a used-furniture store. The seller wants $300 for it, and Greg offers $200. Because the two of them are far apart on the price, Greg suggests "splitting the difference" at $250. A standard form reconstruction will show the unwarranted assumption involved in Greg's argument:

Since you want $300 for the used refrigerator,

and I am willing to pay only $200 for it,

(and the middle position is always the right or best position),

Therefore, the right or best price would be $250.

Although such a compromise may seem fair to Greg, it may not be the best solution to the problem. On the one hand, it is possible that the seller already has $250 invested in it and needs to make some profit. On the other hand, it is possible that it may not even be worth $250 in the used-appliance market. Thus, Greg's original offer of $200 may have been a very fair one. One must also consider the possibility that one or both of the negotiators may have already "built in" the anticipated call for compromise, so that the so-called compromise turns out not to be a compromise at all. In any case, the third premise represents an unwarranted assumption, which renders the premise unacceptable.

Example   "I have difficulty accepting the notion that all human events are the inevitable results of prior causes, but I also have difficulty with the view that human beings can act apart from prior causes in their experience. In other words, I find both determinism and indeterminism untenable. Surely the most defensible view is somewhere between those extremes."

This is the somewhat common dilemma that the introductory philosophy student encounters. The solution does not lie in finding a middle view between these extremes. Determinism and indeterminism are contradictories. Either all events are determined or it is not the case that all events are determined. There is no middle ground.

Example   Consider the following argument that is sometimes put forth regarding the Israeli-Palestinian conflict: "Both the Palestinian and Israeli points of view represent extremes. Therefore, some kind of compromise must be the best solution." Compromise may be the only way that this dispute can be finally settled, but it is a different thing to say that a compromise *per se* is the best solution in that conflict.

Attacking the Fallacy   If an arguer proposes a middle position with regard to an issue, insist that he or she justify the merit of that position, without reference to its middle status. It might also be helpful for all parties to keep in mind that there are two ways of understanding the notion of "best position to take" in any particular situation. A compromise may be the "best" way to resolve a difficult situation. For example, it may prevent continued economic deprivation, bloodshed, or mental anguish. However, it may not be the "best" in the sense of being the most accurate, justifiable, or morally responsible solution to the problem. Even though you may sometimes have to accept the *compromise* position in order to settle an issue, you may want to make it clear that you do not think it is the *most justifiable* position to take.

If your direct attack upon the fallacy of the mean is unsuccessful, you can always try an absurd example. Ask your opponent if the best way to behave in the voting booth would be to "compromise" and divide your vote evenly among all the political parties on the ballot.

Faulty Analogy

> **DEFINITION** *This fallacy consists in assuming that because two things are alike in one or more respects, they necessarily are alike in some other important respect, while failing to recognize the insignificance of their similarities and/or the significance of their dissimilarities.*

One who argues by analogy usually compares a thing about which there is some dispute with another thing that may be less complex and controversial, and argues that because they are similar in certain respects, it is reasonable to conclude that they may be similar in some other important respect that is relevant to the question at issue. For example, if a certain known thing, X, has properties a, b, and c and the thing at issue, Y, has those same properties, then, if X has property d, then it may be concluded that Y probably has that property as well. Suppose that the issue before us is that of whether leaving work early, coming in late, taking long coffee breaks and extra long lunch breaks is morally wrong. To make a strong case for the immorality of such action, one might argue that such behavior is no different from stealing money from the employer. To produce a good analogical argument, the arguer would want to point out as many important and relevant *similarities* as possible between the compared cases and to show that there are no important and relevant *dissimilarities* between them. If important similarities are *not* found and a number of important dissimilarities *are* found, the analogy may be a faulty one

A good analogical argument does more than point out similarities. If a conclusion is drawn about one case based on its similarity to another, then there should be evidence presented to show how the compared cases are alike in the significant way that is relevant to the claim at issue. An observed similarity, by itself, does not constitute evidence. Even if the premises of an analogical argument accurately identify important similarities and find few, if any, dissimilarities, there could still be a problem with the analogy. Because analogies are by nature usually only suggestive, even a good analogy is rarely forceful enough to make a strong case. The arguer should therefore be prepared to offer other evidence for the claim in question.

One who commits the fallacy of faulty analogy simply assumes that things similar in some ways are necessarily similar in other ways. He or she then draws a questionable conclusion from compared cases that may be alike only in trivial or superficial ways and/or are quite different in important ways—that is, in ways that are relevant to the issue at stake in the argument. Hence, the analogy fails to support the argument's conclusion.

The implicit premise that two things alike in one or more respects are also alike in some other respect is a very dubious assumption and thus cannot qualify as an acceptable premise. Therefore, any argument concerning compared cases in which an inference is drawn solely on that assumption cannot qualify as a good argument.

Example   Professor Ray: "If one were to listen to only one kind of music or eat only one kind of food, it would soon become tasteless or boring. Variety makes eating and listening exciting and enriching experiences. So it seems to me that an exclusive sexual relationship with only one partner for the rest of one's life—that is, marriage—does not hold out much hope for very much excitement or enrichment." If we were to convert this analogy into standard form, the unwarranted assumption will be clearly revealed:

Since eating the same food and listening to the same music all the time would soon make those experiences become boring,

and since variety makes those experiences more exciting and enriching,

(and since we wish for similar excitement and enrichment in sexual relationships),

(and in compared cases things that are alike in some respects are alike in other respects),

---

Therefore, variety in one's sexual relationships, rather than the limitation of sexual experience to a single marital partner, would make those experiences more exciting and enjoyable.

Although Professor Ray's argument might have some initial force, in order for it to be a strong argument, he will have to show that the compared cases are alike in significant ways. More specifically, he will have to show that an exclusive sexual relationship is not essentially different from an unchanging food diet or an unchanging musical diet. However, since human relationships are so complex and so full of a variety of possibilities, there is some doubt as to whether Professor Ray will be successful in convincing others that the disadvantages of narrow diets of food and music can be extended to exclusive sexual relationships.

Example Suppose someone defended open-textbook examinations with the following argument: "No one objects to a physician's looking up a difficult case in the *PDR (Physicians' Desk Reference)*. Why, then, shouldn't students taking a difficult examination be permitted to use their textbooks?"

With very little reflection, it will be clear that there is normal similarity between the compared cases. The only thing that seems at all similar is the act of looking inside a book for some assistance in solving a problem. But there the alleged similarity stops. Very different purposes are served by such an act in the two situations. One is specifically designed to test a person's knowledge; the other functions as a means of helping the physician to diagnose a patient's problem. The physician's basic knowledge has already been tested by virtue of his or her status as a licensed physician.

Example "Smoking cigarettes is just like ingesting arsenic into your system. Both have been shown to be causally related to death. So if you wouldn't want to take a spoonful of arsenic, I would think that you wouldn't want to continue smoking."

Although it is true that both the ingestion of arsenic and the smoking of cigarettes have been shown to be causally related to death, there are some significant differences in the character of those causal relations. A single heavy dose of arsenic poisoning will bring about immediate death, whereas the heavy smoking of cigarettes would be likely to bring about premature death only as a result of a long process of deterioration or disease. In one case, then, death is immediate and certain; in the other, death is statistically neither immediate nor certain. Thus, the analogy is a faulty one.

Attacking the Fallacy One of the most effective ways of blunting the force of a faulty analogy is to formulate a counteranalogy that allows you to draw a conclusion in direct contradiction to that of the arguer. For example, you could respond to Professor Ray's argument about narrow diets with the following analogy: "Just as one might want to maintain throughout one's life that sense of comfort and good feeling experienced with those dependable things that are enjoyable and familiar, such as one's relationship to a son or daughter or talking with a lifelong friend, so it is that the dependable, enjoyable relationship with one's life partner, with whom one feels comfortable and toward whom one has good feelings, is something to be cherished and maintained throughout one's life." This counteranalogy may also be flawed, but it would at least suggest that there is an inconclusiveness in Ray's analogical argument.

However, if you are using a counteranalogy to make a serious *counterclaim*, rather than simply providing an absurd example, make sure that you can provide convincing evidence that the compared cases are similar in important or significant ways. If you are not able to come up with a serious counteranalogy or if you are not interested in making a counterclaim, all you may be able to do, when confronted with a weak or faulty analogy, is to point out that since the two compared cases resemble each other only in unimportant or trivial ways, no inference should be drawn concerning the claim at issue. In no case should you allow a clever user of analogies to think that simply pointing out interesting similarities between cases qualifies as evidence for a claim about *one* of them.

ASSIGNMENTS

B. Unwarranted Assumption Fallacies   For each of the following arguments, (1) identify the type of unwarranted assumption fallacy illustrated, and (2) explain how the reasoning violates the acceptability criterion. There are two examples of each fallacy discussed in this section. Arguments marked with an asterisk (*) have sample answers at the end of the text.

*1. People who have to have a cup of coffee every morning before they can function have no less a problem than alcoholics who have to have their alcohol each day to sustain them.

*2. If a physician is justified in deceiving a sick person, and if there is nothing wrong with telling children about Santa Claus, then we simply have to reject the view that "lying is wrong."

3. No one dislikes me enough to slash my tires. I'm sure of it. It must have been an act of random violence or a case of mistaken identity.

*4. I don't see why you have criticized this novel as implausible. There isn't a single incident in it that couldn't have happened.

*5. Anyone who eats meat tacitly condones the killing of animals. We might just as well condone the killing of human beings, for how do we draw the line between one form of animal life and another?

*6. The University of Virginia is one of the best universities in this country, so it must have an outstanding philosophy department. Why don't you apply to do graduate work there?

*7. The way I see it is that we must either spend enough money on our football program to make us competitive with some of the better teams in this region or simply drop the program altogether.

*8. Maxine: Give me some time to think about it, Eugene. Whether to have sex with someone is a very important decision. I want to try to make a rational decision about this.

Eugene: Look, Maxine! Having sex with someone is not something people make rational decisions about.

*9. No one can prove the existence of God. You simply have to believe that He is and accept Him into your life.

*10. Judge: "I have heard contradictory testimony from the two principal witnesses in this case. I can only conclude that the truth must lie somewhere in between."

11. Each of the members of the Board of Trustees has demonstrated superior judgment and skill in handling his or her personal affairs. Therefore, I think we can be assured that the Board will exercise superior judgment and skill in handling the affairs of this institution.

12. Some students want our college dorms to be completely open to members of the opposite sex, 24 hours a day. Others want a closed dorm policy—that is, one that makes the dorms off limits to any member of the opposite sex, anytime. Wouldn't the best solution be to have the dorms open about 12 hours a day—perhaps from noon to midnight?

13. Because the Democratic party supports a program of national health insurance, I assume that Congressman Trent, who is a member of the Democratic party, supports such a program.

14. Because human bodies become less active as they grow older, and because they eventually die, it is reasonable to expect that political bodies will become less and less active the longer they are in existence, and that they too will eventually die.

15. Farmer to son: "Son, if you pick up that newborn calf over there once every day, your muscles should develop to the point that you would be able to lift it when it is a full-grown cow. The calf will gain just a tiny bit of weight each day, and that little bit of weight can't make any significant difference in your ability to lift it. If you can do it one day, you should be able to do it the next day."

16. Resort Manager: I'm sorry, but you cannot bring that dog in here. We have a rule against any pets.

Vacationer: But he's my wife's guide dog; she is blind.

Resort Manager: I'm sorry, but we have to enforce the rule or we would have a whole menagerie here.

17. Did you vote for him for president because he is a Democrat or because he promised to reorganize and simplify the federal bureaucracy?

18. But, officer, you shouldn't give me a parking ticket for parking here! People park here all the time and never get tickets. I myself have been parking here for several months and never once received a ticket. No one pays any attention to the "No Parking" sign in this alley.

C. For each of the following arguments (1) identify, from among all the fallacies studied in this chapter, the fallacy illustrated, and (2) explain how the reasoning violates the acceptability criterion. There are two examples of each of the fallacies discussed in this chapter.

1. Can you believe that Nathan got an A on his history test last week? I also heard that Debbie, who sits directly in front of him, also received an A.

2. *Man* has always been used as a generic pronoun. There's no reason that we should change it now.

3. It is hard for me to see how my neighbors and I can be blamed for discrimination when it comes to deciding who is to live in our neighborhood. We make discriminations all through life. If people are not allowed to discriminate, how can they make decisions in life between right and wrong? Indeed, how can they even act responsibly if they must be indiscriminate in their choices?

4. No, I don't believe you. Barbara would not do that to me. She loves me; she would not be unfaithful. If she has been cheating on me, as you say, it would destroy a beautiful relationship. She's my whole life, Mike. She just wouldn't do that to me.

5. We do not advocate censorship. We are simply protecting students from reading material that is morally objectionable.

6. The phone keeps ringing and ringing. Anita must not be home.

7. We told you to be home at a reasonable hour, Dawn, and you come dragging in here at midnight. We thought you could be trusted, but I guess we were wrong.

8. Student: I don't understand why I have to give you my parents' name and address just to get a phone line put into my apartment.
   Telephone representative: You're a student, aren't you? We have to have parental information on all students. That's company policy.
   Student: But I'm a 43-year-old graduate student.
   Telephone representative: A rule is a rule.

9. Dirk: The changes in the Senate environment bill introduced by the Republicans have improved it considerably.
   Greg: Well, it's good to see that the Democrats are cleaning up the opposition's bad legislation.

10. Lawyer to judge: "Since women are generally more nurturing than men, and since a young child needs a nurturing parent, I think that you should award custody to my client, Ms. Cox."

11. As a defense for his act of cheating on his wife, because she cheated on him, Robert says, "Well, you know what Jesus said, 'An eye for an eye!'"

12. Some people think that there should be no restrictions on gays in the military. Others think that no gays at all should be allowed to serve in the armed forces. The best solution, I suppose, would be to meet halfway and institute a policy of "Don't ask, don't tell."

13. I know that the sign says that the safe speed for these curves is 25 miles per hour, but if 25 miles per hour is safe, then 30 miles an hour shouldn't give me any problem. After all, there's not a whole lot of difference between 25 and 30 miles per hour.

14. Brad is very attractive and so is Nicole. They should have really beautiful children.

15. People who buy stocks are no different from people who bet on horse racing. They both risk their money with little chance of making a big profit.

16. Jamie: Brian, you seem to have been very irritable lately. Is there anything wrong?
   Brian: So you think that *you're* not irritable!

17. Iris: I just don't understand what could have happened to the $50 that I had in my desk drawer.
   Kris: Why don't you ask Denise? She's been out shopping all day. She just came back with a whole bunch of new stuff.

18. Nobody keeps to the 65-mile-an-hour speed limit. Most everybody drives at least 70. The speed limit really ought to be raised 5 miles an hour.

19. Xander: I just drove the new Mazda. You know, these Japanese cars are great cars.

   Victoria: I don't know why you are putting down American cars. There are some excellent cars built in America.

20. I know that you are not a wealthy man, but I hope that does not embarrass you. There's nothing wrong with being poor.

21. An impartial arbitration committee should not take sides when settling a dispute. But the so-called impartial committee that was supposed to arbitrate the issue between the students and the administration decided in favor of the administration and suspended the students. So how can they claim to have been impartial?

22. My father is in intensive care at the hospital. His prognosis is very bad, but I know he will pull through. I can feel it; he *will not* die.

23. I didn't have a date with Della last night. I just took her to dinner, and then we went to a movie.

24. The Biology Department at the University of Virginia has been given national recognition as an outstanding department because of the quality of their undergraduate teaching. One of its recent graduates has applied for our opening in biology here. I think we should hire her immediately. How could we go wrong?

25. Larry: No . . . I don't think that I'll join your group. I'm really not a very religious person.

   Dan: Really? I never knew that you didn't believe in God.

26. Bar hostess: May I see your driver's license, please?

   Taylor: I don't have one. I don't drive, but I have a student ID. Do you want to see my ID?

   Bar hostess: I'm sorry, but you can't order any drinks unless we see your driver's license.

27. Barry: My wife wouldn't go into the grocery store with her sister, because she hasn't washed her hair for more than a week.

   Erik: Your wife could have left her sister in the car, couldn't she?

28. Protestants and Catholics disagree about a number of issues. But I see no reason why they can't get along. Each side is going to have to give a little. The truth surely must lie somewhere in the middle.

29. Mark: Dylan has two daughters. His *older* daughter, Laura, is very bright.

   Matt: The younger daughter must have our friend Dylan's genes.

30. Teresa and Mark are getting married? They are two of the most unhappy people I know. There's no way that can be a happy marriage.

31. This country is like a machine. No matter who operates it, it will behave in essentially the same way. So it doesn't make any difference who is elected president.

32. I'm so mad that I couldn't get into the club last night. After all, I will turn 21 in just two weeks. It seems to me that they could have let me in. It's not as if I were, like, 18 or 19 years old.

D. Submit an argument (different from the ones submitted in previous chapters, but follow the same procedure). Point out any named fallacies that violate the structural criterion, the relevance criterion, and/or the acceptability criterion. Then set forth the best argument possible for the most defensible position on the issue.

E. Following the model used in the text, use a 3 × 5 card to submit an *original* example (found or created) of each of the fallacies that violate the acceptability criterion.

F. Create your own strategies or suggestions for attacking each of the fallacies that violate the acceptability criterion.

VIII
Fallacies That Violate
the Sufficiency Criterion

One who presents an argument for or against a position should attempt to provide reasons that are sufficient in number, kind, and weight to support the acceptance of the conclusion.

The fallacies discussed in this chapter are particular ways in which insufficient evidence can cause an argument to go wrong. Some arguments use too little evidence or no evidence at all; others use biased evidence or only the appearance of evidence; still others omit key or crucial evidence from the mix. Arguments that commit the so-called causal fallacies draw conclusions about causal relationships that are not sufficiently supported by appropriate evidence.

Each of these patterns of reasoning is a way in which an argument may violate the sufficiency criterion of a good argument by failing to provide sufficient grounds for its conclusion. If the premises are not sufficient in number, kind, and weight, they may not be strong enough to establish the truth of the conclusion. Additional and/or different premises may be needed to make the case.

The fallacies that violate the sufficiency criterion are divided into two groups: (1) the fallacies of missing evidence and (2) the causal fallacies.

FALLACIES OF MISSING EVIDENCE

A study of actual arguments reveals that many utilize little or no evidence, which means that numerous arguments violate the sufficiency criterion. There are many different types of such missing-evidence fallacies.

The most common of the missing-evidence fallacies, which might be called the *fallacy of inference from a name or description,* is the kind of fallacy that advertisers and public relations experts hope you will commit over and over again. This *fallacy of advertisers* is committed when descriptive or identifying words or phrases attached to people or things are regarded as constituting sufficient reason for drawing conclusions about those objects. If one infers that a product is the "economy size" based on nothing more than an ad or the product's package that *says* it is the economy size, or if one concludes that a particular college is the best college in the South simply because the college's catalog states that it is, one has come to a conclusion based on no evidence. This fallacy is so lacking in subtlety that little more need be said about it other than to point out that it is probably the most frequently committed of all fallacies, in spite of its lack of subtlety.

The more interesting and somewhat more subtle types of missing-evidence arguments are discussed in more detail in the following section. The first is that of drawing a conclusion from either too small a sample or from data that is unrepresentative. The most interesting and thoroughgoing case of missing evidence is the argument that tries to make a case for a particular claim because of the lack of evidence against it, without regard to whether there is evidence in its favor. Other missing-evidence fallacies make claims on the basis of what didn't happen or has not yet happened, use clichés and aphorisms in place of evidence, or plead for one to be treated as an exception to a rule or principle, without providing any reason for doing so. Finally, there is the kind of argument that inexplicably omits the key evidence needed to make its case.

Insufficient Sample

DEFINITION *This fallacy consists in drawing a conclusion or generalization from too small a sample of cases.*

The evidence used in a case of insufficient sample is usually acceptable and relevant, but there is not enough of it to establish the conclusion of the argument. This fallacy is sometimes called a *hasty generalization*, because an arguer has been too quick to draw a conclusion, given the skimpiness of the evidence. It is not uncommon for an arguer to draw a conclusion or generalization based on only a few instances of a phenomenon. In fact, a generalization is often drawn from a single piece of supporting data, an act that might be described as committing the *fallacy of the lonely fact*.

It is sometimes difficult to determine just what constitutes a sufficient number of instances for drawing any particular conclusion. The sufficiency of a sample is partially determined by each context of inquiry, but it should not be assumed that an increase in the number of instances means that the claim for which they are evidence will be more reliable. There is a point beyond which the increase in the number of instances has a negligible effect on the merit of the claim.

Some areas of inquiry have quite sophisticated guidelines for determining the sufficiency of a sample, such as in voter preference samples or television viewing samples. In many areas, however, there are no such guidelines to assist us in determining what would be sufficient grounds for the truth of a particular conclusion.

Example   "Vitamin C really works. Every member of my family used to have at least one winter cold every year. Last fall each of us started taking 1,000 milligrams of vitamin C a day, and there hasn't been even a sniffle at our house in over nine months." If we convert this argument into standard form, we have the following argument:

Since each member of my family for nine months has been taking 1,000 milligrams of vitamin C daily,

and during that period we have had no colds,

and during the previous cold season, we each had at least one cold,

(and the sample of one family is a sufficient sample to determine what is true for all persons),

---

Therefore, a vitamin C therapy of 1,000 milligrams daily will prevent the common cold.

Such data may be interesting enough to encourage some people to consider experimenting with vitamin C therapy, but the argument hardly makes the case for the program's effectiveness. The claim made in the implicit fourth premise about the sufficiency of a sample limited to one homogeneous family is highly questionable and would not justify drawing any conclusion about the cold-preventing effects of daily megadoses of vitamin C. A number of other factors could possibly account for the no-cold phenomenon in the arguer's family during that particular nine-month period.

Example   It is not unusual to pick up a few items at a grocery store other than the one at which we normally shop and discover that the prices on those few items are lower than the prices on the same items at our regular store. In such a situation we might infer that we should switch grocery stores in order to save on our monthly grocery bill. We could also find the prices on those few items to be higher and infer that we should stick with our regular store. However, neither conclusion would be warranted, because the samples used are too small. Only the results of a more comprehensive comparative survey of the prices on all the items we typically buy during the month could possibly justify a conclusion about the matter.

Example   "My experience with my ex-wife was such a bad one that I have no intention of ever marrying again. In fact, I would not recommend marriage to anyone." This reasoning is obviously based on a very small sample. His one experience with marriage apparently convinced him that marriage was not a worthwhile institution for him, his friends, and probably anyone else. It is quite possible, however, that his one negative experience with marriage could be attributed to his own flaws or to those of his wife, rather than to flaws in the institution of marriage. It can at least be said that the conclusion concerning the value of marriage deserves a larger sample.

Attacking the Fallacy   Those who present you with an argument based on a single case or an insufficient sample are usually quite convinced of the truth of their claim. Perhaps the reason that it seems so convincing to them is that it often comes out of a significant personal experience. You should, however, find some way to make it clear that a personal insight falls far short of being a good argument.

It is possible, in some cases, that what appears to be a one-instance generalization may not be intended as an argument at all; it may simply be the expression of an opinion, accompanied by an illustration. To clarify the matter, you might ask, "Are you just expressing an opinion, or are you presenting an argument?"

If the arguer denies that he or she is just expressing an opinion, a reconstruction of his or her argument may be helpful. A reconstruction of the argument, spelling out the implicit premise that is being used—namely, that one or a few cases constitute sufficient grounds for drawing a conclusion about all cases—should clearly demonstrate to the arguer the flawed character of the argument. If it doesn't, an absurd example might:

"Faculty kids are real brats. I babysat with one the other night, and he was spoiled, rude, and uncontrollable." If necessary, put the argument into standard form:

> Since the faculty child I babysat for recently was a brat,
>
> (and one faculty child is a sufficient sample of faculty children to determine what is true of all faculty children),
>
> _____
>
> Therefore, all faculty children are brats.

It is highly unlikely that your opponent could embrace, without embarrassment, the second premise, once it is spelled out, and therefore he or she could not continue to hold to a similar premise in his or her own argument.

Unrepresentative Data

> **DEFINITION** *This fallacy consists in drawing a conclusion based on data from an unrepresentative or biased sample.*

Unrepresentative data are data that are not proportionately drawn from all relevant subclasses. For example, if one wished to generalize about the opinion of the American people on a particular issue, it would be appropriate to consider data proportionately drawn from subclasses based on race, age, educational status, sex, geographical area, and perhaps even religion and political affiliation. In most cases, data from other subclasses, such as body weight and hair color, would not be relevant.

It is also important to avoid using data that may be biased. This can occur in at least two ways. First, the data collected may be tainted by virtue of the bias of the gatherer. Opinion data gathered by a political party or by an advocacy group should be immediately suspect. Second, data purporting to support claims about any matter are biased data if collected from one or only a few subgroups of the target population—especially if data are collected from groups that might have strong positive or negative opinions about the matter at issue. For example, if one were interested in assessing campus opinions about college athletics, one should not survey just the members of the campus athletic teams. Neither should one survey just the nonathletes.

If you were interested in the quality of a recent film release, you should not form a judgment exclusively on the basis of evaluations collected from readers of a single magazine, since its subscribers are a subgroup with special interests and tastes. Neither should you give much credence to the call-in or e-mail polls frequently taken by virtually every network these days, if you want to know what the American people think about a particular issue.

Another kind of atypical data might be data of differing quality. If one compared statistics gathered with modern techniques of statistical reporting and analysis with statistics gathered under very different methodological and technical conditions, almost any conclusion would be highly questionable. For example, if one were to compare statistics on the number of violent crimes committed in the United States in 2000 with statistics about similar phenomena in 1940, the comparative conclusion would be quite suspect.

Example "It has been concluded from a recent study involving more than 100,000 people in the state of Florida that 43 percent of the American people now spend at least two hours a day in some form of recreational activity." A conversion of this argument into standard form clearly reveals the statistical flaw:

> Since 43 percent of Florida residents spend at least two hours a day in some form of recreational activity,
>
> (and the people of Florida are representative of all other Americans),
>
> ———————————————————————————————
>
> Therefore, 43 percent of all Americans spend at least two hours a day in some form of recreational activity.

To draw such a conclusion about the leisure-time activities of the American people would not be warranted. The state of Florida is populated by a disproportionate number of retired and leisure-oriented people, so data based on a Florida population alone would be unrepresentative.

Example "We had a mock election on campus today, and the Democratic candidate won. So I am pretty confident that she will win the election in November, especially because more than 2,000 students voted. That seems to be a big enough sample. Don't you agree?"

A college population hardly qualifies as a representative sample of voters, even if the size of the sample is actually larger than the number usually polled by sophisticated polling organizations. If it is not drawn from relevant representative subclasses, the size of the sample is of no consequence.

Example "A recent study of how Americans spend their vacations revealed that 52 percent of the people spend five or more days a year at ocean beaches."

This study was based on a sample of 50,000 Virginians, drawn from every relevant subgroup of the population, but it is hardly representative. Most areas of Virginia are close to popular beaches within the state as well as in North and South Carolina. For that reason a disproportionate number of the residents of Virginia, when compared with those from many other states, vacation at the beach.

Attacking the Fallacy Suggestions for responding to arguers who use unrepresentative data are similar to those for dealing with arguers who use too small a sample. If you encounter a case in which someone has used suspect data, you might expose the flawed statistical assumption by making it part of a similar argument with an absurd conclusion. For example:

> Since most of the 1,000 people in attendance at the county dog show own dogs,
>
> (and what is true of the people at the dog show is true of the entire population),
>
> ———————————————————————————————
>
> Therefore, most people own dogs.

If the arguer sees nothing wrong with the second premise, no attack against unrepresentative data may turn out to be very successful, but you might try one other strategy. Threaten the arguer with the possibility of your gathering another set of data of the same size from people living in local nursing homes as support for a claim that most people do *not* own dogs. If samples of equal size can support two contradictory conclusions, it should be clear that there must be something wrong with the representative quality of the data.

Arguing from Ignorance

DEFINITION *This fallacy consists in arguing for the truth (or falsity) of a claim, because there is no evidence or proof to the contrary or because of the inability or refusal of an opponent to present convincing evidence to the contrary.*

Arguing from ignorance is a tactic many people use to defend some of their favorite unsupported beliefs. They simply point out that since a claim has not been *disproved*, it must be true, in spite of the fact that there is no evidence for its truth. Of course, another person could argue that since the claim has not been *proved*, it is false, in spite of the fact that there is no evidence that it is false. But this is hardly an appropriate way of arguing, for if a claim were so absurd or trivial that no one even bothered to address it, an arguer would always win by default.

Nevertheless, many arguers use the lack of evidence *for* a claim as evidence for its being false or use the lack of evidence *against* a claim as evidence for its being true. For example, if I were to argue that the lack of evidence against the claim that all my students like and respect me is evidence that they *do*, I would be arguing from my ignorance of any evidence. In such an argument, the alleged "evidence" for the claim that my students like and respect me is actually no evidence at all. If the absence of evidence *for* a claim does not constitute sufficient evidence for that claim, it most certainly does not constitute evidence *against* the claim.

There are some situations of inquiry in which this kind of reasoning seems to be acceptable. In our judicial procedure, for example, a defendant is assumed to be innocent unless proven guilty. But this is not a case of arguing from ignorance. The principle of *innocent until proven guilty* is a highly technical judicial construct that actually means *not proven guilty*. In other words, a defendant is not proven guilty until he or she is proven guilty.

The fallacy of arguing from ignorance probably gains its *appearance* as a good argument from its similarity to a legitimate way of arguing. For example, suppose that I claimed that there were termites in my house. However, if a professional termite inspection revealed no evidence to support the claim, it would then be justifiable for me to conclude that there are no termites in the house. This sounds like a case of arguing from ignorance, because the lack of evidence *for* a claim ("there are termites') is used as evidence that the claim is false ("there are no termites"), but there is a crucial difference in this case. The negative claim is based not on a lack of evidence, but on a thorough assessment of *all* of the positive and negative evidence relevant to the question of whether there are termites in the house.

Arguing from ignorance also violates the principle that the burden of proof for any claim generally rests on the person who sets forth the claim. For example, if an arguer claimed that "ghosts exist, unless you can prove that they don't," he or she is attempting to shift the burden of proof to another person, usually to someone who is dubious about the claim. This is typically done by insisting that those who are unconvinced of the truth of the arguer's claim have the responsibility to disprove it or to provide support for the contradictory claim. If the doubters don't accept that responsibility, the arguer fallaciously assumes that no proof is needed for the claim at issue.

But proof *is* needed. An argument that employs an appeal to the "evidence" of no evidence does not satisfy the sufficiency condition of a good argument. It obviously fails to provide sufficient grounds for the claim at issue, since evidence is missing altogether.

Example   "What's all this business about equal pay for women? The women who work in my office must be satisfied with their salaries, because not one of them has ever complained or asked for a raise." A conversion of this argument into standard form will reveal clearly the faulty implicit premise:

> Since the women in my office do not complain about receiving less pay than their male counterparts,
>
> (and where there is no expression of dissatisfaction, there is no dissatisfaction),
>
>> (because the lack of evidence against satisfaction is evidence for satisfaction),
>
> ──────────────────────────
>
> Therefore, the women in my office are quite satisfied with receiving less pay than the men in the office.

The arguer assumes that the situation of a group of people must be satisfactory, simply because no complaints about that situation have been expressed. In other words, the absence of evidence *against* the satisfactory character of a situation is regarded as evidence *for* the satisfactory character of that situation. Making such an inference is so distinctive a form of the fallacy of arguing from ignorance that it is often given a separate name—the *fallacy of quietism*. But from the fact that a person or group is "quiet"—that is, makes no complaint—one could not infer that there is nothing to complain about. There may indeed be many good reasons why the complaints are not openly voiced.

Example   "Since my opponent has not clearly indicated his *opposition* to the new federal gun-control bill, he obviously is *in favor* of it." The only "evidence" offered in support of such a claim is the fact that the opponent has not addressed the issue. Interestingly, the arguer could have defended the opposite claim with the same evidence: "Since my opponent has not clearly indicated his *support* for the new federal gun-control bill, he obviously is *opposed* to it." Any evidence that could lead to either a positive or negative conclusion with equal strength cannot be sufficient grounds for *one* of the conclusions.

Example   "I didn't see any 'No Trespassing' sign, so I assumed that it was alright to walk through his field." The fact that there is no sign indicating that an act is *not* permissible does not entitle one to assume that the act *is* permissible.

Example

Connie: Did you get that teaching job at the University of Virginia?
Dot: No. I sent in my application over two months ago, and I never heard a word from them.

Dot is assuming that her application has been rejected by the University, because there is no evidence that she has been accepted. However, she could have just as easily argued from ignorance for the opposite claim. She could have argued that she has been accepted, because there is no evidence that she has been rejected. However, neither inference should be drawn, because it would be inappropriate to conclude anything on the basis of no communication from the University, especially in view of the fact that the institutional procedure required for filling a teaching position is usually a very long and complex one.

Attacking the Fallacy   If the absence of proof against a claim could be regarded as proof for it, then even the most bizarre of claims could allegedly be proved. If an arguer makes what you consider a highly questionable claim and supports it by pointing out the lack of evidence against it, you could show the faulty character of that kind of reasoning by making what you think he or she would consider an equally questionable claim and supporting it by the same method.

You could also show how one could be led to logically contradictory conclusions if the pattern of thinking in question were not fallacious. Suppose someone suggests that because psychokinesis has not been proved false, it must be true. Some other person could argue that because psychokinesis has not been proved true, it must be false. Such reasoning would lead us to the contradictory conclusion that psychokinesis is both true and false.

Contrary-to-Fact Hypothesis

DEFINITION   *This fallacy consists in treating a hypothetical claim as if it were a statement of fact by making a claim, without sufficient evidence, about what would have happened in the past if other conditions had been present or about an event that will occur in the future.*

Because empirical evidence for claims about nonexistent events is obviously not available, any alleged "evidence" must be regarded as part of an imaginative construct. Even though there is usually no way of knowing what might have been the consequences of an event that did not occur or what may be the consequences of an event that has not yet occurred, it is sometimes possible to develop a hypothetical construct about such events. Such constructs are helpful in understanding the past and in planning for, or avoiding undesirable consequences in, the future. However, it must be remembered that such constructs are only speculative and thus quite uncertain. They are at best "likely stories," and their speculative character must always be acknowledged.

This fallacy, insofar as it refers to past "events," is sometimes called "Monday morning quarterbacking." Nearly every avid football fan is known to make claims about what would have happened in last weekend's game if the quarterback had just called a different play or had executed the same play differently. But there is no way of knowing with any degree of certainty what would have happened in the past if something that did happen had not happened, or if something that did not happen had happened. The evidence for a claim that is *contrary to the facts* is simply not available. For this reason, the contrary-to-fact hypothesis violates the sufficiency criterion of a good argument, because it draws a conclusion without sufficient grounds for doing so.

Example   Consider the following contrary-to-fact hypotheses, none of which is provided with any support: "If you had only tasted the stewed snails, you would have loved them"; "If I hadn't goofed around my first year in college, I would have been accepted at medical school"; "If I had only been there for him last night, he wouldn't have killed himself"; or "If only I had practiced a little more on my backhand, I could have won that tennis tournament."

Even if there *were* reasons to accept such claims, we are rarely, if ever, *given* those reasons, and even if we were, there is still the question of whether they could be legitimately counted as "evidence." Let us examine the last of these arguments more closely by converting it into standard form:

> Since I did not win the tennis tournament,
>
> and I had not practiced sufficiently on my backhand before the match,
>
> and my practiced backhand would make the difference between winning and losing,
>
> ———————————————————————————
>
> Therefore, if I had practiced my backhand, I would have won the tournament.

There is no way of knowing what would have been the outcome if the backhand had been practiced. The third premise is simply a claim for which no evidence is available. The most that might be said is that the player's lack of practice on the backhand might have contributed to a few missed or poorly executed backhand plays, but there is no way to know how that might have affected the outcome of the tournament, given the complexity of the game of tennis. In any case, the arguer seems oblivious to the fact that the claim cannot be regarded as a statement of fact.

Example   Consider the number of students who have convinced themselves or their parents of the wisdom of moving out of campus housing with something like the following argument: "If I could just live off campus, I could get a lot more studying done, my grades would improve, and I'm sure I would get a lot more sleep." The student probably thinks that there are reasons to support these claims; yet it is doubtful that those reasons would qualify as evidence. The claims are at best purely speculative.

Example   Most of us have witnessed the fallacy of the contrary-to-fact hypothesis in claims made about historical events: "If Hitler had not invaded Russia and opened up two 'fronts,' the Nazis would have won World War II" or "If the Democrats had won the election of 1860, then the War Between the States would never have erupted." These are such highly speculative claims that it is difficult to imagine how sufficient "evidence" for such claims could ever be found.

Attacking the Fallacy   Because the formulation of imaginative constructs is a vital part of planning for the future and understanding the past, in no way would I encourage readers to pounce on every hypothetical construct or to refrain from exercising their own imagination. However, if you are confronted with a substantive contrary-to-fact claim that is highly questionable, I would suggest that you find some way of getting the arguer to recognize and to admit to the speculative character of the claim. Sometimes the very act of admitting that a claim is speculative will lead one to be more open to counterarguments and to take more seriously the task of supporting the claim.

One effective way of confronting an unsupported hypothetical claim might be something like this: "Well, you may be right, but I would have no way of determining that, as I am not aware of what kind of evidence you might *have* for such a claim." There is, of course, no "evidence" that is likely to be available, but the arguer will at least probably feel obligated to make some attempt to share with you the basis for his or her speculation about the claim, and that might get the discussion on a constructive track.

Fallacy of Popular Wisdom

DEFINITION   This fallacy consists in appealing to insights expressed in aphorisms or clichés, folk wisdom, or so-called common sense, instead of to relevant evidence for a claim.

This fallacy commonly takes the form of using a cliché or aphorism as a premise in an argument as if it were evidence and failing to show that the proposition expressed by the cliché is reliable. Because clichés, like analogies, are at best only suggestive, no argument wholly constituted by a cliché should be treated as a serious one. If the cliché were accompanied by other premises that explained why the cliché or aphorism expressed an important and defensible insight, the cliché itself would add nothing to the argument; it would be, at best, only a clever way of expressing the premise.

The fact that many clichés or aphorisms seem to contradict one another is an additional reason for regarding a cliché as providing insufficient support for a claim. Look at the contradictory advice in the following pairs of aphorisms: (1) "Two heads are better than one" and "Too many cooks spoil the broth." (2) "Where there's smoke there's fire" and "You can't tell a book by its cover." (3) "He who hesitates is lost" and "Fools rush in where angels fear to tread." (4) "Better safe than sorry" and "Nothing ventured, nothing gained." (5) "A new broom sweeps clean" and "Many a good tune is played on an old fiddle." (6) "Where there's a will, there's a way" and "If wishes were horses, beggars would ride." (7) "Birds of a feather flock together" and "Opposites attract." Since aphorisms or clichés are expressions of so-called popular wisdom, and the "wisdom" expressed in many aphorisms can easily be contradicted by the "wisdom" expressed in others, there is no reason, apart from other evidence, to regard an aphorism as reliable support for any claim or course of action.

Another form of this fallacy is to appeal to the insights embedded in the folk wisdom that is perhaps passed on in the culture from generation to generation as if it were evidence for a claim. For example: "Feed a cold, starve a fever" or "An apple a day keeps the doctor away." Such claims are highly questionable and/or misleading pieces of medical or nutritional advice, and the fact that such beliefs may be widely held constitutes no evidence for a particular claim.

A third form of this fallacy often heard is the appeal to "just common sense." The notion of "common sense," however, is usually totally undefined and bereft of any evidence. Even though an arguer may be able to produce some evidence upon request, he or she often seems to believe that such evidence does not need to be presented if it is named "common sense." The words themselves seem to take on an aura that some take as sufficient reason to accept a claim in question, as in "it is just common sense to conclude that exercise is bad for your high blood pressure."

Attempts to argue by means of an appeal to a cliché, a piece of folk wisdom, or "just common sense" are clear violations of the sufficiency criterion of a good argument—that there be sufficient grounds presented for a claim. These substitutes for evidence do not constitute such grounds.

Example   Suppose that a counselor tells a young woman that she can't have a serious relationship with two different men at the same time. In an attempt to convince her, the counselor says, "You just can't have your cake and eat it too." When this argument is seen in a standard format, the questionable premise looks almost absurd:

Since you have a continuing relationship with two different men,

and you cannot have your cake and eat it, too,

(Therefore, you must cut off one of the relationships.)

The principle of charity drives us to articulate what is probably the argument's implicit conclusion. But the obvious question is whether the aphorism is applicable in this particular instance. Having or keeping a piece of cake and consuming that same cake are logically incompatible, but there is nothing logically incompatible about being in a serious relationship with two people at the same time. It certainly does not apply in the case of friendship or nonromantic relationships. To make the case, the counselor would have to demonstrate why the two are unworkable or practically incompatible. Even though in some cases it might be *wise* to confine one's romantic life to a single serious relationship, that cannot be inferred from the aphorism.

Example   A typical campus cliché expressed by one student to another the night before an important test is "Well, if you don't know it now, you never will." No evidence is usually given for such a questionable claim; indeed, there is considerable evidence to suggest that the claim is false. As far as performance on tests is concerned, it is probably safe to say that a conscientious student might learn a significant amount of material during the hours immediately before a test.

Example   Suppose that a couple is discussing the question of whether they should use a recent inheritance to pay off a large mortgage on their house:

Jackie: Now we can pay off our house loan.
Tim: No. I don't think so. I think it would be better to invest it in something that can pay a higher yield than the cost of the mortgage.
Jackie: What? That's crazy! It's just common sense to pay off a mortgage if you have the money to do it.

In what way is it "just common sense"? Tim just explained to Jackie an idea that seemed to make *fiscal sense* to him and to most professional financial advisers. Can an action make *fiscal* sense and not make *common* sense? If so, to what does "common" refer? To call something "just common sense" does not necessarily mean that it actually makes sense. In the absence of any supporting evidence, the claim may well be an empty one.

Attacking the Fallacy   In no way should you be intimidated by the alleged wisdom of a popular cliché. A cliché or aphorism, like any other not so cleverly expressed opinion, requires evidential support to make it worthy of acceptance. If an arguer attempts to use a cliché rather than evidence to support a claim, challenge it directly; or better yet, counter it, if possible, with a cliché that gives contradictory advice. The arguer would then have to show why his or her cliché is better founded than yours.

You should also not let yourself be intimidated by appeals to folk wisdom or "just common sense." There should be no embarrassment in simply asking, "What evidence leads you to believe that this bit of popular wisdom is true?" It is also always appropriate to ask, "Just how is it 'just common sense'?" The very fact that you are in a serious discussion with the arguer indicates that you are not prepared to accept a proposed claim as "just common sense." If it were obvious that it was just common sense, the discussion would be over.

Special Pleading

DEFINITION   *This fallacy consists in applying principles, rules, or criteria to another person while failing or refusing to apply them to oneself or to a situation that is of personal interest, without providing sufficient evidence to support such an exception.*

Almost every example of special pleading occurs in a context in which it is assumed or understood that a rule, principle, or law applies to all persons alike in the situation. The special pleader usually accepts the principle, but wishes to make himself or herself an exception to it. However, exceptions to rules or principles must be justified. If a double standard is to be applied, some reason must be given for treating differently what appear to be similar cases. Special treatment is sometimes called for, but not unless a case for it can be successfully made.

Appropriate evidence for making an exception of oneself is simply missing from a special pleading argument. For that reason, the argument violates the sufficiency criterion of a good argument that says that the grounds must be sufficient in number, kind, and weight to establish the truth of the conclusion. Hence, any argument for special treatment that fails to provide sufficient evidence for that claim cannot qualify as a good argument.

Example   James claims that he is too tired to share in the chores of cooking, cleaning, or caring for the children after working all day. If he claims that his wife should do those domestic jobs, even though she too is tired from her full-time job outside the home, he is engaged in special pleading. Let us look at this argument in standard form:

Since I work hard all day and am tired at the end of the day,

and you work hard all day and are tired at the end of the day,

(and the governing principle in such a situation is that each partner should share in the domestic chores),

(and the principle applies to you but not to me),

Therefore, you should do all the domestic chores.

Being tired from a full day's work outside the home presumably excuses him from domestic chores, while it apparently does not excuse his wife. James is applying a principle to his wife that he is not willing to apply to himself, and, as can be clearly seen, he has presented no evidence for making that exception.

Example Sometimes we make a special case of ourselves through a subtle use of language: "I am confident, you are arrogant; I am aggressive, you are ruthless; I am thrifty, you are cheap; I am frank, you are rude; I am flexible, you are inconsistent; I am clever, you are conniving; I am thorough, you are picky; I am curious, you are nosy; I am excited, you are hysterical; I am firm, you are pig-headed; I am friendly, you are flirtatious; I am a free spirit, you take license."

But if the behaviors in these cases are the same, how can we justify assessing our own behavior positively and another's negatively, without being inconsistent? When charged with inconsistency, special pleaders often respond with "Well, this is different!" But if they cannot convincingly make the distinction stick, they are clearly guilty of special pleading.

Example Jane and Joyce are roommates who come into conflict over the use of their dorm room. Jane wants to play her music, and Joyce wants to take a nap. Whose interest should take precedence? The principle that roommates assume is that neither one's interest is more important than the other's. If Joyce claimed that her interest was more important than Jane's, we would probably say that she was engaged in special pleading, because there is no obvious reason why one of the roommates should be granted special treatment.

Attacking the Fallacy An attack that is most effective is to accuse your special-pleading opponent of applying a double standard, playing favorites, or being inconsistent. Each of these charges is commonly understood outside logical circles and has strong negative connotations, with which the arguer will not want to be associated. But you will need to explain carefully how you think the double standard has been employed and to scrutinize carefully any defense your opponent may make against the change.

There may be some situations that call for making oneself a special case, but these are rare, so the careful thinker should always be suspicious of any preferential treatment claim. Ask the arguer to spell out the reasons why he or she should be treated differently from others or why the principle should not apply in a particular case. The arguer, of course, will almost always have reasons. The question is whether he or she can provide sufficient reason to support the preferential treatment desired. For the hard to convince, try an absurd example:

> Since the law with regard to the payment of income tax should be applied in all cases,
>
> and I am an exception because my case is not like that of others, for I need that money for other things,
>
> ---
>
> Therefore, the income tax law should not be applied to me.

The second premise should sound absurd to even the most inveterate special pleader, and the arguer should be prepared to show why the special treatment he or she is requesting is not equally absurd.

Omission of Key Evidence

DEFINITION *This fallacy consists in constructing an argument that fails to include key evidence that is critical to the support of the conclusion.*

The sufficiency criterion of a good argument is perhaps most clearly violated when crucial or key evidence that is necessary to support a particular conclusion is simply absent from the premises of an argument. It is not unlike the situation of preparing a mixed drink and leaving out the alcohol. The mistake that is made is not a failure to provide evidence that might make the argument stronger; it is simply a failure to supply the evidence necessary to make the case *at all*. It is like the missing piece of a puzzle. Without it, the argument will not work.

Example   "Let's get married, Jessica. We like the same things, we both love your dog, we go to the same church, we share the same tastes in food and movies, and we can save money on living expenses. So, what do you say, huh?" Let us look at this argument in standard form:

Since we like the same things,

and we love your dog,

and we go to the same church,

and we share the same tastes in food and movies,

and we could save money on living expenses,

_____

Therefore, we should get married.

The reasons given in the actual argument might support equally well a proposal to marry your sister or your best friend. What most people think are key issues to be considered in a marriage decision—whether they love each other and whether they want to spend the rest of their lives together—are completely omitted.

Example   Suppose you wanted to nominate a professor for "Teacher of the Year." The reasons that you might give for why Professor Pour should receive the award are many: She is bright, she is widely published, she is dedicated to her job, she is always willing to talk to students, she is always kind and caring toward students, and she is excited about her discipline.

These are all very good reasons for giving her an award, but the list does not even mention what is surely the most important or key reason for such an award—her teaching ability. Do the students learn from her? A successful case for giving her the award must include at least a positive answer to that question.

Example   "I think we should buy the Tudor-style house in Emory Hills. It is the right size for our family, it is close to school, it has a big yard for our dog, an attic for all our junk, and a huge eat-in kitchen. It has the fireplace that we have always wanted. Indeed, it is the only house that everyone in our family has liked. It is just the ideal house to buy."

These may all be good reasons to buy the house, but one of the key premises in an argument for buying the house is whether the house is in the right price range. And that information is entirely missing.

Attacking the Fallacy The best way to address this fallacy is directly. Point out the evidence that you must have in order to be convinced of the conclusion. It is quite possible that the omission is simply the result of the arguer's carelessness and that it can be easily produced. In that case, the argument could perhaps be quickly made into a successful one.

It is possible, however, that the evidence was omitted for some other reason. For example, the arguer may not even be aware of the crucial nature of the missing evidence. In such cases, the glaring omission must be pointed out to those who are obviously not blinded by its glare. But whatever may account for the missing key evidence, it must be made clear that the argument, as it stands, is not a good one.

ASSIGNMENTS

A. Fallacies of Missing Evidence For each of the following arguments, (1) identify the type of missing-evidence fallacy illustrated, and (2) explain how the reasoning violates the sufficiency criterion. There are two examples of each fallacy discussed in this section. Arguments marked with an asterisk (*) have sample answers at the end of the text.

*1. I know that my term paper is due today, Professor Raines, but would you please give me a two-week extension? You see, I have had a lot of work to do in my other classes, and I just haven't had time to start on the paper yet.

*2. If you ever ate in our school cafeteria, you would see that institutional food is never very good.

3. A recent telephone survey of randomly selected people revealed that 75 percent of the American people watch at least one soap opera a day. Indeed, to ensure accuracy in the data, the way they conducted the study was to make the calls between 1:00 and 4:00 in the afternoon, and then ask what show the respondent was actually watching at the time.

4. **Daughter:** But, Mother, I have given you several good reasons why you should let me go to Susan's party. Why won't you let me go?
   Mother: Just remember, dear, that "Mother knows best."

*5. This timeshare deal looks like a good one. If I buy a timeshare at this resort, all I have to pay is an annual maintenance fee and I'll be guaranteed a vacation week every year at the same time at a place I and my family really like to go.

*6. If I just hadn't dropped out of college, I'd be working now rather than standing in this unemployment line.

7. **Laura:** John, you said that you wanted to be free to date other women. I don't understand how you can get angry when I date other guys.
   John: But every time I see you with someone else, it really hurts. Maybe it would be better if you didn't look like you were having such a good time. In fact, you look like you really like the guy. That can't be good for our relationship.
   Laura: But you date other women.
   John: But you know that when I date other women, it's not serious. You know that you are the one I really care about.

*8. The black people in this country must be happy with their situation now. There haven't been any protest marches or any loud voices of dissent for several years.

9. All three sex offenders arrested this month by the city police had previous records for the same crime. It seems that once a sex offender, always a sex offender.

10. Hey, look at this ad, Julie. They have a sale on selected paint at Emory Hardware at half off the regular price. We said that we were going to paint our house this spring. Why don't we go get some of the paint while it lasts.

11. I'm sorry, Ms. Robinette, but we cannot approve your loan application. We must assume that your credit is no good, because there is no record indicating that you have ever met any monthly installment or credit card payments.

12. If I had gone with him to the party, I could have kept him from making a fool of himself.

*13. From a recent survey of a large number of representatively selected people in New York City, it has been discovered that less than 2 percent of Americans engage in hunting for sport.

*14. **Marsha:** If that were a child of mine, I would have given him a good spanking rather than sitting down and talking with him about his behavior as you did.

　　　David: Why do you think that your method is better?

　　　Marsha: I just think that "if you spare the rod, you spoil the child."

CAUSAL FALLACIES

Trying to understand the notion of cause has been a difficult philosophical problem for a long time, and this difficulty also underlies a number of problems in reasoning. A causal fallacy, more than any other type of fallacy, requires that we draw from the entire reservoir of our knowledge and understanding of the world. The more we know about the nature of complex causal relationships, the more likely we will be able to detect a faulty causal analysis.

The fallacies in this section represent various ways of inferring faulty causal explanations from premises that do not provide sufficient support for such explanations. Hence, the causal analysis is misapplied in particular situations. There may be a confusion between a necessary condition and a sufficient condition, or the causal factors in a situation may be too few to account for the effect in question. Some faulty causal analyses claim that because something happened after another event, it was caused by that initial event, while others confuse an effect with a cause or fail to recognize that there may be a third or common cause that accounts for two events that were thought to be causally related. Finally, faulty causal analyses often inappropriately claim that a series of events leading to an inevitable end will follow from a single event or that it is possible to make predictions based on the past performance of chance events.

Confusion of a Necessary with a Sufficient Condition

DEFINITION　*This fallacy consists in assuming that a necessary condition of an event is also a sufficient one.*

A *necessary condition* of an event is a condition, or set of conditions, in the absence of which the event in question cannot occur. Even though a necessary condition of an event must be present in order for that event to occur, in most cases it alone is not sufficient to produce the event. For example, since electrical power is necessary for a vacuum cleaner to work, the absence of electrical power guarantees the absence of a functioning vacuum cleaner. But electrical power alone is not sufficient for the event of a functioning vacuum cleaner.

A *sufficient condition* of an event is a condition, or set of conditions, in the presence of which the event in question will occur. For example, a sufficient condition of a functioning vacuum cleaner would include not only a source of electrical power, but also a vacuum cleaner that is in good working order, a bag or canister that is not completely full, and a functioning connection between the vacuum cleaner and the power source.

It is not uncommon for some arguers to claim that an event will occur simply because one of its necessary conditions is present. But such thinking mistakes a necessary condition for a sufficient one. The necessary condition must be there, but its being there does not alone provide sufficient grounds for drawing any inference about the event in question. For example, it is necessary to read a book in order to understand it, but reading it will not guarantee understanding it. Additional conditions would have to be present to bring the reader to understanding. To assume that merely reading a book will guarantee an understanding of it is to confuse a necessary condition with a sufficient one. Therefore, to make a claim that an event will occur, based solely on the presence of a necessary condition, is to draw a conclusion based on a faulty causal anaysis. A premise that contains such an analysis fails to provide sufficient evidence for the conclusion, which is a violation of the sufficiency criterion of a good argument.

Example   "This flashlight should work; I just bought new batteries for it. I'm going to take these batteries back and get some different ones." If we put this argument into standard form, the fallacy is clearly revealed:

Since I just put fresh batteries in the flashlight,

and it doesn't work,

(and having fresh batteries is a sufficient condition of a working flashlight),

_____

Therefore, the batteries are defective.

The batteries may be defective, but the more likely causal explanation is that some other factor accounts for the nonworking flashlight. Although the batteries are a necessary condition for a working flashlight, they are not a sufficient condition. The argument's implicit premise, however, assumes that they are. The arguer has therefore confused a necessary with a sufficient condition of an event.

Example   "You said that I would have to run the mile in less than six minutes to be on the track team, and I did. So why did I get cut from the team?"

The arguer has assumed that meeting the eligibility requirement of being able to run a mile in less than six minutes would be a sufficient condition of being on the track team. Meeting the requirement, however, was only a necessary condition. The sufficient condition for being on the track team would probably include the meeting of many other requirements.

Example   Consider the situation in which a professor tells the students at the beginning of the term that, in order to pass the course, they will have to come to class regularly, read the daily assignments, participate in class discussions, take all tests and examinations, and submit a research paper. Some students have faithfully met such conditions and then have experienced genuine surprise when they failed the course. Such puzzlement could possibly be eliminated if the students understood the difference between the necessary and the sufficient condition for passing the course. In the case in question, the professor mentioned the necessary but not the sufficient condition for passing the course. The sufficient condition would presumably include getting *passing grades* on the tests and the research paper.

Attacking the Fallacy   Many people reason in a way that confuses a necessary condition with a sufficient condition because they do not understand exactly how the two differ. Hence, it might be helpful to clarify that distinction carefully when confronting such confusion. One of the most effective ways of doing this is to use an example that makes the difference unmistakable. Suppose a young woman were to argue that she would become a great concert pianist because she had been practicing two hours a day for 15 years. It should be plain that, although practicing the piano regularly is a necessary condition of becoming a concert pianist, it alone is not a sufficient one. The set of sufficient conditions would include not only the long hours of practice, but having a considerable amount of talent, and perhaps a good manager. When the difference between a sufficient and a necessary condition becomes clear, the arguer should recognize the problematic character of his or her own argument, which exhibits the same form as the argument in the example.

Causal Oversimplification

DEFINITION   *This fallacy consists in oversimplifying the causal antecedents of an event by specifying causal factors that are insufficient to account for the event in question or by overemphasizing the role of one or more of those factors.*

In causal explanations, it is a common practice to point to a very obvious antecedent of an event and to designate it as the cause. However, a careful analysis of the notion of cause would show that the cause, or sufficient condition, of an event in most cases includes a considerable number of antecedents that only together are sufficient to bring about the event. To point to only one of those factors in a causal explanation might very well be a case of oversimplification.

Since the typical explanation of an event rarely includes all the literally hundreds of antecedent conditions that constitute the sufficient condition of that event, it is almost always possible to question another's causal explanation. However, one should not expect a causal explanation to include every antecedent condition of the event in question. To do so would be unnecessary and an inefficient use of time and energy. Nevertheless, an argument should include enough of those factors to escape the charge of oversimplification. Otherwise, the argument fails to provide sufficient grounds for its conclusion and thus fails to satisfy the sufficiency condition of a good argument.

Example   "Corporal punishment is no longer allowed in public schools. This is why children have no self-discipline and are losing respect for authority." We will put this argument into standard form to make the faulty causal analysis more blatant:

> Since corporal punishment is no longer allowed in public schools,
>
> and children now have less self-discipline and respect for authority than in the past,
>
> (and the lack of corporal punishment is by itself sufficient to explain the difference in the behavior of today's children),
> ──
> (Therefore, corporal punishment should be brought back to the public schools.)

The problems of self-discipline and loss of respect for authority are not new issues. The ancient Greeks used to wring their hands in anguish over such problems. But even if these were new problems, it is very unlikely that they could be traced directly to the abandonment of corporal punishment in the schools. These are very complex issues, and it is highly unlikely that they have a single cause. For that reason, the conclusion should be rejected, because there is not sufficient evidence to support the implicit and crucial premise.

Example "Children today spend an average of five hours per day watching television—time that used to be spent in physical activity and reading. That explains why young people today are fatter and dumber than kids used to be."

Even if the facts presented were true, it is unlikely that television viewing alone is sufficient to account for higher weights and lower test scores. An increase in the time devoted to daily TV watching may well be one of the causal antecedents of the alleged effect on the body weight and test scores of children, but to assign that heavy a role to one factor would seem to oversimplify a causally complex phenomenon.

Example A radio preacher recently argued in the following way: "Marriage would be greatly helped if husband and wife would read the Scriptures together and pray together every day. No wonder divorce has increased so much! Family worship has dropped almost 50 percent in just the past 15 years."

Apart from questions that might be raised about the reliability of the facts regarding the drop in the rate of family worship, it does not seem that the rise in the national divorce rate could be sufficiently accounted for by such data—even if the data were true. Because the reasons for the dissolution of a marriage are usually quite varied and complex, it seems highly questionable to reduce them to a change in worship patterns.

Attacking the Fallacy It is always appropriate to remind the arguer who commits this fallacy that events are almost always the result of many factors. This is an important feature of the dialogue, because it is unlikely that the arguer would disagree with that general claim. Hence, the door is at least opened for him or her to entertain other contributing causes and even to adjust earlier inferences that he or she may have drawn.

If you suspect that a causal analysis is oversimplified, because it seems insufficient to account for the event in question or because you think it overemphasizes the role of one or more specific factors, point out these problems to the arguer and request some further justification of the analysis. You may help, of course, by suggesting additional factors that you think should be considered in the causal analysis. Be sure to ask the arguer what he or she thinks of your suggestions, so that they cannot be ignored and the arguer will be forced to consider their merit.

Post Hoc Fallacy

DEFINITION   *This fallacy consists in assuming that a particular event, B, is caused by another event, A, simply because B follows A in time.*

Establishing the temporal priority of one event over another is not a sufficient condition for inferring a causal relationship between those events. One cannot assume *post hoc, ergo propter hoc*—that an event that occurs *after* another event therefore occurs *because* of that other event. A chronological relationship is only one of the indicators of a possible causal relationship. Other indicators might include a spatial connection or perhaps some history of regularity. If temporal priority alone were sufficient to establish a causal relationship, then virtually any event that preceded another could be assumed to be the cause of it. This kind of thinking has contributed to the creation of many superstitions. Something was often considered "bad luck" for no reason other than the fact that it preceded a misfortune. Such thinking mistakes a sheer coincidence for a causal relation.

The *post hoc* fallacy is sometimes confused with the fallacy of causal oversimplification. The *post hoc* fallacy, however, is not a special case of causal oversimplification. Causal oversimplification usually occurs when a particular causal antecedent is mistakenly regarded as constituting the sufficient condition of an event when it is not by itself adequate to account for that event. In the case of the *post hoc* fallacy, a causal factor is not being oversimplified; rather, the question is whether the events have any causal relationship at all.

One who commits the *post hoc* fallacy has clearly argued in a way that fails to comply with the conditions of a good argument. The flaw is that of using insufficient grounds for the conclusion drawn. What purports to be a causal argument has a premise that expresses no clear-cut causal factor—only the temporal priority of one event in relation to another. But this is not a sufficient reason to infer any causal connection between the two.

Example   "It was only three months after Harold got married that he started smoking pot. His wife must have gotten him started on the stuff." If we convert this argument to a standard format, it looks like this:

Since Harold recently got married,

and having a new wife preceded the event of starting to smoke pot,

(and what precedes another event is the cause of that event),

Therefore, Harold's wife is the cause of his pot smoking.

The only evidence offered for the causal explanation of the event in question is the temporal priority of Harold's marriage. However, temporal priority fails to provide sufficient evidence for any causal claim, so the argument fails the sufficiency criterion of a good argument.

Example   "I can't help but think that you are the cause of this. We never had any problem with the furnace until you moved into the apartment." The manager of the apartment house, on no stated grounds other than the temporal priority of the new tenant's occupancy, has assumed that the tenant's presence has some causal relationship to the furnace's not working properly.

Example   "Ever since we quit going to church, business has been getting worse. If we want to keep from going completely bankrupt, we'd better get started back to church." Again, the claim is that one event was brought about by another event simply because of the temporal relationship.

Attacking the Fallacy   It is difficult to believe that anyone would really conclude that B is caused by A simply because B follows A in time. In most cases, there are probably additional factors that lie behind the causal claim. For example, the manager of the apartment house may have reason to believe that the tenant has tampered with the furnace, or the operator of the business may have strong beliefs about divine punishment. However, the arguments themselves focus simply on the temporal character of the relationship of events. Insofar as other factors or assumptions are not specified or even mentioned, it is appropriate to point out the *post hoc* character of such a claim and to indicate that you will regard such a causal explanation as adequate only if it is supplemented by other convincing evidence.

You should have no trouble finding absurd examples that could demonstrate the fallaciousness of *post hoc* thinking. Pick out any two temporally related events and claim that the prior one caused the succeeding one. For example, you might argue that the garbage truck must have caused the phone to ring, since the phone rang right after the truck passed. It would be wise to select events that the arguer knows to be temporally related but causally *unrelated*, so that he or she will be more likely to recognize the faulty analysis involved in your causal claim. If the arguer regards temporal priority as insufficient evidence for your causal claim, then perhaps he or she may be encouraged to abandon such grounds in his or her own argument, or at least to supplement the temporal priority with additional causal factors.

Confusion of Cause and Effect

DEFINITION   *This fallacy consists in confusing the cause with the effect of an event or in failing to recognize that there may be a reciprocal causal relation between the two events in question.*

When the Scarecrow asks the Wizard of Oz for a brain, the Wizard answers that he cannot give him a brain, but that he can give him a diploma from the University of Kansas. The Wizard has confused the brain with the effect of a brain, but nobody really cares, least of all the Scarecrow, because *The Wizard of Oz* is just an interesting story. In the real world, however, resolving such confusion can be very important; it can assist us in coming to an accurate understanding of our experiences and in anticipating the future.

An argument that confuses the effect with the cause of an event and then draws a conclusion about the causal relationship does not provide sufficient grounds for that conclusion. The grounds are not sufficient because the evidence is constituted by a faulty causal analysis.

Example   One prison inmate to another: "Governor Warner always seems to know when we're having a good meal. He times his annual inspection visit here on the one day of the year that we have steak." A look at this argument in standard form will help us to see the faulty causal analysis:

> Since Governor Warner always comes to visit the prison on the one day a year that we have steak,
>
> (and either the Governor has intuitive powers or the prison officials are informed of his visit in advance and serve steak because of his visit),
>
> (and it is not likely that prison officials are informed of the Governor's visit in advance),
>
> ---
>
> Therefore, Governor Warner must have an intuitive way of knowing such things.

The inmate has it backwards. The third premise is surely constituted by a faulty causal analysis. It is much more likely that prison officials are given advance notice of the governor's visit than that the governor has intuitive powers that he uses to pick a day when he can get a good meal.

Example   "It's no wonder that Sela makes such good grades. She's the teacher's pet."

It is more likely the case that Sela is the teacher's pet *because* she makes good grades. Or perhaps there is a reciprocal causal relationship between Sela's being the teacher's pet and Sela's good grades. The teacher's positive attention causes Sela to make good grades, and Sela's good grades cause the teacher to give Sela positive attention.

Example   Many theologians claim that an act is right because God approves of it. This is one of two possible answers to the ancient Socratic question about the relationship between God and morality: Is a thing good because God approves of it, or does God approve of it because it is good? Socrates suggests that there is a confusion of cause and effect in the theologians' claim. Socrates himself takes the alternative position that "God approves a thing because it is good." Does God's approval cause the good, or does the good cause God's approval? One of these claims must be false, for they are incompatible positions and since each view has very different and serious moral and theological implications, it is important to determine which is the confused causal analysis.

Attacking the Fallacy   Any causal confusion that obscures the truth should be avoided or challenged. For that reason, even if a young child were to say, "Look, Daddy, that tree moving over there is making the wind blow," it should be considered less an occasion for being amused than an opportunity for giving the child a more accurate understanding of the nature of wind.

When the thinking of adults exhibits a confusion of cause and effect, then it is all the more dangerous, because the claims of adults are more likely to have an effect on the thinking of others. Hence, any kind of causal explanation that represents what you believe to be a confusion of cause and effect should be challenged in a way that would be helpful in eliminating the confusion.

If an arguer draws a conclusion based on a confusion of cause and effect, the absurd example method may be the easiest way of exposing the error. If *The Wizard of Oz* example doesn't work, try the following somewhat more subtle example. One staff member to another at the unemployment office: "No wonder these people can't get jobs. Have you noticed how irritable they are?" If the arguer is able to recognize that reversing the cause and effect creates a more plausible causal understanding of the factors in this situation—that the unemployed are irritable because they can't find a job—then maybe he or she will be able to do the same with regard to the faulty causal claim in question.

A confusion of cause and effect is sometimes not at all easy to detect. Even the absurd example method will not always ensure an acknowledgment by the arguer of a confusion in his or her own causal analysis. The arguer may acknowledge that there is a clear confusion in the absurd example but still insist that no such confusion exists in the case at issue. In these cases, of course, it will be necessary to explain carefully why the reversal of the cause and effect makes more sense.

Neglect of a Common Cause

DEFINITION *This fallacy consists in failing to recognize that two seemingly related events may not be causally related at all, but rather are effects of a common cause.*

When two events are found together in what appears to be a causal relation, we tend to assume that one is the cause and one the effect. Such thinking, however, can obscure another possible understanding of the relationship. One should be open to the possibility that both events may be effects of another event or common cause. However, in order to identify such a common cause, it is often necessary to draw on one's general store of knowledge or other information not provided in the situation.

An argument that causally connects two obvious events while neglecting a third, less obvious factor or event that may be the underlying cause of each of the other events does not provide sufficient grounds for its causal claim. Neglecting what appears to be a common cause means that the arguer has failed to produce the best explanation of the event in question. Hence, the argument cannot qualify as a good one.

Example If it were discovered that most elementary school teachers have children of their own, it might be concluded either that teaching stimulates an interest in parenthood or that being a parent stimulates interest in working with children. We will now convert this argument into standard form:

Since most elementary school teachers have children of their own,

---

Therefore, teaching must stimulate an interest in being a parent, or being a parent stimulates an interest in working with children.

However, a more likely analysis of the situation is that another factor, the love of children, causes many people to become both parents and elementary school teachers.

Example Suppose that a young college student is both obese and depressed. A hasty, but typical, analysis of the situation might be that the obesity is causing the depression or that, because of the depression, the student tends to overeat. However, a more likely explanation is that some underlying psychological or physical problem is causing both effects.

Example   We often hear that current movies and television programming are bringing about a "moral degeneration" in our country. However, it seems probable that a number of other factors at work in our culture are producing both the contemporary trend in films and our changing moral standards. Because these factors are more difficult to detect or to isolate in a causal analysis, it is simpler, although fallacious, to blame the filmmakers or the television programmers.

Attacking the Fallacy   Great care should be taken not to charge a person falsely with neglect of a common cause. In almost any causal relationship there will be peripheral factors common to the events in question, the neglect of which would constitute no fallacy. For example, if the explanation of the alleged causal relation between being an elementary school teacher and being a parent failed to mention that being an adult was causally necessary to both effects, it would not be appropriate to charge the arguer with neglecting a common cause. The common cause in this case is not a significant one. However, if one is attempting to explain an allegedly causal relationship between two things by reference to only those two things, and a more adequate account could be provided by appealing to an additional factor causally common to both, then it would indeed be fallacious to neglect that alternative explanation.

If you believe that the primary problem with a proposed explanation is its neglect of a common cause of the events in question, you should demonstrate just how that common factor could provide a more adequate explanation. The arguer should then feel obligated to scrutinize your proposal and to show, if possible, why it is not a more adequate explanation.

Domino Fallacy

DEFINITION   *This fallacy consists in assuming, without appropriate evidence, that a particular action or event is just one, usually the first, in a series of steps that will lead inevitably to some specific, usually undesirable, consequence.*

The name *domino fallacy* derives from the child's game of lining up dominoes on end about an inch apart and then pushing the first one over, causing a chain reaction of falling dominoes. The chain reaction works in the child's game, but not all events are arranged so that a falling-domino effect ensues. For each event in any so-called series of events, an independent argument must be presented. In no case should one assume that one event will lead to or cause another event or series of events without making a separate inquiry into the causal factors that might be involved in each of those events.

The domino fallacy has sometimes been referred to as the *fallacy of the slippery slope*. As the name suggests, when we take one step over the edge of a slope, we often find ourselves slipping on down the slope, with no place to dig in and stop the sliding. While this image may be insightful for understanding the character of the fallacy, it represents a misunderstanding of the nature of the causal relations between events. Every causal claim requires a separate argument. Hence, any "slipping" to be found is only in the clumsy thinking of the arguer, who has failed to provide sufficient evidence that a single event can serve as an adequate causal explanation for a whole series of other causal events.

Example "If we allow gay and lesbian marriages, next there will be some who want group marriages, and soon no one will even bother to get married." Let us convert this argument, with its domino-thinking feature, into standard form:

Since allowing gay and lesbian marriages will lead to group
marriage,

> (because there is a causal relationship between these two things),

and group marriages will lead to no marriage at all,

> (because there is a causal relationship between group marriage
> and the abandonment of the marriage practice),

(and no marriage at all is not a good idea),

(Therefore, we should not allow gay and lesbian marriages.)

This arguer is not likely to be able to show that there are any causal relationships between the events cited, as asserted in the two implicit subpremises. These subpremises exhibit faulty causal analyses and are therefore not good ones. Because the argument does not provide sufficient evidence to support the claims about these causal relationships, it fails to meet the sufficiency criterion of a good argument and the conclusion does not follow.

Example "If we allow the government to limit the number of guns a person can buy each month, what's next? If they can limit guns, they can limit how much liquor, how much food, or even how many cars you can buy. They already tell us how many deer we can shoot. Next thing you know, they will even be telling us how many kids we can have. They'll keep on until they totally control us."

There is no evidence here that any of these events are causally connected with one another. In fact, it is difficult to imagine how such a connection might be made. While it is conceivable that good reasons might be found for putting limits on some of the things mentioned, it is not because they are causally connected to each other.

Example Examine the following hypothetical argument against allowing students to become members of faculty committees: "If you let students serve on faculty committees, the next thing they will want is to be members of departments, and then members of the Board of Trustees. Before you know it, they will be hiring and firing the faculty."

The proposal to put students on certain faculty committees is one for which a number of very good reasons can be given. Whether it is wise to elect students as departmental members or to appoint students to the Board of Trustees would require separate arguments, because presumably different issues would be involved in each case. There is little reason to believe that students would not or could not distinguish between these issues and recognize that one event bears no logical or causal relationship to the other.

Attacking the Fallacy If you suspect a bit of "domino thinking," insist that the arguer give an independent causal explanation for each event about which a claim is made. Another strategy might be to counter with an unsupported claim about the connections between events in some obviously absurd series of events. For example, suggest that if you use a credit card to buy things, you will soon buy more than you can afford, you won't be able to pay your bills, the bank will repossess your car because you are behind in your payments, you'll lose your job because you'll have no way to get to work, and you'll be so unhappy you will kill yourself, all because you used a credit card. It should be obvious to the arguer that there is no reason to believe that using a credit card will necessarily lead even to the second event, let alone to suicide. Each causal connection would need a separate causal analysis. Likewise, it should become obvious that each causal relationship between the events in the arguer's predicted series of events requires a separate treatment.

Gambler's Fallacy

DEFINITION *This fallacy consists in arguing that because a chance event has had a certain run in the past, the probability of its occurrence in the future is significantly altered.*

This fallacy is typically committed by gamblers, who erroneously think that the chances of winning are better or significantly altered in their favor because of a certain run of events in the immediate past. Remember the loser who says, "I can't lose now, I'm hot," or the big loser who says, "My luck has got to change. I haven't had a single win all night. I'm betting everything on this one." Such people seem to be unaware that a chance event, such as the outcome of a coin toss or a roll of the dice, is totally independent of all the tosses or rolls preceding it. To commit the gambler's fallacy, then, is to draw an inference on the assumption that the probability of a chance event's turning out in a particular way is affected by the series of similar chance events preceding it.

Even though this fallacy is common among gamblers, it is not unique to them. Consider the parents who already have three sons and are quite satisfied with the size of their family. However, they both would really like to have a daughter. They commit the gambler's fallacy when they infer that their chances of having a girl are better, because they have already had three boys. They are wrong. The sex of the fourth child is causally unrelated to any preceding chance event or series of such events. Their chances of having a daughter are no better than 1 in 2—that is, 50–50.

This fallacy, which seduces virtually every one of us from time to time, is nevertheless an argument that grossly violates the sufficiency criterion of a good argument. One cannot infer anything about the probable occurrence of a single, genuinely chance event based on what has occurred with regard to similar chance events in the past. The grounds for such a claim are simply nonexistent. The fallacy confuses, among other things, a claim about statistical probability in a whole sequence of chance events with a predictive claim about a *single* chance event.

Example Reflection about romantic concerns often involves use of the gambler's fallacy. Consider the college student who argues that since the last three blind dates worked out so badly, the chances of something more positive occurring on the next match are better. If we reconstruct the argument in standard form, it looks like this:

Since I have had three bad blind dates in a row,

(and the outcome of the fourth will be altered positively by the negative nature of the three preceding it),

---

Therefore, my next blind date is likely to be a good one.

Unfortunately for this person, there is no causal connection between the first three bad "matches" and the next one. The odds do not change with regard to any particular date. Each event stands alone. The implicit second premise represents a faulty causal analysis of chance events and provides no support for the conclusion. The argument therefore fails to meet the sufficiency criterion of a good argument.

Example "It seems that every time I open my mail I get an offer of chances to win a lot of money or other prizes in some kind of sweepstakes. I almost always mail back the entry form to see if I have won anything. Since I haven't won anything yet, I figure my time is coming." As long as this person sends in only one entry for each contest, the chances of winning any particular contest do not improve because there is no causal connection between the results of independent sweepstakes.

Example "It's been heads five times in a row. I'm sticking with tails." There is no more likelihood that the next toss of the coin will be tails than that it will be heads, in spite of the fact that most of us are inclined to believe that the odds would be in favor of its being tails.

Attacking the Fallacy An attack on this fallacy is peculiarly difficult. You could demonstrate repeatedly that in the case of a genuine chance event, the chances of correctly predicting a single event are no better than 1 in X (whatever the number of theoretical options happens to be). But such demonstrations are not likely to be effective until you can adequately explain to the arguer how almost all of us, perhaps unwittingly, tend to conflate two very different concepts—statistical probability and causality. It is your job to show that even though statistical probabilities *do* operate for the *totality* of chance events, no chance event is causally related to another. Each chance event stands alone.

Let us assume that you may be able to get the arguer to agree that chance events are not causally affected by previous chance events. You may even get the arguer to agree that statistical probabilities that operate in the context of chance events are entirely separable from the notion of a causal relation between such events. But such distinctions become fuzzy in an actual case. For example, if one were to flip a fair coin 30 times, it would probably be "heads" approximately 15 times and "tails" 15 times. Suppose that you want to demonstrate this statistical probability and start flipping a coin. If you have a run of nine "heads" in a row, someone might be sorely tempted to infer that the next flip is more likely to be "tails," simply because he or she would be thinking it must be about time for the "heads" and "tails" to start evening out so as to reach that statistically probable balance of 15 "heads" and 15 "tails" at the end of 30 flips. After all, there is only room for 6 more "heads" out of the next 21 flips. But by making that inference, the arguer is importing the notion that previous flips causally affect the outcome of subsequent flips *back* into the mix under the guise of statistical probability. These two notions must be kept separate. You must make it clear that while it is *not* a case of the gambler's fallacy to anticipate the 15–15 split, it *is* a case of the gambler's fallacy to assume that the 10th flip is more likely to be "tails" because of the previous nine "heads."

Another strategy that may work on some gamblers is to show how using the gambler's fallacy can lead to contrary conclusions. Consider the once-a-month poker player who has had poor hands all evening. The longer this series of unfortunate events continues, the more such a player might be led to conclude, "This just isn't my night."

But one could just as well conclude, "Surely my time is coming; I'm bound to get a good hand soon." Neither conclusion is warranted, because both derive from a misunderstanding of the character of chance events. Moreover, there is apparently no good reason why a person should draw one conclusion rather than the other. The choice appears to be wholly arbitrary. At best, it would depend on what one's mood happened to be.

ASSIGNMENTS

B. Causal Fallacies   For each of the following arguments, (1) identify the type of causal fallacy illustrated, and (2) explain how the reasoning violates the sufficiency criterion. There are two examples of each fallacy discussed in this section. Arguments marked with an asterisk (*) have sample answers at the end of the text.

*1. The reason you caught such a cold is that you didn't wear a hat to the football game. I told you you'd be sick when you went out the door without a hat on.

*2. Senator Lane came out in favor of the budget bill just one week after he had a meeting with the president at the White House. The president must have really applied some pressure.

*3. You said that if I'm going to make more friends, I'd have to learn to control my temper. Well, I haven't lost my temper in over six months, and as far as I am able to tell, I haven't made a single new friend.

*4. Son, all it takes is one drink to start you on the road to alcoholism. The same is true with marijuana; it's that first smoke that is crucial. If you try it and like it, you'll want more, and the more you smoke, the more dependent you'll become. Then you'll try the harder stuff and finally end up completely "freaked out." Take my word for it and stay away from that stuff.

*5. We haven't shot a deer in three seasons. We're due to bag one this trip.

*6. Recent studies show that most successful executives have very large vocabularies. So if you wish to have a successful business career, I would suggest that you develop as large a vocabulary as possible.

*7. I think that the reason that Yoko and Liam have been so rude and irritable is that the customers have not been giving them many tips lately.

8. You told me a year ago that in order to get a loan at this bank I would have to have stable employment. I've had this job I now have for over a year, so I don't understand why I was turned down for a loan.

9. Medical records show that alcoholics tend to be undernourished. These data strongly suggest that a poor diet contributes to alcoholism.

10. Our study shows that 80 percent of the young people who are users of hard drugs have serious difficulties in relating to their parents. So I think that a stricter enforcement of our drug laws could significantly reduce the domestic problems of these young people.

11. Sally and John were the happiest couple I knew, until Sally started working outside the home. It just shows how the wife's abandonment of the traditional role can destroy a marriage

12. I'm not going to invite Herb to my party tonight. If I invite him, he'll bring all his friends, and they'll bring their friends, and before you know it, the party will be out of control, the neighbors will call the police, and we'll all end up in jail.

13. If you speak softly but firmly to your children, they will not be boisterous or undisciplined. That is the way I have brought up my children, and they have always been well behaved.

14. We won't be here this weekend. We'll be up in the mountains enjoying the pleasures of fishing and hiking. Rain has caused us to postpone our camping trip for the past two weekends, so this weekend is bound to be a pretty one.

C. For each of the following arguments (1) identify, from among all the fallacies studied in this chapter, the fallacy illustrated, and (2) explain how the reasoning violates the sufficiency criterion. There are two examples of each of the fallacies discussed in this chapter.

1. The high rate of divorce can be directly traced to the feminist movement. It has encouraged women to be more independent and assertive in relationships.

2. Professor Stainback, you clearly said that an argument has to be understood to qualify as a good argument. You admitted that my argument is perfectly understandable. So why isn't it a good argument?

3. Those who major in philosophy and take the LSAT or the MCAT do statistically better than those from any other discipline. Therefore, if you want to do well on one of those exams, I suggest that you major in philosophy.

4. No, I don't think you should invest your money in real estate or stocks. You know, "a bird in the hand is worth two in the bush."

5. I dated a blond once, and you know, they really are dingbats.

6. I know why our club meetings are so boring; no one shows up for them.

7. Sharon: As treasurer of our sorority, you made the rest of us pay our dues weeks ago, but you have yet to pay your own dues. Why?
Sandra: Well, I needed to pay some other bills at the time. Besides, as treasurer, I can pay anytime; I'm fully aware of who's paid and who hasn't.

8. There's got to be a good movie on HBO tonight, because there hasn't been a good one on for weeks.

9. Emory & Henry is the best college for me. It's the only school I ever had an interest in. If I get accepted, that's where I'm going.

10. A recent poll of more than 2,000 adults conducted in the Southeast revealed that more than 65 percent of Americans believe strongly in their religious faith and attend worship services weekly.

11. No wonder children are joining gangs. When both parents work and spend so little time with their children, the children tend to look for some sort of family-like support.

12. I worked in Judge Thomas's office for over a year. Not one woman voiced a complaint of sexual harassment. Judge Thomas is not guilty of sexual harassment, because if he were guilty, other women would have said something about it.

13. If only my parents hadn't divorced while I was in junior high school, I would be a happy, self-confident person today.

14. No wonder she can run 5 miles so fast; she's in great shape.

15. Karen: I'm in real trouble, Christine. I'm pregnant and my parents will hit the ceiling. I don't want to get married, and I don't want to have to take care of a baby. Jeff wants us to get married and have the baby. What do you think I should do?
Christine: Well, "you've made your bed. Now you'll just have to lie in it."

16. I can't understand why I suddenly am having problems with my car. I never had a bit of trouble with it until I had it serviced by that new mechanic. He must have messed up something.

17. If students don't stand up to the administration on this issue, they will begin to take away more and more of our rights until we have none left.

18. I don't understand why my car stopped; I have *plenty* of gas.

19. I've driven while I was drunk many times and have never been caught, so I know that my luck is wearing thin. Somebody else better drive us home.

20. Whatever happened to southern hospitality? The people in Atlanta are not friendly at all. I got lost while I was visiting there last weekend and had to stop several times to ask people for directions. And they were not the least bit friendly.

21. If you have some money to invest, I suggest that you put it in bank certificates of deposit. That way your money is safe. CDs are insured by the federal government.

22. The majority of the members of Congress and state legislatures are lawyers. There must be something about law school or the practice of law that prompts people to run for office.

23. Why should I be arrested like a common criminal just because I had a few glasses of wine at the restaurant before I drove home? I am an upstanding citizen of this community.

24. Since the defendant did not take the stand to defend herself, she must have something to hide. She must be guilty.

25. It has been discovered from a survey of over 100,000 female college students that 1 in every 5 women in America has some kind of eating disorder.

26. If we allow them to impose censorship on our school newspaper, they will soon censor the books and magazines in the library, our textbooks, and even the dictionaries and encyclopedias. Eventually, they will be telling the teachers what they can say and the students what they can think.

27. Professor Purifoy said that if there had been TV in 1896, William Jennings Bryan would have won the presidential election.

28. Right after I wrote the mayor about the property tax increase, she came out in favor of it. She must have been persuaded by my argument.

D. Submit an argument (different from the ones submitted in previous chapters, but follow the same procedure). Point out any named fallacies that violate the structural criterion, the relevance criterion, the acceptability criterion, and/or the sufficiency criterion. After setting forth the best argument possible for the position that you think is the most defensible, evaluate that new argument in accordance with the five criteria of a good argument.

E. Following the model used in the text, use a 3×5 card to submit an *original* example (found or created) of each of the fallacies that violate the sufficiency criterion.

F. Create your own strategies or suggestions for attacking each of the fallacies that violate the sufficiency criterion.

IX
Fallacies That Violate
the Rebuttal Criterion

One who presents an argument for or against a position should attempt to provide an effective rebuttal to all serious challenges to the argument or the position it supports and to the strongest argument on the other side of the issue.

The fallacies in this chapter are ways of arguing that fail to provide an effective rebuttal to the criticisms of one's own argument and of the position that it supports and to the strongest arguments on the other side of a controversial issue. This rebuttal feature of good arguments is perhaps the most neglected feature in the construction and evaluation of arguments. For that reason, we have focused attention on it in this text in a way that is not likely to be found in any other text on arguments.

An argument is not a good one if it does not satisfy the rebuttal criterion. To meet that criterion, an argument should anticipate the criticisms that might be brought against the position being defended and block the force of those criticisms by addressing them in the so-called rebuttal premises of the argument.

Each of the fallacies treated in this chapter violates the rebuttal criterion of a good argument in a distinctive way and belongs in one of the following categories: (1) the fallacies of counterevidence, (2) the *ad hominem* fallacies, or (3) the fallacies of diversion.

FALLACIES OF COUNTEREVIDENCE

The fallacies in this section are committed by one who is attempting to escape the requirements of an effective rebuttal by failing to deal honestly with the counterevidence. The arguer either refuses to consider or unfairly minimizes the counterevidence to the view being defended, or simply ignores or omits reference to the counterevidence or arguments on the other side.

Denying the Counterevidence

> **DEFINITION**   *This fallacy consists in refusing to consider seriously or in unfairly minimizing the evidence that is brought against one's claim.*

A method of thinking that allows blind adherence to claims or to assumptions from which such claims may be inferred without proper attention to counterevidence obstructs the discovery of truth. Such thinking also violates the principle of fallibility, which says that every nondefinitional claim has the inherent possibility of being false.

Rather than denying the counterevidence outright, the arguer will sometimes simply refuse to take it seriously or will unfairly minimize its strength. Since the arguer has to consider the possibility that counterevidence might seem credible, he or she has to find some way of "explaining it away." The counterevidence is not really evidence against the arguer's position, it is often claimed; it only appears to be counterevidence, for which there is some simple explanation.

The most radical form of this fallacy is an unwillingness to acknowledge any conceivable evidence that might count against one's position. It is at this point that the critic will sometimes ask: "What it would take to cause you to reconsider your position or to change your mind?" The critic is here attempting to get the arguer to identify some possible counterevidence that might be damaging to his or her position. If the arguer is willing to identify that conceivable evidence, the critic then knows what evidence has to be produced. If the arguer claims that no conceivable evidence could convince him or her of being wrong, then it is clear that the argument is not being conducted on evidential grounds at all and that further discussion would be fruitless.

Example   "I couldn't care less what is in your biology textbook. I know that I didn't come from some monkey or lower form of life or whatever you call it. The Bible says that God created man in his own image. And unlike the Bible, your textbook was written by a mere human being. What's in those textbooks is just somebody's opinion." Let us put this argument into a standard form:

Since your biology textbook says that humans evolved from a lower form of life,

and your text was written by a flawed human being,

and the Bible says that humans were created by God as humans,

and the Bible was written by a nonflawed being,

(and a nonflawed being does not make mistakes),

Therefore, the Bible expresses the correct view about how humans got here.

It is fairly clear that there is no evidence that could convince such a person on the matter of biological evolution, because any evidence offered would have been marshaled by a "mere human being." The rebuttal premise fails to take the evidence seriously and is therefore an ineffective one. Moreover, it "explains away" virtually any evidence that could conceivably be presented by attributing it to "mere humans," which is the source of *all* empirical evidence. Further discussion of the issue would therefore seem to be a waste of mental energy.

Example   Suppose that Debbie is discussing with her college roommate the possible legalization of marijuana. As a part of the discussion, Debbie calls attention to a number of recent government studies concerning marijuana use. These reports conclude that there is no strong evidence to suggest that moderate use of marijuana is in any way harmful. The roommate retorts, "I don't care what the conclusions of your government studies or any other studies are. Marijuana is obviously harmful and should not be legalized under any circumstances."

In this argument there is not even an attempt to address the counterevidence. There is apparently no evidence that she would accept as weakening her position. Indeed, if Debbie were to ask her directly if there were any evidence that she might accept, she would probably reply, "Nothing could convince me that I am wrong."

Example   "Homosexuality is a learned trait. You don't have to be a homosexual," says Reverend Carroll. "Your so-called studies that say it is something you're born with were fabricated by the radical left to try to force us to accept the gay lifestyle. I'll tell you one reason it's not true: God did not create any homosexuals. I know that!"

This arguer denies, in effect, that there is any credible counterevidence to her claim, but she also takes the evidence that is offered and tries to "explain it away" for any who may be taken in by it, by saying that it is the work of leftist radicals. Not only is such an attempt at rebuttal not effective, it seems likely that no evidence against the arguer's view would be taken seriously.

Attacking the Fallacy   To demonstrate whether the arguer is genuinely open to counterevidence, you could ask what particular kind of evidence, if it could be produced, might seriously weaken the claim. If the arguer cannot or will not specify such evidence, it would probably be more productive and less frustrating to shift the discussion to some other issue. However, you might want to point out to the arguer the fruitlessness of carrying on a discussion with one who will entertain no counterevidence and who refuses to take seriously the principle of fallibility. However, if the arguer specifies some conceivable evidence that might tend to alter his or her opinion, then you should make a reasonable effort to find that evidence and bring it to the table.

If you are successful in getting the arguer to listen to counterevidence, ask him or her to respond to it or to evaluate it. If there is a serious attempt to do so, the discussion will have moved forward.

Ignoring the Counterevidence

DEFINITION   *This fallacy consists in arguing in a way that ignores or omits any reference to important evidence unfavorable to one's position, giving the false impression that there is no significant evidence against it.*

None of us wants to lose an argument, mainly because we think we are correct in what we are saying. However, most of us would not want to win an argument by "cheating"—that is, by deliberately ignoring evidence that we knew was damaging to our case—just as we would not want to win a tennis game by cheating—for example, by calling a close but "in" ball "out." It is quite possible that we might think we are really a better player than our opponent, but we could hardly justify cheating to prove it. In tennis, the best player is the one who wins the game. In reasoning, the best position is the one that is best supported in view of all the evidence. Nevertheless, if one holds very strongly to some position, it is tempting to ignore evidence that could possibly throw that judgment into question.

There are at least two situations in our culture in which deliberate "slanting" or "one-sided assessment" of evidence seems to be acceptable. One is in our adversarial method of judicial procedure. In a criminal case, for example, it is acceptable for the arguments of both the defense and the prosecution to be presented with a very deliberate neglect of counterevidence. However, it is *not* acceptable for the *jury* or the *judge* to neglect any evidence in coming to a fair judgment.

The other situation in which slanting, unfortunately, seems to be acceptable is in debating clubs and tournaments on the high school and college level. In this context, the issue is not primarily that of arriving at the best answer to the question on which the debate is focused. The more important issue is that of evaluating the relative forensic abilities of the opposing debaters. It should be noted, however, that in both judicial and debate procedures, the opposition is specifically charged with the responsibility of presenting contrary evidence. Hence, evidence from all sides will be heard in each of those contexts.

However, winning a court case or winning a debate tournament is not the principal concern of one who is interested in the truth. The truth-seeking principle requires that one investigate all sides of an issue and accept the position that is best supported by the evidence. Indeed, as truth-seekers, we should welcome the presentation of any evidence that might weaken our position. If that evidence can be shown *not* to be damaging in any way, we can be all the more assured of the merit of our position. On the other hand, if the counterevidence is significantly damaging to our position, we should be grateful, for it may lead us closer to the truth by steering us away from an indefensible or questionable conclusion.

An argument that ignores relevant counterevidence fails to satisfy the rebuttal criterion of a good argument, because it fails to address effectively the possible downside of the position being defended. "Stacking the deck" by ignoring counterevidence renders a conclusion questionable, because important evidence has not been properly evaluated.

Example   "Swift capital punishment for those found guilty of committing capital crimes would be a very good idea, because it would quickly rid society of undesirables, thereby reducing the fears of the citizenry; it would lower by an enormous amount the costs involved in maintaining them in our penal institutions during long appeal procedures; and it would be a considerable deterrent to would-be criminals. The whole issue seems clear-cut to me." If we look at this argument in standard form, it will be clear that it contains no rebuttal premises:

Since killing immediately those who are convicted of capital crimes would reduce the fears of the citizenry,

because it would rid the society of undesirables,

and it would save a great amount of money required to maintain convicts during long appeals procedures,

and it would be an effective deterrent to would-be criminals,

---

Therefore, we should swiftly carry out capital punishment for those convicted of capital crimes.

Anyone familiar with the capital punishment debate should be aware that this "swift punishment" argument ignores a number of relevant considerations, not the least of which is the injustice that might be done by precluding the right of appeal. This constitutionally guaranteed procedure is a standard and defensible part of our legal system that helps to assure that justice is done. Because the argument fails to address this and other important considerations, it cannot be a good one.

Example   "Motorcycles are dangerous; they are noisy; only two people can ride at once; you can't ride them in cold or rainy weather; in most states you are required to wear an uncomfortable helmet; and the grease from the motor can completely ruin your clothes. I can't see why anyone would want to buy one."

The arguer has neglected to consider many other factors relevant to the desirability of owning a motorcycle. For example, the motorcycle is a relatively inexpensive form of transportation; it is more maneuverable than a car; it is easier to find a place to park it; and many people simply find it more enjoyable than a car. A good argument would contain rebuttal premises that address these and other features of the motorcycle/auto debate.

Example   "I can't see why anyone would want to go to the movies rather than watch television. After all, with television you can sit in the privacy of your own home; you don't have to pay high prices for the movies you see; you don't have to get dressed up; and you don't have to pay those exorbitant prices for food and drinks. You also don't have to fight the traffic or buy gasoline."

This kind of argument might possibly persuade a number of people to stay home and watch television, but for many others it ignores a number of important factors. Television does not usually run movies until a year or so after they are first shown in theaters, and some films that are shown at theaters *never* make their way to the television set. Moreover, many people find it enjoyable to dress up and go out for an evening. Finally, can one really ignore the "big-screen effect"? One ought at least to consider these and other factors when evaluating the relative merits of watching films on television and going to see them in movie theaters.

Attacking the Fallacy   Do not be surprised if someone who presents an argument fails to accompany it with all the evidence *against* its conclusion. It is quite possible, of course, that the arguer has considered such evidence and is of the opinion that it does no damage to the claim at issue and therefore deserves no mention. However, in view of our general tendency to ignore evidence damaging to our favorite opinions, such an assumption would probably not be warranted. Hence, it is legitimate to ask an arguer to give at least some indication that all relevant factors have been seriously evaluated.

Be careful not to be misled by some of the tactics of the deck-stacker. One clever device is to acknowledge and then dispose of a very weak objection to one's position before going on with a one-sided assessment of the evidence. This gives the impression of objectivity and can sometimes be very disarming to the victim of this fallacy. The alert critic, however, will not let the arguer ignore the serious objections to the question at issue.

ASSIGNMENTS

A. Fallacies of Counterevidence   For each of the following arguments, (1) identify the type of fallacy of counterevidence illustrated, and (2) explain how the reasoning violates the rebuttal criterion. There are two examples of each fallacies discussed in this section. Arguments marked with an asterisk (*) have sample answers at the end of the text.

*1. I don't care what the *Report of the President's Commission on Pornography* says. I know that the viewing of pornographic materials *does* encourage people to commit sex crimes. We must not allow the supporters of this report to give free rein to the pornographers.

*2. Even if I were in great shape, I would have no interest in climbing Mount Everest. The slope is steep, treacherous, and barren; the temperature is unbelievably cold; and one takes considerable risk to one's life. Besides, what can you do after you get to the top—just turn around and come back down. The whole thing seems worthless.

3. Why should the president set up a commission to find out the causes of poverty in the United States? They're not going to find anything other than what we already know. We know what causes it. It's just laziness! That's all it is!

4. I don't want to discuss my religious beliefs with you. I'm an atheist, and there is nothing that you could say that might make me change my mind.

AD HOMINEM FALLACIES

The fallacies in this section fail to meet the requirement of an effective rebuttal by unfairly attacking the critic of his or her argument instead of the critic's criticism or counterargument. This may be done by attacking the critic in a personal, abusive way, by claiming that the critic acts or thinks in a way similar to the way being criticized, or by claiming that the criticism is poisoned by the impure motives or questionable circumstances of the critic. While personal attacks are primarily ways of avoiding the obligation of providing an effective rebuttal to another's criticism or counterargument, they also attempt to raise considerations that are irrelevant to the truth or falsity of the claim under review—a clear violation of the relevance criterion as well.

Abusive *Ad Hominem*

DEFINITION   *This fallacy consists in attacking one's opponent in a personal or abusive way as a means of ignoring or discrediting his or her criticism or argument.*

An *ad hominem* argument is an argument directed "toward the person." The personal attack often takes the form of calling attention to some distasteful personal characteristic of an opponent. What that might be in any particular situation depends on what the arguer finds repugnant. A person may be abused for being messy, an "intellectual," fat, thin, foreign, an atheist, a lawyer, a feminist, liberal, conservative, ugly, physically uncoordinated, a smoker, or any number of other things. However, the abusive *ad hominem* is not just a case of directing abusive language toward another person. There is nothing fallacious about calling people names or saying ugly things about them. The fallacy is committed when one engages in a personal attack as a means of ignoring, discrediting, or blunting the force of another's argument.

It is very important, however, that a distinction be made between the *argument* and the *testimony* of a person. For example, if a known liar or psychotic is testifying as a *witness*, the fact that he or she is a liar or psychotic is indeed relevant to the credibility of his or her testimony. However, if the liar or psychotic formulates and presents an *argument*, that argument can and should be evaluated independently of its source. It makes no difference whether it comes from a demented mind, a convicted felon, a child, or a Nazi; an argument can and must stand on its own. After all, even the most despicable of persons may be able to construct a good argument. We could conclude, then, that although there may be personal characteristics of a person, such as his or her bias, psychotic nature, or lack of truthfulness, that might rightly affect our assessment of his or her testimony, it should have nothing at all to do with our evaluation of the person's arguments.

The abusive *ad hominem* obviously fails to meet the rebuttal criterion of a good argument, since it is primarily a device to *avoid* complying with the rebuttal requirement. Some abusers, however, apparently believe that such characteristics actually provide good reasons for ignoring the arguments of those who have them. If so, the abusive *ad hominem* could also be construed as a violation of the relevance criterion, because the personal characteristics of a critic have no bearing on the merit of his or her criticism or counterargument. For these reasons, any argument that uses what the arguer finds personally distasteful about an opponent as a reason for ignoring or rejecting his or her idea cannot be a good one.

Example   "No wonder you think promiscuity is all right. You know you've never had a really good relationship with a woman. So it's not strange that you'd resort to recreational sex." If we put this argument into standard form, the abusive *ad hominem* should become quite clear:

Since you think that sexual promiscuity is morally acceptable,

and you have never had a really good relationship with a woman,

(and because your position stems from your own lack of a good sexual experience),

---

(Therefore, your position or argument about promiscuity is a bad one.)

Rather than addressing the merit of the opponent's position on sexual promiscuity, the arguer abuses his or her critic. The arguer uses what he or she considers to be a negative personal fact about the critic as a reason for not seriously considering the critic's argument or claim. To abuse a person rather than rebut his or her criticisms or argument is a violation of the rebuttal criterion of a good argument. Therefore, the conclusion of the argument does not follow.

Example

Sara: Professor Elliott gave an excellent lecture last night on sculpture and the creative process. She suggested that one of the best ways for a sculptor to make a piece of stone or metal come alive is to imagine himself or herself inside the piece being sculpted—trying to get out.

Phillip: I have no interest in Professor Elliott's opinions. I'd be surprised if any piece of her sculpture has ever even "placed" in an art show. Have you ever seen any of her junk?

An attack on Professor Elliott's artistic ability is simply a means of ignoring the substance of her insights about the creative process.

Example

Cynthia: I think we need to clean up this place tonight, Denise. The landlord wants it to look decent when he shows it to a prospective tenant tomorrow. He said that he lost the prospective tenant he showed it to last week because we had it so messy in here—especially the kitchen. He reminded us that we had agreed in our contract that once we have given notice to vacate, we would keep the apartment clean for showing to prospective tenants.
Denise: What does he know about "clean"? He's been wearing the same shirt for a week.

Denise is not responding to the landlord's argument about keeping the apartment clean during the "show" period; she is using her negative assessment of the landlord's personal habits as a device to avoid dealing with the substantive claim at issue.

Attacking the Fallacy   When we are abusively attacked, there is a great temptation to counterattack in the same abusive way. Yielding to that temptation will not help advance the debate on the real issue. Indeed, it could slow the debate down considerably. The most constructive response is to point out to the arguer that he or she is being abusive and then politely ask for a response to your criticism or counterargument. Sometimes a simple "But what do you think of my *argument*?" will do.

If an arguer persists in a personal attack on you rather than responding to your criticisms or arguments, you should try to find a way to encourage him or her to separate evaluation of a person from evaluation of the merit of that person's ideas or arguments. You might point out that all of us are likely to encounter many unlikable people in our lifetime, many of whom will have good ideas, and if we cannot separate the person from those ideas, we will probably fail to reap the benefit of many good insights.

If possible, take the first step and acknowledge, if appropriate, any merit that you might find in the abuser's position. Such behavior just might encourage similar behavior on his or her part.

Poisoning the Well

DEFINITION   *This fallacy consists in rejecting a criticism or argument presented by another person because of that person's special circumstances or improper motives.*

This fallacy is called "poisoning the well" because its intended effect is to discredit the source of an argument or point of view in such a way that it precludes any need to consider the merit of that position. In other words, it "damns the source," so that nothing that comes from that source will be or can be regarded as worthy of serious consideration. Insofar as the arguer fails to address the criticism, counterevidence, or counterargument that may come from that source, he or she has violated the rebuttal criterion of a good argument.

An argument that exhibits the fallacy of irrelevant authority tries to get us to accept *testimony* from a questionable source as one of its premises. Poisoning the well, however, tries to get us *not to accept* an *argument* from a questionable source. Both are inappropriate argumentative moves. While we should *not* accept testimony from a questionable source, there is no reason not to consider an *argument* that comes from a questionable source. A person's sex, age, race, religion, profession, economic status, or political persuasion might, in some cases, prevent him or her from being a credible witness, but it should not in any way interfere with our willingness to consider his or her argument on the matter at issue. An argument, unlike testimony, is entirely separable from its source. For example, if an argument in opposition to the death penalty comes from a death-row inmate, the source would not make the argument any less or any more worthy of our consideration.

Similar things can be said concerning the charge of improper motives. A person whose motives are suspect might not be a credible witness, but that should not prevent us from giving serious consideration to the merit of his or her argument. For example, the fact that a particular landowner stands to gain financially from a new highway that would go through her property does not make her argument in support of the project unworthy of consideration.

A good argument must provide an effective rebuttal to the criticism of or counterargument to the position it supports. Therefore, an argument that inappropriately poisons the source of a counterargument or criticism, thus preventing it from even being heard or seriously entertained, cannot be a good one.

Example "You're not a woman, so anything you might say about abortion is of no significance." Let us look at how this argument appears when converted into standard form:

(Since you have presented your argument on the subject of abortion),

and you are not a woman,

and no man could have anything of importance to say on the subject,

---

Therefore, your argument is not worthy of my consideration.

The special circumstance of not being a woman should not preclude a male from defending a position on the question of abortion that is worthy of serious consideration. But the arguer does not allow us to hear the argument, let alone evaluate the arguer's response to it.

Example "You can't believe what Professor Roberts has to say about higher salaries for teachers. As a teacher herself, she would naturally be in favor of increasing teachers' pay."

The fact that Professor Roberts is in favor of higher salaries for teachers is of no concern to us. The issue is whether she has a good argument in support of her claim.

Example "Since you are not a member of a sorority or fraternity, you are in no position to tell us how our pledges should be treated."

The frequency with which this attempt to poison wells is used should not deter us from pointing out its fallacious character. An argument for any action or change of action stands on its own. If the argument is a bad one, we should be shown what makes it bad. But if it is a good one, it matters not that it comes from one who is not a member of a sorority or fraternity.

Attacking the Fallacy   It is sometimes quite difficult to attack the poisoning the well fallacy, especially if it is your well that has been poisoned, because even your attack on such reasoning supposedly comes from a contaminated source. Perhaps the most constructive approach in such cases is to confront the issue directly: "Okay, you have decided that anything I might say is contaminated, even before I've said it. That is a very clever device, and there's not a whole lot that I can do about it. But I do not intend to be silenced so easily. One reason you might want to silence me is that you think that what I have to say might seriously damage your position. I think I *do* have something significant to say on this issue, and I'd be interested in your response to it." It is possible, of course, that such a forceful response will not be necessary, for you may find some way of convincing your opponent that there can be no real debate if there is only one speaker.

Two-Wrongs Fallacy

DEFINITION   *This fallacy consists in rejecting a criticism of one's argument or actions by accusing one's critic or others of thinking or acting in a similar way.*

The Latin name of this fallacy, *tu quoque*, translates as "You [do it] too." The arguer who commits this fallacy is implicitly saying to the critic, "Because you are guilty of doing the same thing or thinking the same way that you are criticizing me for, your argument is no good and/or I don't have to listen to you." This counterattack on the critic functions as a way of avoiding the obligation to rebut his or her criticism or counterargument. While this response is primarily a violation of the rebuttal criterion, it is also a violation of the relevance criterion, for the fact that some other person engages in a questionable practice or thought process is irrelevant to whether such a practice or way of thinking merits our acceptance.

Almost all children feel entirely justified in antisocial behavior if they can respond to the scolding parent, "But he (or she) did it first." But there are also adults who seem to feel absolved of any guilt for their behavior if they can say to a critic, "You do the same thing!" Even though most of us would agree that "two wrongs don't make a right," it almost always seems to make us feel better, when our own behavior is questioned, if we can point out that our critic, or some other person, acts in a similar way. But there is no logical way that another's fault can absolve our own guilt for the same fault, nor does the behavior of another person or group constitute any logical justification for us to behave in a similar manner.

However, those who commit this fallacy are not primarily concerned with justifying their behavior by the behavior of a critic. They are using the behavior of the critic as a reason for abdicating their responsibility to address the substance of the critic's questions or counterargument. They may indeed want us to "practice what we preach" or even think that we are hypocrites, but the inconsistency between what we say and what we do is in no way relevant to the merit of our criticisms of the arguer's position or argument. Counterarguments and criticisms deserve to stand on their own, and if the argument being criticized is to qualify as a good one, it must effectively blunt the force of those criticisms.

Example

Thurman: At your age, you really shouldn't work so hard, Roy. You're going to exhaust yourself completely and end up in the hospital.
Roy: You work just as hard as I do, Thurman, and you are not one bit younger than I am.

Roy has not really responded to Thurman's claim that if he continues to work at the same level, he is likely to develop some serious physical problems. Instead, he has used the "you do it, too" argument as a way to draw attention away from himself and to avoid dealing with the issue. In standard form, Roy's argument looks like this:

Since you have made an argument against my way of acting,

and you act the same way that I do,

Therefore, your argument is a bad one and/or I do not need to address your argument.

No! Roy's argument is the bad one. It miserably fails to meet the conditions of the rebuttal criterion.

Example

Father: Owen, I really don't think that you should be drinking. Alcohol tends to dull your senses, reduces your physical control, and may even become psychologically addicting.
Son: That's not a very convincing argument, Dad, when you're standing there with that glass of bourbon in your hand.

Although it may be tempting for Owen to point out to his father the apparent inconsistency between what he is saying and what he is doing, the proper action is to assess the merit of the father's argument. The father's failure to practice what he preaches does not neutralize that argument.

Example Suppose that the golf pro tells you in your first golf lesson that the first and most important thing to do in learning to become an effective golfer is to "keep your head down and your eye on the ball." It would be fallacious to conclude that you are not being given sound advice, simply because the golf pro doesn't always keep *her* head down when *she* plays tournament golf.

Attacking the Fallacy If an arguer points out an inconsistency between your criticism and your own behavior, there is no reason to be intimidated or silenced by such a charge. It may be best to admit the charge, if true, and to confront the arguer who commits this fallacy by insisting that he or she set aside concerns about your possible inconsistency and evaluate the merits of your criticisms or counterargument. A perceived inconsistency between a critic's words and deeds does not relieve an arguer of the responsibility to effectively rebut criticisms or counterarguments to his or her argument or to the position it defends.

Few people would defend, in principle, the view that indefensible behavior by one person justifies similar behavior by another. After all, most of us have been taught since childhood that "two wrongs don't make a right." But the real issue here is whether or not an arguer will treat the inconsistency between the words and behavior of a critic as a sufficient reason for abandoning the obligation to address his or her criticisms or counterargument. The inclination to dismiss that obligation is a common and very powerful psychological response to the critic who says one thing and does another. Indeed, because such thinking is so emotionally convincing, its fallacious character is usually not fully recognized until it is pointedly brought to one's attention. And that, of course, is your job.

ASSIGNMENTS

B. *Ad Hominem* **Fallacies**　For each of the following arguments, (1) identify the type of *ad hominem* fallacy illustrated, and (2) explain how the reasoning violates the rebuttal criterion. There are two examples of each fallacy discussed in this section. Arguments marked with an asterisk (*) have sample answers at the end of the text.

*1. Claudia: Just stop yelling at me! The only way that we're ever going to solve any problem is to sit down and talk calmly about it. Screaming at me will not help in any way!

　　Mike: Well, you don't yell! You just cry all the time! Do you think that's any better?

*2. Parishioner to priest: "You've never been married, so why should I listen to your advice concerning my marital problems? How could you possibly know what you're talking about?"

3. Do you really expect me to dignify your comments against my proposal by responding to them? They simply confirm what I've always thought about you, anyway. Your thinking is shallow, naive, and uninformed. And I feel that you're wasting my time.

4. Sue: You know, Betty Lou, with all this stuff about AIDS, you really should be more careful about the guys you sleep with.

　　Betty Lou: Me? Be careful? You've had at least a half dozen partners since Christmas!

*5. Ms. Phillips: My political opponent, Representative Abbott, is not telling the truth when he says that he has never missed a single roll-call vote in the House of Representatives during his long tenure. According to the Congressional Record, Mr. Abbott missed eight roll-call votes during his first term.

　　Mr. Abbott: Ms. Phillips, is the Congressional Record the only piece of reading material that they would allow you to read at the mental hospital in which you were a patient during my first term?

6. Don't tell me how to raise my children! I don't care how much you've studied child psychology; if you don't have any children of your own, you can't possibly understand kids.

FALLACIES OF DIVERSION

The fallacies in this section fail to meet the rebuttal criterion by attempting in various ways to divert attention away from the weakness of their own argument and/or the strength of their opponent's criticism or counterargument. These are argumentative devices that help to maneuver one into a more advantageous or less embarrassing position by directing attention away from the actual issue. In this way, the arguer can avoid responding to the criticism or the counterargument. Some common diversionary tactics are distorting or misrepresenting the criticism or counterevidence, attacking only trivial points of the criticism or counterevidence, trying to distract discussants to a side issue, or ridiculing the critic or making a joke related to the criticism or counterevidence.

Attacking a Straw Man

DEFINITION *This fallacy consists in misrepresenting an opponent's position or argument, usually for the purpose of making it easier to attack.*

"Straw man" is a metaphor used to describe the caricature of an opponent's argument that the faulty arguer substitutes for the flesh-and-blood original version. But a successful attack on this straw-like substitute is not a successful attack on the *actual* position or argument of the opponent. According to the rebuttal criterion, a good argument must effectively address the *strongest* version of a position or argument on the other side of an issue. Since the arguer has attacked a deliberately weakened version of that argument, he or she has failed to satisfy the rebuttal criterion.

One may misrepresent another's argument in several ways. First, one may *distort* it. This is often done by paraphrasing it in words that trivialize it or that subtly include one's own negative evaluation of it.

Second, one may *oversimplify* it. A complex argument can be made to look absurd when it is stated in a simplified form that leaves out important qualifications or subtle distinctions.

Third, one may *extend* it beyond its original bounds. This can be done by drawing inferences from it that are clearly unwarranted or unintended.

The principle of charity obligates us to represent fairly the arguments of others. Indeed, we are obligated to give their arguments the best possible interpretation. Since a misrepresentation of another's argument or position hardly qualifies as a fair treatment of it, the straw man attack should be regarded as a violation not only of the rebuttal principle but of the principle of charity as well.

Example Misrepresentation or deliberate distortion is a clever and typical technique of politicians. If Senator Coulthard argues for a decrease in the national defense budget by suggesting that billions can be saved by cutting out waste and mismanagement, her political opponent might respond, "My opponent wants to undercut our defense posture around the world by cutting our defense spending. A cut could only mean reduction of our forces in strategic defense positions in Europe and Asia. I say that America cannot become a second-rate military power and still keep her commitments abroad." Let us convert this argument into standard form so that we can see more clearly how it has been misrepresented:

Since Senator Coulthard wants to decrease defense spending,

and this is to be done by cutting out waste and mismanagement,

and by weakening our military position in Europe and Asia,

and by becoming a second-rate military power,

(and since we should not weaken our position in Europe and Asia and become a second-rate military power),

---

(Therefore, Senator Coulthard's idea is a bad one.)

This example shows not only how a position may be misrepresented but also how it may be extended beyond its original bounds. Cutting out waste in defense spending does not necessarily entail a reduction of armed forces in Europe and Asia nor America's becoming a second-rate military power, but the opponent has tried to make it appear that those things are a part of the Senator's plan and then proceeds to attack those added straw-like parts. If Senator Coulthard had been given the opportunity to review the reconstruction of her argument, it would not have looked like this argument.

Example   A very clear case of misrepresentation that involves drawing unwarranted inferences can be seen in this short exchange between a proponent and an opponent of a plan to construct a new dam.

> **Proponent:** Unless we construct a power plant in this area within the next ten years, we will not be able to meet the significantly growing demand for electrical power.
>
> **Opponent:** What you're saying is that you couldn't care less what happens to the plant life and wildlife in this area or even to human lives that might be dislocated by the building of this dam.

The opponent has drawn an inference from the proponent's argument that is clearly unwarranted. In no way could one conclude from the argument that the proponent was unconcerned about the possible environmental dangers and other disruptions that would be created by the construction of a power plant in a particular area. Indeed, it is possible that every precaution would be taken to ensure that very little harm to living things would occur.

Example   Critics of the Supreme Court's school prayer decision either deliberately or unknowingly distort the view of its defenders by claiming that it prohibits any prayer in public schools, while in fact it only prohibits a public school from *endorsing* or *requiring* a religious ceremony. But that important qualification is left out by the critics. Similarly, some critics regard the display of the Ten Commandments in public buildings as compatible with the separation of church and state, by claiming that the Ten Commandments are simply moral guidelines, a public display of which would serve a public good. However, to refer to the Ten Commandments simply as moral guidelines is a misrepresentation of their character, since the first four deal with very specific *religious* demands, including one that requires commitment to the God of the Hebrew people. In both cases, these arguers have constructed straw men to attack rather than to evaluate the real arguments of their opponents.

Attacking the Fallacy   It is not always possible to know if an opponent has deliberately distorted your argument or has simply failed to understand or interpret it in the way that was intended. For that reason, it might be helpful to recapitulate the basic outline of any lengthy argument you present or, better yet, ask your opponent to summarize it for you. If he or she is willing to do so, that will put you in a better position to correct any misinterpretation, misrepresentation, or omission.

If you have the opportunity, you should insist that a fruitful or constructive debate is not possible unless every attempt has been made to understand what is being said on both sides. If your opponent insists on continuing to misrepresent your position, call attention to that fact and correct the distortion in each counterresponse. In no case should you debate the issue on the distorter's terms, by allowing yourself to be forced into defending a misrepresented version of your position.

Trivial Objections

DEFINITION *This fallacy consists in attacking an opponent's position by focusing critical attention on some minor point in the argument.*

The most likely time for the appearance of trivial objections is when the basic argument appears to be a strong one. Indeed, one may take it as a good sign that one has a decent argument when trivial objections rear their heads.

Trivial objections can take many forms. It may be an attack against a premise that bears no significant weight in an argument—a support that can be easily knocked down without doing any serious damage to the argument. It may be an attack on a minor or insignificant detail that has no important bearing on the main point of the argument. It may even be a criticism of an illustration used. In such cases, the basic argument remains intact, because even if the objection has some merit, it is a trivial one.

The fallacy of trivial objections is not an attack on a misrepresentation or a weakened version of an opponent's argument; it is simply an attack on a minor flaw in it. But those who commit this fallacy treat the flaw as if it were a major one. These nitpickers seem to think that any flaw found in an argument is sufficient to destroy it.

But the one who resorts to making trivial objections is the one who has a flawed argument, for such an argument is a violation of the rebuttal criterion. By trying to dismiss an opponent's argument on the basis of trivial objections, the arguer has failed to address the strongest evidence or arguments on the other side of the issue.

Example "It's not that I haven't looked carefully at Christianity, Joe, but I just can't swallow that stuff about Jesus walking on water or turning water into wine. You and I both know that's empirically impossible." The argument, when put into standard form, looks like this:

Since the New Testament includes some stories of miracles as a part of its expression of the Christian faith,

and miracles are empirically impossible,

Therefore, the Christian faith is an indefensible perspective.

The speaker is surely raising trivial objections, for these are clearly some of the least significant features of the Christian perspective—at least for most nonliteralists. Indeed, they would probably not even qualify as weak supports. A successful attack on these features, then, would have no significant negative effect on the argument for the Christian faith. Because the arguer has not satisfied the rebuttal principle by addressing the strongest features of the case for Christianity, the conclusion does not follow.

Example

Eleanor: Walking is one of the best kinds of exercise you can get. One should walk rather than ride whenever possible. For example, rather

than drive over to the cafeteria to eat lunch, it would be more benefi-
cial to your health to walk.
Margaret: But I don't eat at the cafeteria.

Margaret is attacking an illustration that Eleanor used to make her point. The fact that
the specific illustration does not fit in Margaret's case is irrelevant to the basic thrust of
the argument about the benefits of walking.

Example

Larry: I don't understand why you failed me in philosophy this term.
Professor Provost: I think I can explain that very well. As you know,
you failed the first test I gave, you were caught cheating on the last
test, and you neglected to turn in any of the written assignments. Besides, I don't think you ever contributed anything to class discussion.
Larry: I thought you knew why I didn't talk in class. My physician
gave me strict orders to keep my talking to an absolute minimum because of some growths on my vocal cords.
Professor Provost: Oh, I didn't know about that. I can see now why
you didn't speak up in class, and under the circumstances, you could
not have been expected to. How is your throat now?
Larry: Fine. But the important point is that you have admitted that
your evaluation of my performance in your course was based on a
false understanding, so I should not have failed the course. Right?

Wrong! Larry has blunted only the weakest point in Professor Provost's argument for
failing him—his contribution to class discussion.

Attacking the Fallacy   If a critic points out a minor problem in your argument, you should probably acknowledge it. But do not hesitate to point out that the
strongest supports for your position are still intact and that you would be interested in
hearing a response to them. If the critic insists that the objections raised are not trivial
and do indeed damage the argument, ask for an explanation of exactly how the matters
raised have any significant bearing on the merit of the basic position being defended. As
always, you might remind the arguer that the rebuttal criterion puts him or her under
obligation to effectively rebut the strongest feature of your position or argument.

One way to effectively disarm an opponent is to make clear in advance which
are your strongest and which are your weakest supports for your claim. If the arguer
then chooses to attack one of your weaker supports, you will have already acknowledged that it is a weak support, so whatever damage it may cause will probably not significantly affect the quality of your argument.

Red Herring

DEFINITION   *This fallacy consists in attempting to hide the weakness of a position
by drawing attention away from the real issue to a side issue.*

The strange name of this fallacy comes from the sport of fox hunting. A herring
is cooked to a brownish-red color and its strong smell is used to train dogs to follow a

scent, but it is also dragged *across* the fox's trail in order to test the dogs' ability to follow the fox scent. Dogs that can be easily pulled off are not ready for the real hunt. In argument, using a red herring means consciously or unconsciously steering a debate away from one issue to a different, perhaps related issue in such a way as to make it appear that the related issue is relevant to the issue at hand, but primarily as a means of avoiding the obligation of addressing the main issue or criticism.

A very common form of red herring is *empty consolation*, which seeks to draw attention away from a complaint or criticism by claiming that the complainant should be satisfied with an undesirable situation, because "things could be worse" or because the situation of some other person or group is worse. Although it is true that "things" could almost always be worse than they are, that is not the issue, and drawing attention to such a notion is simply a way to avoid dealing with the initial criticism or complaint.

Example

Senator Clark: Why are you not willing to support my antiabortion amendment? Don't you have any feelings at all for the unborn children whose lives are being indiscriminately blotted out?

Senator Rich: I just don't understand why you people who get so worked up about lives being blotted out by abortion don't have the same feelings about the thousands of lives that are blotted out every year by the indiscriminate use of handguns. Is not the issue of the sanctity of human life involved in both issues? Why have you not supported us in our efforts at gun-control legislation?

Let us convert Senator Rich's argument into standard form:

Since you wish me to join you in support of an antiabortion amendment to the constitution,

and you do not join me in support of gun-control legislation,

and because they both deal with the issue of the sanctity of human life,

---

Therefore, your nonsupport of gun control suggests some unexplained inconsistency on your part.

Senator Rich's concern here is no doubt a very important one, and her "conclusion" or observation about inconsistency may be very insightful, but she does not answer the question at issue set forth in the first premise, which is why she is not supporting the antiabortion amendment. The issue of gun control and its possible connection to the issue of sanctity of life may be addressed on another day, but in this context it should be seen as a red herring, in that it inappropriately directs attention away from addressing the primary issue.

Example

Many of us have had the experience of complaining about the low or unfair wages we receive for our labors, only to be told by a parent or some other older person, "Well, you could be making $35 a week as I did when I was your age." Such empty consolation diverts our attention in a way that often precludes dealing seriously with our concern.

Example

Dorothy: I'm convinced that your proposal to adopt an honor code here at Mason College just won't work. We don't have a tradition for it. Even institutions like West Point that have had a long history with an honor code are finding it difficult to maintain. Public school teachers, I understand, even refuse to listen to so-called tattletales. In fact, it is the tattletale who is now considered to be at fault if he or she informs the teacher about the behavior of another student.

Vladimir: But don't you agree that the honor code has worked well in the past for many institutions that have used it? And you can't deny that those who have lived under such a code have a genuine respect for it. If we had such a code here at Mason, we would be numbered among some of the most elite institutions in this country.

Vladimir has not addressed Dorothy's concerns or criticisms. The issue is not whether the honor code has worked well in the past in certain institutions or whether it would place Mason College among the most elite institutions in the country. Those are red herrings that are made to appear to be relevant considerations in the discussion of the real issue, which is whether the honor code should now be initiated by an institution that has no tradition for it.

Attacking the Fallacy To "hold the reins" on a heated argument or discussion is not an easy task. Red herrings creep very subtly into many counterarguments. Detecting when the focus of an argument has been maneuvered from the main issue to a side issue requires constant surveillance.

Moreover, a frequent reminder of "that's not the issue" may not always be understood by your opponent. Therefore, you should be prepared to explain how the issue has been sidetracked or why a certain issue is appropriately classified as a red herring.

Since red herrings are often not consciously, or at least not deliberately, dragged into a discussion, one should perhaps be cautious about accusing an opponent in such cases of engaging in fallacious reasoning. If the swerve to the side is innocent, you should perhaps treat it as such. You would do well to save the charge of "red herring" for those who use it as a deliberate diversionary device to avoid addressing the strongest points of an argument or counterargument.

Resort to Humor or Ridicule

DEFINITION *This fallacy consists in injecting humor or ridicule into an argument in an effort to cover up an inability or unwillingness to respond appropriately to an opponent's criticism or counterargument.*

Humor is a very effective diversionary tactic, because a clever and well-delivered remark can quickly blunt the force of an opponent's argumentative advantage in the minds of an audience, toward whom such humor is primarily directed. Moreover, it can quickly bring an audience over to one's own side, even though there is no logical justification for such a shift.

Diversionary humor can take a number of different forms. It may be a pun created from a remark in an opponent's proposal or argument, a not-so-serious response to a serious claim or question, a humorous anecdote, or just plain ridicule of an opponent's position or remarks. Ridicule of another person is an effective device only if it is not overly cruel—that is, it must be good-humored enough to elicit some spontaneous laughter. If it is too sharp, it may tend to weaken the position of the one who uses it by creating sympathy for the target.

Most arguers who use this tactic are very much aware of its diversionary effect. They are, in effect, using a joke, pun, or bit of ridicule as a means of ignoring or discrediting the criticism or argument. By doing so, they violate the rebuttal criterion, which requires that they effectively *rebut* the substance of the criticism or argument. Making fun of or ridiculing an argument or its author is clearly not a way of meeting the rebuttal criterion of a good argument.

Example   Imagine the following conversation between a third-party, or minor, presidential candidate and a young reporter at a news conference.

> **Reporter:** It seems to me that if you were elected president, the Congress with which you would have to work would not be very cooperative at all. How could you, as president, bring about any reform or help enact any beneficial legislation with a Congress that was almost totally opposed to your programs?
>
> **Candidate:** Well, if I were elected, about half the members of Congress would drop dead of heart attacks, and half of my problem would be solved from the outset.

Let us attempt to convert the candidate's humorous response into the standard form of an argument:

> Since I would have a problem dealing with an uncooperative
> Congress if I were elected president,
>
> and since half the members of Congress would die of heart attacks if
> I were elected president,
> _____
> Therefore, half of my problem of dealing with an uncooperative
> Congress would be solved.

The candidate's conclusion does not follow from the joke premise. He is simply trying to use humor to dodge the reporter's question, although it seems to be one that deserves a serious response.

Example   During the 1984 presidential race, President Reagan's age was an issue of concern to many people. During one of the presidential debates on television with the younger former vice-president Walter Mondale, Reagan was asked by a panelist whether he might be too old to handle a nuclear war. "Not at all," replied Reagan, and then added that he did not want to make age an issue in this campaign. "I am not," he said, "going to exploit my opponent's youth and inexperience." The extended laughter from the panel of reporters and the audience had the effect of defusing the age issue and prevented any further questioning about it.

Example   When a philosophy student noticed that his political science professor had used a questionable contrary-to-fact hypothesis in her analysis of a particular issue in class, he confronted her with it. Rather than examining the charge to determine whether it was justifiable, the professor tried to blunt the force of the charge by saying, "Well, class, Socrates must have slipped into our class while we were not noticing. Now what did you say I did? Used a contrary-to-fact what? I didn't think philosophers were concerned about facts." Since the other class members were amused by her ridicule of the student, the professor was able to avoid facing squarely the charge against the soundness of her reasoning.

Attacking the Fallacy   If a humorous intrusion into an argumentative context is a genuinely clever one, you could perhaps show appropriate appreciation of it, for sound arguments need not be totally cheerless. A response in kind might even be an effective move, as a means of leveling the field of play. However, at the appropriate moment you should reiterate the basic claim or criticism at issue and insist on a serious response.

ASSIGNMENTS

C. Fallacies of Diversion   For each of the following arguments, (1) identify the type of diversionary fallacy illustrated, and (2) explain how the reasoning violates the rebuttal criterion. There are two examples of each fallacy discussed in this section. Arguments marked with an asterisk (*) have sample answers at the end of the text.

*1. Student: The opinions of the students are completely ignored in the process of determining both curricular changes and social programs. The students should have a much greater voice in campus governance, because we have a very great stake in this institution, and we think that we have a positive contribution to make.

Professor Little: The faculty are the ones who need a greater voice. Professors can be fired without explanation, and they have no control over who is promoted or given tenure. Their opinions about budgetary allotments are completely ignored. Why aren't you concerned about the injustice the faculty is experiencing?

*2. Diana: Dan, I'm tired of staying home every day, washing dishes, cleaning house, chasing the kids, and fixing meals. I would like to do something different with my life. I'd like to feel I am making some significant contribution. As it is, I feel worthless. How would you like to have to stay home and do the things I do every day—day after day?

Dan: Look, Diana, into everyone's *wife* a little pain must fall.

*3. Professor Lang: It doesn't make much sense any more to prepare for a specific vocation in college. In a technological age, change takes place so rapidly that job training usually becomes obsolete within eight years. I suggest that we maintain a strong nonvocationally oriented, liberal arts curriculum. That way our students will be prepared to go in a number of different vocational directions.

Professor Reid: I'm not so sure, John. I think there are a lot of technological jobs that last longer than eight years.

4. You shouldn't complain! You're lucky that women on this campus can stay out until 1 A.M. Women here used to have to be in by 10 P.M.

5. **Mother:** I think it would be a good idea for us to encourage the children to watch less television and to get more physical exercise.
Father: You think I've let the kids become a bunch of lazy, unhealthy television addicts, don't you?

*6. **Daughter:** If two people really love each other and have committed themselves to each other, I don't see any reason why they shouldn't live together. Philip and I really do love each other, Mother. Someday we may get married, but right now we simply want to be close to each other.
Mother: The way I see it is that you're just looking for an excuse to go to bed together. Your whole attitude about this thing makes sex something cheap!

7. **Challenger:** If I am elected, I promise to do everything I can to make our streets safe enough that our wives can walk the streets at night.
Incumbent: Is that what you want to do—make hookers out of our wives?

8. **Professor Roper:** I think the administration is entirely justified in dismissing Professor Frederick. He's never prepared for his lectures, he makes off-color remarks to his female students, he grades arbitrarily, and he isn't even friendly toward his students.
Student: I disagree with you. He always says "hello" to me every time I see him.

D. For each of the following arguments (1) identify, from among all the fallacies studied in this chapter, the fallacy illustrated, and (2) explain how the reasoning violates the rebuttal criterion. There are two examples of each of the fallacies discussed in this chapter.

1. **Sofia:** People would be a lot healthier if they used fish and poultry as their main sources of protein.
Taylor: But some people are allergic to fish and poultry.

2. If I had a choice, Joan, I would take a nice apartment over a house anytime. House payments are much higher than apartment rents for about the same amount of living space. But even more important, you don't have to cut the grass, rake the leaves, or get out the old paintbrush when the paint begins to peel. If anything breaks, you just call "maintenance" to fix it. You don't have to buy and repair appliances; they usually come with the apartment. Neither do you have to pay taxes or insurance. And the best thing of all is that you don't have to deal with obnoxious vinyl siding or replacement windows salespeople. Why would you want to buy a house?

3. I don't see why you want a raise. You know, don't you, that you already have the biggest, nicest office on this floor of the building.

4. **Teresa:** Aren't you going to put on some sunblock before you go out on the beach? Recent articles in a number of prestigious medical journals say that the sun's rays, whether they burn or not, can cause cancer of the skin.
Kathleen: I don't care what the doctors say. The doctors can be wrong. Unblocked sun gives me a great tan, and anything that makes me look and feel this good has to be good for me.

5. **Joe:** I believe that if we create a minority seat on the council, there would be equal representation and diversity of opinion expressed. We African Americans do not feel adequately represented here as it is.

Fred: Why did you come to a predominantly white school in the first place, when you knew how things were?

6. **Dr. Carmack:** You really shouldn't be smoking that much, Ms. Lowe. Not only is it likely to cause you to have cancer, but since you smoke around others, it is damaging to the health of family and coworkers.

   Ms. Lowe: I noticed that you put out your cigarette just as you were entering the examining room, Dr. Carmack.

7. **Supervisor:** I'm going to have to let Joan go. She is almost always late for work, she makes frequent errors that turn out to be very costly, she spends a lot of time making personal phone calls, and personally, I don't think she dresses appropriately for our kind of business.

   Employee: I don't think that wearing blue jeans once in a while is reason enough to fire someone.

8. **Mother:** Have a good time, son, and don't forget to wear your bike helmet.

   Son: Why should I? You ride with me sometimes, and you don't even own a helmet.

9. The army certainly doesn't seem like an attractive option to me, Jerry. You have to be up at the crack of dawn, and you are under someone's direct command 24 hours a day. Rarely are you allowed to think for yourself; most things are already decided for you. Besides, the physical demands can be awful. Have you thought about that?

10. **Father:** I think Grandma might be better cared for in a nice nursing home.

    Son: What you're saying is that you are tired of taking care of her—that she's a burden to you.

11. The lieutenant governor's plan for reform of the procedures for dealing with victims in rape trials cannot be taken seriously. You know that his wife was raped last fall, don't you?

12. **Ms. Cox:** Your position about birth control is just not realistic. Parents need to talk seriously to their children about birth control and about alternative contraceptives.

    Ms. Powers: Well, it seems to me that if you were a little shorter and had an accent, you would be a regular Dr. Ruth.

13. **Prosecution expert witness:** It is my considered opinion, as a practicing psychiatrist, that the defendant is as sane as any member of the jury.

    Defense attorney: How many of these insanity defense trials do you do a year, Dr. Qualls? How much do you get paid for each gig? How many days a year are you on the road traveling around the state from courtroom to courtroom? When do you have time to practice your profession, Doctor? Aren't you getting a little rusty? No more questions, your honor.

14. You have never been in military service, so how can your argument about gays in the military be taken seriously?

15. **Ed:** But all studies and every expert says that you cannot get the AIDS virus from casual contact.

    Mark: I don't care what the studies say. I'm not going to touch anyone who has AIDS. I don't intend to die because of what some study says.

16. **Scott:** The Supreme Court was wrong in allowing sodomy in the Texas case. The state laws against sodomy should stay just as they were. Sodomy is against the laws of nature. Sodomy never produced a single human life.

    Dan: Oh yeah? Then where do you think lawyers came from?

17. **Senator Kobler:** I think that to impose these standards on the automotive industry by next year would put the American auto industry at a disadvantage in the world automobile market.

    Ms. Chen: It's not surprising that you would side with the automakers in their fight against tougher environmental standards. You've never really cared about the environment, anyway. You only pretended that you were concerned about the environment to get elected. You couldn't care less, could you?

18. **Joy:** After listening to both candidates, I think that Ms. Gaia is better qualified for the job.

    Bob: In other words, you're voting for her because she's a woman.

E. Submit the best argument possible (in essay form) that represents your own position on a current controversial issue selected by the class. Be particularly careful to provide a rebuttal to the strongest arguments against your argument or the position it supports and/or against the argument for an alternative position. Bring photocopies of your argument to give to each of the other students. After all position arguments have been read, use class time to conduct a rational discussion in accordance with the principles outlined in the "Code of Conduct for Effective Discussion," with the goal of coming to some rational consensus about the most defensible position on the issue.

F. Following the model used in the text, use a 3 × 5 card to submit an *original* example (found or created) of each of the fallacies that violate the rebuttal criterion.

G. Create your own strategies or suggestions for attacking each of the fallacies that violate the rebuttal criterion.

H. As one of the assignments at the end of Chapter IV, you were asked to read a fictional "Letter to Jim" in the Appendix. You were asked to try to identify, without benefit of the knowledge of particular names of fallacies, the 60 violations of the criteria of good reasoning embedded in the letter. You should now be able to name those fallacies. Return to the Appendix, name each of the fallacies, and bring your numbered list to class.

X
Writing the Argumentative Essay

The ability to construct an argument that convinces not only ourselves but also others is a desirable skill. Without that skill, we are at a great disadvantage in most contexts. In whatever role we play in our society, we are repeatedly called on to construct an argument defending a view on important issues. We have found or will find ourselves defending a proposal in a committee or group meeting, deciding whether to make a major purchase, changing jobs, casting votes, or getting married. We construct arguments as a means of resolving disagreements with parents, spouses, children, neighbors, parents, bosses, teachers, students, and customer service representatives. We construct arguments for ourselves and/or others on moral, religious, political, and entertainment issues almost daily. This text has presented insights and strategies for performing that constructive task effectively. It now behooves us to bring those ideas together in one place for the particular task of writing an argumentative essay.

Writing an argumentative essay entails five basic steps: researching the question, stating a position, arguing for that position, rebutting objections to that position, and resolving the question. The outline of such an essay might look like this:

1. Statement of the question

2. Position on the question and its importance

3. Argument in support of the position and replies to anticipated criticisms of the premises

4. Objections to the argument and/or position and replies to those objections

5. Arguments against alternative positions

6. Resolution of the question

RESEARCHING THE QUESTION

The first step in constructing an extended argument or writing an argumentative essay is to become thoroughly acquainted with the complexity of the issue at stake.

Your concern should not be that of defending the position that you might already have on an issue; your goal is to discover which of the available positions on the question is the most defensible one. It is not unlikely that researching the question might cause you to change your mind about which position to support.

Good preparation involves looking at all sides of an issue. Not only does this guide you in determining which position to defend, it acquaints you with the strongest reasons that might be used in support of that position. It also acquaints you with the alternative positions on the question and the reasons that are used in support of them. Most importantly, you will become aware of the major criticisms of your argument and/or objections to your position, which you must effectively rebut as a part of your essay.

In preparation for writing an argument, it might be a good idea to start a file in your computer, dividing it into the six sections of the suggested outline of your essay. As you read articles or books, conduct research on the Internet, and talk with others about the topic, write down ideas as they occur to you and place them in the appropriate section of the file. You may then reorganize these notes from time to time, with the help of your "cut and paste" tool. If you return often to the file, you will begin to expand or amend the ideas in your notes, to make connections between your ideas, and to see the major features of your essay slowly emerge.

STATING YOUR POSITION

When presenting an argument for a position, the most forceful way of starting the essay is to state your position up front, similar to the way a prosecutor does at the beginning of the state's opening statement. Your research has already led you to the conclusion whose truth you now want to demonstrate, so you should declare it as quickly and as simply as possible. There is no need to waste time introducing the subject. While you may need to distinguish the question at issue from any other question with which it might be confused, the nature of the question and your position on it will be become sufficiently clear as you elaborate on your position and present your argument in support of it.

Prior to presenting your argument, it would be a good idea to indicate why the question at issue is an important one. The very fact that you are writing an argumentative essay suggests that there is an important unresolved or open question to be addressed. If it is a problem to be solved, you should make it very clear what that problem is, and how your proposal will help to solve it.

In stating your position on the question, you should be careful to be very precise in the way you state it. You will want to use language that is free of vagueness, not subject to multiple interpretations, and no more technical in nature than is absolutely necessary. Key terms or concepts referred to in your stated position should be defined and/or carefully explained. Finally, the claim in the statement of your position must be properly qualified. Failure to do so could make an otherwise good argument a very poor one. For example, the claim must not be so narrowly defined that it becomes a trivial or inconsequential one. Nor should it be so broadly defined that it overlooks or neglects legitimate exceptions. If there are possible exceptions that you are willing to make, those should be identified as a part of the position. Such qualification tends to strengthen the position and makes it less vulnerable to the counterexample attack or criticism by your critics. Your position should also not be so broadly defined that it promises more than it can deliver, in terms of solving the problem addressed.

As a general rule, do not assume anything about the person reading your essay other than that he or she is an adult who is reasonably acquainted with the world. Explain all concepts, terms, and ideas that are not necessarily part of a high school graduate's general knowledge. Above all, do not write as if only your professor were reading the essay, and do not assume that you don't have to explain certain terms or concepts because you think the reader "already knows them." Instead, envision the reader as a fellow student who is not necessarily familiar with your course or discipline.

ARGUING FOR YOUR POSITION

This section is the most critical part of your essay. Here is where you will present the argument in support of your stated position. You may even want to introduce this section by saying something like: "And the main argument for my position is. . . ." In most cases, the stated position and the conclusion of the argument supporting it are the same claim. However, if you have more than one argument for your position, present them one at a time and make it clear to the reader each time you move to a different argument. Typically, you should use one paragraph for each premise in your argument, so that the reader is less likely to confuse the parts of the argument. Keep in mind that everything you say should help advance the argument, so no extraneous material should be included, even if it would make the essay more entertaining or colorful.

Set forth the strongest evidence you have in support of your conclusion, making all your premises as explicit as possible and arranged so that they flow from one to the next in logical order. Avoid weak premises altogether if they are not needed to support the conclusion. Use examples sparingly, so that the reader is less likely to confuse an illustration with an argument or premise. Also, make it clear to the reader whether your argument is a deductive or an inductive one, so that he or she knows with what degree of certainty to accept the conclusion. Finally, if your conclusion or position is a moral one, support the argument with an articulated moral premise. Otherwise, you cannot legitimately draw a moral conclusion.

If you think that one of your premises may be a weak one and/or if you anticipate that a critic may raise an objection about a particular premise, you may want to provide some additional support to the premise by means of a subargument. If you believe your critic's objection is not a damaging one, point out what you believe to be the weakness in the objection and/or show that the premise in question violates no criterion of a good argument. If it is a powerful criticism, and you have no effective response to it, you should not be using that premise in the first place. Eliminate it and replace it with a stronger premise. Objections to the argument's *conclusion*, which is usually the same as the stated position, are best addressed in the rebuttal section of the essay.

In presenting the argument for your position you should always be guided in the construction of the argument by the five criteria of a good argument. A good argument for a position must satisfy every one of them. The first of these is the *structural criterion*. A good argument must meet the fundamental structural requirements of a well-formed argument, using premises that are compatible with one another, that do not contradict the conclusion, that do not assume the truth of the conclusion, and that are not involved in any faulty deductive inference.

The second criterion of a good argument is the *relevance criterion*. A good argument should attempt to set forth only reasons that are directly related to the merit of the conclusion or position at issue. A premise is relevant if its truth or acceptance provides some reason to believe, counts in favor of, or has some bearing on the truth of the conclusion.

The third criterion of a good argument is the *acceptability criterion*. A good argument uses premises that are likely to be accepted by the audience or at least likely to be accepted by a rational person in the face of all the relevant evidence. Since arguments use premises that are *more* acceptable to an audience to bring them to a conclusion that is initially *less* acceptable, a good argument would try to find common grounds or shared premises that would be more likely to bring others to the desired conclusion.

The fourth criterion of a good argument is the *sufficiency criterion*. A good argument should provide a sufficient number of relevant and acceptable premises of the appropriate kind and weight to prove its conclusion. Each argumentative context is different and thus creates different sufficiency demands. The more experienced we are in a particular context the more likely it is that we will have a feel for what constitutes sufficient evidence in that situation.

REBUTTING OBJECTIONS TO YOUR POSITION

The fifth criterion of a good argument, which deserves a special status in the argumentative essay, is the *rebuttal criterion*. A good argument should provide an effective rebuttal to all serious challenges to the argument or the position it supports and to the strongest arguments in support of alternative positions on the question. This is the most neglected feature of arguments in general and argumentative essays in particular. Almost any argument can find relevant, acceptable, and even sufficient premises to support a conclusion, but such an argument would not be a good one unless it could also effectively answer those who challenge its merit. It must also be able to identify the flaws in those arguments supporting alternative positions.

Criticisms of your argument or position should be anticipated and your effective rebuttal to them should be included as a part of your essay. If you do not have an effective response to these criticisms of your position, you probably should not be defending that position. That was something that you could have discovered in the research phase of the argumentative essay. .

A good argument is also one that can effectively rebut the strongest arguments in favor of alternative positions on the question at issue. This suggests, of course, that only one position can be the most defensible position on the question. However, since it may not be possible to give a knock-down argument against each of the others, the most appropriate way of dealing with the situation is to defend the position that is supported by arguments that come closer to successfully meeting all the criteria of a good argument than any of the arguments for the alternative positions.

RESOLVING THE QUESTION

Since the conclusion of the essay will have been stated at the beginning of the essay in the the stating of the position, there is probably no reason to state it again in your conclusion. However, you probably *will* want to show how the position you have defended resolves the question, solves the problem, or settles the conflict—which was the impetus for writing the essay. You might also point out how the argument successfully meets all the conditions of a good argument, including the effective rebuttal of criticisms and arguments for alternative positions. Finally, you may wish to suggest areas related to the question where further inquiry may be usefully conducted; but do not, in any case, leave the reader with any doubt about where you stand on the issue.

SAMPLE ARGUMENTATIVE ESSAY

A Married Woman's Name
by T. Edward Damer and Nancy Jean Bradford

We have made great progress toward the goal of becoming a nonsexist society. However, there is one sexist feature of our culture that remains relatively unchanged. The overwhelming majority of women still take their husbands' names when they marry. We believe that this custom of a woman's taking her husband's name is a morally questionable one that should be abandoned in favor of a woman's keeping her own name.

Contrary to the opinion of many, the practice of taking one's husband's name at marriage is merely custom—not law. No state or local government requires such an action. That custom, however, has had a relatively short history. Women in England began taking the surnames of their husbands as recently as the seventeenth century. The trend reflected prevailing property and inheritance laws, in that it evolved concurrently with the erosion of a married woman's right to own property or to handle her own business affairs without the consent and assistance of her husband. A woman did not really need a separate name, for she had no legal identity of her own. Although such laws were never a part of our own legal history, the custom has been carried over to the present.

More Than a Personal Preference
The fact that it is a custom, however, does not determine whether it is morally acceptable. That question must be decided on other grounds. There are obviously some who insist that a woman should have the option to keep her own surname *or* take her husband's as a matter of personal choice. We would point out, however, that other sexist practices are *not* treated as optional. It would not be argued, for example, that it should be optional for an employer to pay women less than men. In fact, most institutional practices that have come to be recognized as clearly sexist have been removed from the category of "optional," just as we have removed from the "optional" category those practices that are clearly racist.

We believe that a married woman's choice of surname is not simply a matter of personal taste. To change or not to change her name is a serious moral question, and it must be clearly focused in moral terms. The practice of a woman changing her name to that of her husband violates a number of moral principles and results in harmful consequences for at least half of our society. Our argument goes like this: Since sexist practices are immoral, and the practice of changing one's name at marriage to the name of one's husband (whether by choice, expectation, or custom) is a sexist practice, therefore the practice of a woman's changing her name to that of her husband at marriage is immoral.

Since the first premise has been sufficiently established in public debate and in other contexts, we will concentrate primarily on the task of defending the second premise: that the custom of a woman's changing her name at marriage is a sexist one. A sexist practice is one that exploits the feature of gender or discriminates on the basis of gender in situations where gender is, or should be, irrelevant. To support our claim that the custom of women changing their names at marriage is a sexist practice, we will show how it is both discriminatory and exploitive. It is discriminatory in the sense that it imposes a requirement on women but not on men; and it is exploitive in the sense that it is used not to serve the interests of the women involved, but of the men.

A Matter of Fairness

Any attempt to focus an issue in moral terms requires some criterion or standard that can be used to determine whether or not a practice is immoral; for if something is immoral, it violates some rule or standard of conduct. The question, then, is: Does the practice of a woman's changing her name to that of her husband violate any moral principle? We believe that it does indeed violate a number of generally held moral principles. Consider, for example, the theory of justice outlined by John Rawls, a well-known contemporary moral philosopher. Rawls suggests that in order to determine whether a practice is immoral, you should imaginatively blind yourself to such things as your own social, economic, racial, or sexual status in the world. In other words, for the purpose of engaging in ethical deliberation about an issue, you simply pretend, as best you can, not to know whether you are rich or poor, black or white, male or female. In such a state of mind, says Rawls, rational beings should be able to determine a fair way of devising moral rules or societal laws. If we were blinded to our own present status, whatever laws or norms we might propose and adopt would not be biased toward ourselves or the traditional way we do things. Instead they would be designed so that, whatever we "turned out to be" (male or female, black or white, or whatever), we would regard the proposed rules as both fair and rational.

If we want to be fair and unbiased in our assessment of the practice of a woman's changing her name at marriage, we might ask: Is this system one that we *now* would devise if we were trying to find a fair way of determining how names should be handled when two people marry? If we were to start from scratch and redesign the whole marriage naming system, would we design a plan similar to our customary way of doing it? We think not. The customary practice is not one that would be proposed by rational people attempting to design an ideal world. It simply does not make sense, for example, that we would arbitrarily decide that it should be the woman, and not the man, who changes her name at marriage. Indeed, we are convinced that rational people in that imaginative state would propose that all parties simply maintain their own names throughout their lives.

A Surrender of Identity

Our name is usually treated as one of the most important things about us. It is the primary mark of our identity and the vehicle for establishing our heritage. Notice, for example, how upset we get when someone misspells or mispronounces our name, for our name is very closely tied to our awareness of ourselves as unique individuals. It symbolizes who we are. That is why keeping our own name is so very important to us—particularly in the marriage partnership. A woman's name is a symbol of who she is and a man's name is a symbol of who he is, but a woman who takes her husband's name is no longer who she was, for she is now "Mrs. Him."

When the justice of the peace or the minister pronounces a couple "husband and wife," only one of the two identities changes—the woman's. Traditionally, a woman at this moment officially changes her identity to that of her husband and begins to live through him, being "known as" his wife. The two have become one, and the one is *he*. It is perhaps this naming tradition that has contributed to the fact that many women in our society have low self-esteem. A young girl is encouraged by that tradition to regard her own name as only temporary; she will keep it only until she gets married. Indeed, a common "doodle" for young girls is to combine their own first name with the last name of a male to see how a possible new name will look or sound. A woman cannot be expected to have a secure sense of self-worth if that which identifies who she is, is always subject to change—depending on the man to whom she is currently legally attached. But why should only women be subjected to such crises of identity? No man is required or expected to change his name with every change in his marital situation.

A woman who keeps her own name is symbolically rejecting the notion of being identified primarily by the identity of her husband. She is saying that she is not half of him—not even "his better half." It seems very strange for a couple to profess to have an egalitarian marriage while consciously adopting "Mr. and Mrs. Him" as a symbol of their relationship. A married woman who *retains* her own name, however, will *not* find it necessary to explain to others that she is in an egalitarian marriage. Her name makes that point for her.

A Symbol of Patriarchy

No other feature of our culture calls attention to male dominance with more directness and frequency than does the custom of calling a married woman by her husband's name. Moreover, every woman who displays this sexist symbol helps perpetuate the patriarchal character of the society. Every time she is introduced or introduces herself as "Mrs. Him," she and the culture give their approval to the underlying implications of that sexist act. They are saying: The husband is clearly more important than the wife in our culture.

To use a woman's birthname in place of the sexist symbol of "Mr. and Mrs. Him" makes a powerful egalitarian statement. The adoption of the alternative symbols of "Ms. Her" and "Mr. Him" says: This is no longer to be a male-dominated society, in which the male offspring will assume the mantle of control. Name retention thus has the potential to help destroy patriarchy by contributing significantly to the balancing of the power relationship in marriage and ultimately in the society.

A Double Standard

The cultural expectation (and sometimes insistence) that a married woman take the name of her husband is a clear case of a double standard. A double standard is a principle or a set of principles that is applied to one person or group differently from how it is applied to others, when there are no relevant reasons for doing so. A well-known way of exposing double standards is to employ the reversibility test: "Would you find the action or practice in question acceptable if the situation were reversed?" Applied to our issue, it asks: "Would you, as a man, find it acceptable if the practice in our society were for a man to change his name to that of his wife?" Most men who are asked this question assert very emphatically that they would not change their names. Yet our society expects a woman to do just that. Perhaps the most disturbing kind of male response that we hear to the suggestion that a woman keep her own name is: "No woman of mine would ever do something like that." Such a response shows just how deeply ingrained the sexist attitude toward this issue has become. A man who can speak of a potential partner in such terms of ownership obviously does not regard her as an equal.

A Lack of Self-Respect

One of the first indications that we give others of our own attitude toward ourselves is the way we introduce ourselves. But when a woman replaces her own name with that of her husband, she deliberately devalues herself. For example, a person who telephones us and introduces herself as "Mrs. Him" has already told us a great deal about herself. She has told us that she wants to be known primarily as the "wife of Him" and that she does not consider herself to be an equal with him. She thinks highly of her husband—but not as highly of herself.

Not only does such a woman devalue herself, she also encourages a lack of respect for other women—especially those who are married. If a woman is willing to accept a subservient role, she is saying that women are inferior and is encouraging a sexist attitude toward all women. Moreover, when she waives her own right to equal status with her husband, she is more likely to underestimate, or even disregard, similar rights of other women.

Those who think a woman should take the name of her "equal" do not really regard her as an equal. However, for those who believe in equal marriage, a woman's birthname is one of the most powerful symbols available for making that egalitarian assertion. Every time she is introduced or addressed, her very name says: "I'm equal; I am no more and no less important than my husband; we really are co-partners."

A Sexist Lesson for Children

One of the most serious moral consequences of the name-changing tradition in marriage is the sexist lesson that it teaches the children of that marriage. It teaches that the man is the more important member of the team. As soon as children are old enough to understand that Mommy used to have a different name, they typically ask: "Why do you and I have Daddy's name?" Neither Mommy nor Daddy can give a very satisfactory answer to that question. Any answer that they come up with is going to say to the child that Daddies are more important. However, if a mother has retained her own name in the marriage, like the father has done, the children will see clearly that their parents have equal status in the family. Since example is a very effective pedagogical device, retaining separate names could play an important role in reversing, if not in preventing, sexist attitudes in children.

In our most fair-minded moments, most of us do not believe that men are better than women. We cannot rationally defend the view that some people deserve better, different, or more special treatment than others, unless there is some morally relevant reason for such treatment—and gender, according to virtually all moral analyses, is not such a reason. Hence, those who are aware of the discriminatory character of expecting or requiring a woman to change her name should find participation in such a practice troubling to the moral conscience.

Answering the Objections

There are a number of strongly voiced arguments in support of the tradition of a woman's taking her husband's name. Typically these arguments are offered in the form of objections to the idea of a woman's retaining her own name in marriage. But none of them stand up under the light of careful scrutiny. They fail to blunt the force of our argument for name retention. We will review the major arguments by first stating each argument in its strongest possible form and then by pointing out its flaws.

Unity of the Family

The Argument: Marriage is a new entity—an identity that didn't exist before. A common name publicly symbolizes this union of two people.

The Response: Marriage, to be sure, is a new venture and represents the commitment of two people to a relationship of mutual responsibility and trust. However, it is neither desirable nor accurate to describe it as a new entity or identity. Many of us who are married find it important to maintain some sense of our own independence. We make special efforts not to treat our mates as extensions of ourselves. We have different tastes, ambitions, backgrounds, families, experiences, personalities, and possessions. And these differences should be respected. To belittle them would not make for a healthy marriage. Personal independence within marriage also helps us to maintain our own sense of individual worth—an individuality that is further enriched through one's special commitment to another person and to some common goals. Hence, the description of marriage as a submerging of the self into a larger whole seems antithetical to both the facts and the ideal.

Carry on the Family Name

The Argument: If the wife takes the husband's name, the family name will be carried on through the children. This practice gives a sense of continuity to the family—connecting it to its past and future.

The Response: The "family name" that the arguer has in mind is, of course, the *husband's* family name. Hence, the argument is actually an argument for carrying on *his* name through the children. But the question at issue is whether there are good reasons why a *woman* should take her husband's name, and the carry-on-the-family-name argument has little to do with that matter. There are at least two reasons for this.

First, if a couple were not planning on having children, then presumably, according to this argument, it would not make any difference what name the wife used. Second, even if they did have children, the argument would still be irrelevant. A woman's keeping her own name would not preclude giving the children the father's name or the so-called "family name." In other words, the husband's family name could still be carried on through the offspring, even if the wife did not adopt it.

It seems fairly clear that the focus of the traditional concern to carry on the family name is on the *male* offspring. Since the female offspring are expected to abandon the family name at marriage, the tradition seems to have no concern about what happens to the family name taken by the female offspring. Are we so committed to the tradition that we are willing to abide its negative feature of ignoring our female progeny in this way? It is likely that our strong sense of patriarchy simply blinds us to this very repugnant consequence.

In any case, the issue of carrying on the family name probably deserves much less attention than it gets. Indeed, in some ways, it is a bogus issue. If you have doubts about it, take careful note of the names of those relatives who come to your next family reunion. You will probably find that those who share a common name will clearly be in the minority. After all, if females continue to constitute half of those born, and if they continue to marry and change their names, the percentage of people with the original family name will be halved in each generation. After five generations, less than 13 percent of the members of a family would bear the original name. Hence, under the traditional system, the desire to carry on the family name over a long period of time seems to have little chance of fulfillment.

What About Naming the Children?

The Argument: Women who do not take their husbands' name when they marry cause a problem in naming their children.

The Response: Of all the arguments we have encountered, this is the one that is most frequently mentioned. But this argument actually has little direct bearing on the question of what name a married woman should choose. If a couple is among the twenty-five percent or more of those who neither have nor plan to have children, the argument should carry no weight at all in trying to decide whether to take a husband's name or to keep one's own. Consideration for the children would be beside the point.

Even if a couple plans to have children, it is still beside the point. What to name the children should not be seen as a problem created by the *woman's* decision to maintain her own name in marriage. That issue should be treated independently of the issue of what name a married woman should use. Wives, just as husbands, should be able to use their own name, and then the husband and wife *together* can work on the problem of what to name the children. And there are a number of nonsexist ways to do it.

It's Just Tradition

The Argument: Women have always taken their husbands' names at marriage and this is a socially valuable tradition to follow. We ought to continue with a practice that has had such a long and respected history.

The Response: Unquestionably, many traditions help to stabilize our lives and generate a sense of continuity with our past. But we must not forget that there is also a dark and negative side to many traditions. Powerful traditions can perpetuate ancient injustices, they can stifle creative approaches to life, and they are sometimes the largest obstacles on the path to better ways of doing things. To reveal a particular practice as having the status of a tradition therefore sheds no light on whether it is a good one or a bad one. Whether a tradition deserves to be maintained or abandoned must be determined by weighing its positive and negative features. If the tradition is one that threatens values that enlightened reflection supports, then any positive aspects it may embody will have to be weighed against the damage it inflicts. If the damage is serious, as we have demonstrated in the case of a woman's taking her husband's name, then one must be willing to forsake that tradition.

It is therefore false or at least misleading to argue that following the tradition of taking a husband's name at marriage is a socially valuable way of doing things. Such a claim fails to acknowledge that any socially useful features that the practice might have are far outweighed by what we have identified as its negative features. Not only did the woman's traditional title of "Mrs. Him" have an inglorious beginning, it still suggests that she is in some sense the property of Him, that she is an extension of Him, and that she is identified by and through Him. Far from being the distillation of wisdom from previous generations, the practice is a relic from earlier sexist days, as well as the leading symbol of contemporary sexism. We should therefore get on with the business of establishing a new tradition—one that responsible and informed people can gladly embrace.

We have attempted in this essay to set forth a positive argument for why we think a woman should keep her own name when she marries. We also think that we have effectively answered the main objections to our position and to the argument that supports it. Finally, we have attempted to point out serious flaws in the main alternative to our view that a woman should retain her own birthname as her "married name."

ASSIGNMENTS

A. Write an argumentative essay in accordance with the guidelines suggested in the present chapter. The essay should set forth your own personal position on a current controversial issue.

B. Make a photocopy of your argumentative essay for each person in the class, so that it can be evaluated by other class members.

C. In the last chapter you were asked to identify by name each of the fallacies committed by Dad in his "Letter to Jim." Now, assume the role of Jim and write a "Letter to Dad" that responds to or attacks his poor reasoning in one of the letter's paragraphs. However, try to attack each fallacy committed without using the actual *name* of the fallacy. Use the skills you have learned from the "Attacking the Fallacy" sections throughout the text to make your point without being disrespectful or insensitive to his feelings of self-worth. After all, he *is* your Dad!

D. Evaluate the essay "A Married Woman's Name." Does the essay follow all the suggestions for writing an effective argumentative essay? Does it meet all the criteria of a good argument? Does it commit any known fallacies?

Appendix
Letter to Jim

Dear Jim,

When you were home last weekend, you told me how excited you were about your philosophy class, but you assured me that you had not begun to question your *moral* beliefs. I assume, then, that you *have* begun to question some of your other beliefs. I just pray that some of those other beliefs you are questioning are not your religious beliefs. **(1)** As you have probably discovered, philosophers think that reason should apply to all things—including religion. So I am sure that your philosophy instructor believes that also. **(2)** In all fairness, reason is indeed a very good tool to use when examining all other important issues, but it just doesn't apply to religion. **(3)** Any fool knows that you cannot prove the existence of God. **(4)** You just have to accept God on faith. That's just the way it is with religion. **(5)** And that way of understanding faith has enjoyed a very long and rich history, which I am sure you appreciate. **(6)** Those who claim that they can defend their faith with reason obviously do not have real faith. Real faith is something that doesn't need to be supported by reason. **(7)**

Neither can real faith be half-hearted or lukewarm, Jim. That's like being "somewhat " pregnant. **(8)** Anything less than total faith is no faith at all. It's all or nothing! **(9)** And faith is no small matter. The Bible says that without faith, you cannot enter into the kingdom of heaven. In other words, if you have faith, you will go to heaven. **(10)** And it is worth whatever it takes. Escaping the horrors of hell for even one minute is reason enough for you to take the leap of faith. **(11)** I don't mean to wish them any harm, but the philosophers will eventually find out that wearing a white toga and a condescending smirk is not going to get them through the pearly gates. **(12)**

Philosophers, of course, try to intimidate us by claiming that we believers are often inconsistent in what we believe. But you will perhaps remember what Ralph Waldo Emerson said about that. "Consistency," he said, "is the hobgoblin of little minds." **(13)** I'm not saying, of course, that faith should be totally divorced from rational thought. Faith has to be tempered by reason. In order to prevent people from believing something that might be totally absurd, it's appropriate to use some reason about the things that one accepts on faith, but you don't need to go overboard about it—like the philosophers do. The best way to treat it would be to see reason and faith meeting each other half way. **(14)** However, if reason leads you to some view that is inconsistent with faith, then reason is just wrong. **(15)**

Philosophers also claim that you have to have evidence to believe something. What I say is that you have all the evidence you need when you experience God in your heart. **(16)** Anyway, the philosophers are clearly involved in a contradiction here. Even though they claim that one shouldn't accept something simply on faith, they clearly base their whole approach on their total faith in science and reason. So we should hardly take their criticism of our particular faith seriously. **(17)** You need to keep in mind that these philosophers who demand that you have evidence for your beliefs are just atheists who couldn't care less about you or your eternal destiny. **(18)** And they *are* atheists. Since both atheists and philosophers question the existence of God, it is reasonable to conclude that philosophers really are atheists, whether they admit it or not. **(19)** It is simply a matter of logic. We know that most philosophers question the existence of God, and no persons of faith question the existence of God, so no philosophers could be persons of faith. **(20)** That means that they also probably support the Supreme Court decision that prevents public schools from having prayer at the beginning of each day. **(21)** I just don't understand how things have gotten so messed up in our society. I remember when I was a kid, we had a prayer in school every day, and nobody complained at all. There's no reason why things can't be the same today. **(22)**

If having evidence is so important, just look at the miracles God performs every day. As you know, your mom's brother, Neal, was diagnosed with terminal cancer two years ago, but in faith he asked God to heal him, and God did. Neal went to his doctors, and they could find no sign of his cancer at all. The doctors were amazed. **(23)** Actually, you need look no further than the latest Gallup Poll, published last Sunday in the *New York Times*. Ninety-seven percent of the American people believe in the existence of God. **(24)** My view, however, is that we should not respond positively to the philosopher's demand for evidence at all, and I'll tell you why. If you agree to the demand that *any* evidence be provided for faith, the philosopher will demand more and more evidence until eventually you find yourself trapped into playing by the philosopher's rules and giving in to the demand for *complete* evidence, since there is no point along the way that a particular amount of the evidence can be declared to be sufficient. **(25)** It's better to stay out of the fray altogether. If you accept the principle that faith is self-authenticating and therefore needs no evidence to support it, any use of evidence at all is a rejection of that principle. **(26)**

When I was in college, Jim, I held fast to that principle. If I had questioned my faith as my philosophy professor tried to get me to do, I wouldn't be enjoying God's blessings today. **(27)** Please remember that when dealing with philosophers, "If you give them an inch they will take a mile." **(28)** As you can tell, I just don't trust them in any way. In fact, if I were you, I would try never to be alone with one of them. It wouldn't have surprised me at all if I had learned that my philosophy professor had been charged with sexual harassment by some of his male students. **(29)**

One of the most serious problems with giving up belief in God is that if you don't believe, you will have no basis for morality. Only God can tell us what is right and wrong. An act is right or wrong because God says it is. **(30)** The philosophers will try to prove otherwise by trotting out that Abraham-Isaac story about how Abraham was willing to abandon his own sense of morality to do what God told him to do. They think that the story shows God endorsing the killing of an innocent person and therefore illustrates their point about the absurdity of the view that an act is right because God says it is. But you and I know that God wouldn't let Abraham do something that was *wrong*. **(31)** He was just trying to test Abraham's faith. So the philosophers have no case at all. **(32)**

Just in case there is any doubt about what we are dealing with here, let me remind you that atheists are those who deny that God plays any role in determining right or wrong. Therefore, if your professor denies that God plays any role in determining right or wrong he or she is clearly an atheist. **(33)** So beware! Don't listen to those who tell you something different from what I'm telling you. They are wrong! I have looked at this whole issue very carefully, and there is nothing to suggest there is any serious doubt about the existence of God. **(34)** Just listen to what the Bible says, and I mean what it actually says—not somebody's interpretation of what it says. **(35)** If you listen to some of those so-called interpreters, you will start questioning your religious beliefs, you will then abandon religion altogether, and you will eventually end up as some kind of moral nihilist—with no morality at all. **(36)** So you can understand why your philosophy professor is not likely to give any credence to any other than his own views about God. **(37)**

Perhaps this all boils down to a very simple question. Do you really want to risk spending eternity in hell? **(38)** The Bible makes it very clear that if you don't believe in God, He will send you to hell. **(39)** And if you have read how the Bible describes that place, you don't want to go there. **(40)** And every day that goes by with you in a state of doubt makes it all the more likely that some fatal accident may occur with you ending up in hell. **(41)** Fortunately, God has promised those who remain faithful to Him an eternal paradise, and it must be true. Why else would all people desire it so much? **(42)**

Look at this way, Jim. If God exists, He would have revealed Himself in various ways to His creatures. And, as I have shown, He has indeed revealed Himself by His miraculous acts and through the personal religious experiences of believers throughout the span of history. It follows that God must therefore exist. **(43)** Of course, the best argument for believing that God exists is the fact that the philosophers have not proved that He doesn't. **(44)** Nevertheless, if thousands of miracles had not occurred and thousands of people had not had personal religious experiences, then maybe even I might have some reason to question God's existence, but those things have happened, so there is no question that He exists. **(45)** Even the force of such logic fails to persuade the philosophers. It is not that they have nothing to say about religious experience; they have plenty to say about it. The problem is that just because they have never had religious experiences (or at least find other explanations for them) they then deny the authenticity of any other person's religious experience. **(46)** My view is that if philosophers have never had a religious experience, we really shouldn't even be listening to what any of them say on the subject. **(47)** In any case, I would be willing to bet that not a single point that your professor makes in his criticism of belief in God is a conclusive one. Therefore, his whole atheistic argument should be regarded as inconclusive. **(48)**

I must confess that in a moment of doubt, many years ago, I myself asked God to give me a sign that He existed. The very next day God blessed me with a job promotion—and I had no idea that I was even being considered for the position. It came right out of the blue. **(49)** In any case, if there is no God, how could one explain the intricacies of nature? The only explanation for such marvels is that God exists and that He made it all happen. (50) I know that some scientists and atheistic philosophers claim that evolution can account for all that, but the only reason they are saying that is that they are just desperate to win converts to secularism. (51) There is no way that the human mind could just happen. (52) Reverend John Clausen, Minister of the Boston Trinity Congregational Church, has shown that it would take trillions of years of trial and error for something like the human mind to "just happen." (53) I've actually done some research on this issue. During the last several years, I have surveyed everything that has been written about evolution in *Religious Digest*, and not a single article indicates any merit in the evolutionists' theory. (54)

The simple truth is that God asks us to trust in Him, and I do. That means that He will keep me from harm, answer my prayers, and provide a final home for me in heaven. (55) If sometimes bad things happen to me and God doesn't appear to answer my prayers, then that doesn't mean that God doesn't exist or isn't hearing my prayers or doesn't care about my welfare. It's just that the answer is no. (56) Whatever He does, there is a good reason for it. (57)

Jim, I believe in God because He brought your mother and me together, gave us a son like you, and has blessed us all with a rich and wonderful life. (58) I know that you will do the right thing and not give us cause to think that we have failed to raise you properly. Jim, promise me that you are not going to disappoint your family by bringing home any of your philosophical doubts about religion. When I talked with your mother yesterday, she was in tears over what you could be doing to yourself—and to her—with this philosophy course of yours. We're counting on your returning home as steadfast in the faith as you were when you left for college last fall. (59)

I'm looking forward to talking to you more about these matters while you're here during the Christmas holidays. As you might suspect, I love talking about these things more than your mother. (60)

Love,
Dad

Glossary of Fallacies

Accent, Misleading This fallacy consists in directing another person toward an unwarranted conclusion by placing improper or unusual emphasis on a word, phrase, or particular aspect of an issue or claim. It is sometimes committed by taking portions of another's statement out of its original context in a way that conveys a meaning not intended. (p. 109)

Ad Hominem, **Abusive** This fallacy consists in attacking one's opponent in a personal or abusive way as a means of ignoring or discrediting his or her criticism or argument. (p. 176)

Affirming the Consequent This fallacy consists in affirming the consequent of a conditional statement and then inferring the affirmation of the antecedent. (p. 68)

Ambiguity This fallacy consists in directing another person toward an unwarranted conclusion by presenting a claim or argument that uses a word, phrase, or grammatical construction that can be interpreted in two or more distinctly different ways, without making clear which meaning is intended. (p. 107)

Abusive Ad Hominem *See* Ad Hominem, Abusive

Appeal to Common Opinion *See* Common Opinion, Appeal to

Appeal to Force or Threat *See* Force or Threat, Appeal to

Appeal to Self-Interest *See* Self-Interest, Appeal to

Appeal to Tradition *See* Tradition, Appeal to

Arguing from Ignorance *See* Ignorance, Arguing from

Arguing in a Circle This fallacy consists in either explicitly or implicitly asserting, in one of the premises of an argument, what is asserted in the conclusion of that argument. (p. 53)

Argument by Innuendo *See* Innuendo, Argument by

Attacking a Straw Man   This fallacy consists in misrepresenting an opponent's position or argument, usually for the purpose of making it easier to attack. (p. 183)

Authority, Irrelevant   This fallacy consists in attempting to support a claim by appealing to the judgment of one who is not an authority in the field, the judgment of an unidentified authority, or the judgment of an authority who is likely to be biased. (p. 79)

Causal Oversimplification   This fallacy consists in oversimplifying the causal antecedents of an event by specifying causal factors that are insufficient to account for the event in question or by overemphasizing the role of one or more of those factors. (p. 158)

Common Cause, Neglect of a   This fallacy consists in failing to recognize that two seemingly related events may not be causally related at all, but rather are effects of a common cause. (p. 163)

Common Opinion, Appeal to   This fallacy consists in urging the acceptance of a position simply on the grounds that a large number of people accept it or in urging the rejection of a position on the grounds that very few people accept it. (p. 81)

Complex Question   This fallacy consists in formulating a question in a way that presupposes that a definite answer has already been given to an unasked question about an issue that is still open or that treats a series of questions as if it involved only one question. (p. 57)

Composition, Fallacy of   This fallacy consists in assuming that what is true of the parts of some whole is therefore true of the whole. (p. 123)

Confusion of Cause and Effect   This fallacy consists in confusing the cause with the effect of an event or in failing to recognize that there may be a reciprocal causal relation between the two events in question. (p. 161)

Confusion of a Necessary with a Sufficient Condition   This fallacy consists in assuming that a necessary condition of an event is also a sufficient one. (p. 156)

Continuum, Fallacy of the   This fallacy consists in assuming that small movements or differences on a continuum between a thing and its contrary have a negligible effect and that to make definite distinctions between points on that line is impossible or at least arbitrary. (p. 120)

Contradiction Between Premise and Conclusion   This fallacy consists in drawing a conclusion that is incompatible with at least one of the premises. (p. 64)

Contrary-to-Fact Hypothesis   This fallacy consists in treating a hypothetical claim as if it were a statement of fact by making a claim, without sufficient evidence, about what would have happened in the past if other conditions had been present or about an event that will occur in the future. (p. 148)

Counterevidence, Denying the   This fallacy consists in refusing to consider seriously or in unfairly minimizing the evidence that is brought against one's claim. (p. 172)

Counterevidence, Ignoring the   This fallacy consists in arguing in a way that ignores or omits any reference to important evidence unfavorable to one's position, giving the false impression that there is no significant evidence against it. (p. 173)

Denying the Antecedent   This fallacy consists in denying the antecedent of a conditional statement and then inferring the denial of the consequent. (p. 66)

Denying the Counterevidence   *See* Counterevidence, Denying the

Distinction Without a Difference This fallacy consists in attempting to defend an action or position as different from some other one, with which it might be confused, by means of a careful distinction of language, when the action or position defended is no different in substance from the one from which it is linguistically distinguished. (p. 117)

Division, Fallacy of This fallacy consists in assuming that what is true of some whole is therefore true of each of the parts of that whole. (p. 124)

Domino Fallacy This fallacy consists in assuming, without appropriate evidence, that a particular action or event is just one, usually the first, in a series of steps that will lead inevitably to some specific, usually undesirable, consequence. (p. 164)

Drawing the Wrong Conclusion *See* Wrong Conclusion, Drawing the

End Term, Illicit Distribution of an This fallacy of syllogistic reasoning consists in drawing a conclusion that includes a distributed end term that is not distributed in one of the premises. (p. 73)

Equivocation This fallacy consists in directing another person toward an unwarranted conclusion by making a word or phrase employed in two different senses in an argument appear to have the same meaning throughout. (p. 105)

Fallacy of Division *See* Division, Fallacy of

Fallacy of Popular Wisdom *See* Popular Wisdom, Fallacy of

Fallacy of the Continuum *See* Continuum, Fallacy of

Fallacy of the Mean *See* Mean, Fallacy of

False Alternatives This fallacy consists in restricting too severely the number of proposed alternatives and in assuming that one of the suggested alternatives must be true. (p. 126)

False Conversion This fallacy consists in exchanging the subject and predicate terms in a universal affirmative or particular negative categorical statement or in reversing the antecedent and consequent of a conditional statement and then inferring that such converted statements retain their original truth value. (p. 69)

Faulty Analogy This fallacy consists in assuming that because two things are alike in one or more respects, they necessarily are alike in some other important respect, while failing to recognize the insignificance of their similarities and/or the significance of their dissimilarities. (p. 134)

Force or Threat, Appeal to This fallacy consists in attempting to persuade others of a position by threatening them with some undesirable state of affairs instead of presenting evidence for one's view. (p. 92)

Gallery, Playing to the This fallacy consists in attempting to persuade others of one's position by exploiting their strong emotions or by manipulating their positive and negative attitudes toward certain groups or ideas, instead of presenting evidence for one's view. (p. 97)

Gambler's Fallacy This fallacy consists in arguing that because a chance event has had a certain run in the past, the probability of its occurrence in the future is significantly altered. (p. 166)

Genetic Fallacy This fallacy consists in evaluating a thing in terms of its earlier context and then carrying over that evaluation to the thing in the present, while ignoring relevant changes that may have altered its character in the interim. (p. 83)

Humor or Ridicule, Resort to   This fallacy consists in injecting humor or ridicule into an argument in an effort to cover up an inability or unwillingness to respond appropriately to an opponent's criticism or counterargument. (p. 188)

Ignorance, Arguing from   This fallacy consists in arguing for the truth (or falsity) of a claim, because there is no evidence or proof to the contrary or because of the inability or refusal of an opponent to present convincing evidence to the contrary. (p. 146)

Ignoring the Counterevidence   *See* Counterevidence, Ignoring the

Illicit Contrast   This fallacy consists in a listener's directly inferring from another's claim some related but unstated *contrasting* claim by improperly placing unusual emphasis on a word or phrase in the speaker's or writer's statement. (p. 111)

Illicit Distribution of an End Term   *See* End Term, Illicit Distribution of an

Incompatible Premises   This fallacy consists in drawing a conclusion from inconsistent or incompatible premises. (p. 62)

Innuendo, Argument by   This fallacy consists in directing another person toward a particular, usually derogatory, conclusion by a skillful choice of words that implicitly *suggests* but does not *assert* that conclusion. (p. 113)

Insufficient Sample   This fallacy consists in drawing a conclusion or generalization from too small a sample of cases. (p. 142)

Irrelevant Authority   *See* Authority, Irrelevant

Is-Ought Fallacy   This fallacy consists in assuming that because something is now the practice, it ought to be the practice. Conversely, it consists in assuming that because something is not now the practice, it ought not to be the practice. (p. 127)

Mean, Fallacy of the   This fallacy consists in assuming that the moderate or middle view between two extremes must be the best or right one, simply because it is the middle view. (p. 132)

Middle Term, Undistributed   This fallacy of syllogistic reasoning consists in inferring a conclusion from two premises, neither of which distributes the middle term. (p. 71)

Misuse of a Principle   *See* Principle, Misuse of a

Misuse of a Vague Expression   *See* Vague Expression, Misuse of

Neglect of a Common Cause   *See* Common Cause, Neglect of a

Omission of Key Evidence   This fallacy consists in constructing an argument that fails to include key evidence that is critical to the support of the conclusion. (p. 154)

Playing to the Gallery   *See* Gallery, Playing to the

Poisoning the Well   This fallacy consists in rejecting a criticism or argument presented by another because of that person's special circumstances or improper motives. (p. 178)

Popular Wisdom, Fallacy of   This fallacy consists in appealing to insights expressed in aphorisms or clichés, folk wisdom, or so-called common sense, instead of to relevant evidence for a claim. (p. 150)

***Post Hoc* Fallacy**   This fallacy consists in assuming that a particular event, B, is caused by another event, A, simply because B follows A in time. (p. 160)

Principle, Misuse of a   This fallacy consists in misapplying a principle or rule in a particular instance by assuming that it has no exceptions. Conversely, it consists in attempting to refute a principle or rule by means of an exceptional case. (p. 130)

Question-Begging Definition This fallacy consists in using a highly questionable definition as a premise, which has the effect of making the claim at issue "true by definition." (p. 59)

Question-Begging Language This fallacy consists in discussing an issue by means of language that assumes a position on the very question at issue, in such a way as to direct the listener to that same conclusion. (p. 55)

Rationalization This fallacy consists in using plausible-sounding but usually fake reasons to justify a particular position that is held on other, less respectable grounds. (p. 84)

Red Herring This fallacy consists in attempting to hide the weakness of a position by drawing attention away from the real issue to a side issue. (p. 186)

Resort to Humor or Ridicule *See* Humor or Ridicule, Resort to

Self-Interest, Appeal to This fallacy consists in urging an opponent to accept or reject a particular position by appealing solely to his or her personal circumstances or self-interest, when there is some more important issue at stake. (p. 95)

Special Pleading This fallacy consists in applying principles, rules, or criteria to another person, while failing or refusing to apply them to oneself or to a situation that is of personal interest, without providing sufficient evidence to support such an exception. (p. 152)

Tradition, Appeal to This fallacy consists in attempting to persuade others of a point of view by appealing to their feelings of reverence or respect for some tradition instead of to evidence, especially when there is some more important principle or issue at risk. (p. 93)

Trivial Objections This fallacy consists in attacking an opponent's position by focusing critical attention on some minor point in the argument. (p. 185)

Two-Wrongs Fallacy This fallacy consists in rejecting a criticism of one's argument or actions by accusing one's critic or others of thinking or acting in a similar way. (p. 180)

Undistributed Middle Term *See* Middle Term, Undistributed

Unrepresentative Data This fallacy consists in drawing a conclusion based on data from an unrepresentative or biased sample. (p. 144)

Using the Wrong Reasons *See* Wrong Reasons, Using the

Vague Expression, Misuse of a This fallacy consists in attempting to establish a position by means of a vague expression or in drawing an unjustified conclusion as a result of assigning a very precise meaning to another's word or phrase that is quite imprecise in its meaning or range of application. (p. 115)

Wishful Thinking This fallacy consists in assuming that because one wants something to be true, it is or will be true. Conversely, it consists in assuming that because one does not want something to be true, then it is not or will not be true. (p. 129)

Wrong Conclusion, Drawing the This fallacy consists in drawing a conclusion other than the one supported by the evidence presented in the argument. (p. 86)

Wrong Reasons, Using the This fallacy consists in attempting to support a claim with reasons other than the reasons appropriate to the claim. (p. 88)

Answers to Selected Assignments

Chapter V: Fallacies That Violate the Structural Criterion

A. Begging-the-Question Fallacies (p. 61)

2. Question-begging definition. Sean is using a question-begging definition in his argument about criminal rehabilitation. The reason he does not let any evidence count against his claim is that he *defines* a criminal as someone who cannot be rehabilitated. It is a violation of the structural criterion of a good argument to use a premise that is the same as the conclusion that it allegedly supports. A premise that provides the questionable definition that makes the conclusion true by definition is no different from the conclusion.

4. Arguing in a circle. Dorothy has engaged in circular reasoning. She claims that the Bible is the inspired word of God, and the reason she offers is that the Bible *says* that it is the inspired word of God. Using a premise that is the same claim as the conclusion is a violation of the structural criterion of a good argument.

5. Complex question. The constituent's question is a complex one. Senator Fisher is actually being asked two questions: (a) whether he will vote for the proposed cut and (b) whether the budget cut will weaken the U.S. military posture around the world. It is obvious that the questioner has already implicitly assumed the truth of a positive answer to the second question, by the way the question is asked. This complex question violates the structural criterion of a good argument, because it illegitimately assumes that the same answer can be given to both questions and assumes the truth of an important claim still at issue—whether the bill, if passed, will weaken our military posture. That question should be answered independently of the other, with no assumption being made about the truth of one of the answers.

8. Question-begging language. The real estate broker uses question-begging language to bring Elijah to the conclusion that he does not want to see any more houses, by referring to the house as "tacky." Since the "tacky" premise assumes the truth of the conclusion—namely, that Elijah does *not* want to see other houses—the argument violates the structural criterion of a good argument.

B. Fallacies of Inconsistency (p. 65)

1. Incompatible premises. This argument uses as its premise the claim of skepticism, which means that *no* claim can be known to be true. However, by concluding that the search for truth should be given up, the arguer obviously believes that the claim of skepticism itself is true. To claim that skepticism is true contradicts the very position of skepticism that nothing can be known to be true. To set forth incompatible premises creates a situation in which no conclusion can be drawn and thus violates the structural criterion of a good argument that in a well-formed argument, the premises must be compatible with one another.

2. Contradiction between premise and conclusion. In the premises of this argument, the arguer defends the view of individual moral relativism, the view that the only determiner of what is morally right or wrong is the individual himself or herself. The arguer then declares that smoking marijuana is not morally wrong. But then the arguer *concludes* that his or her opponent, who has determined that smoking marijuana *is* morally wrong, has an incorrect judgment about it. The conclusion contradicts the premise asserting the moral relativist position that an individual (including one's opponent) cannot be wrong when making a moral judgment. This argument violates the structural criterion of a good argument, which requires that in a well-formed argument, the conclusion cannot contradict a premise.

C. Fallacies of Deductive Inference (p. 75)

4. False conversion. This argument violates the structural criterion of a good argument. A well-established rule of deductive logic that governs the treatment of categorical statements says that the subject and predicate terms in an A statement may not be exchanged without altering the statement's truth values. But that is exactly where this argument goes wrong. From the claim that those who obey the law will not get in trouble with the police, the arguer infers that those who do not get in trouble with the police are those who obey the law. While the first claim may be true, there is no reason to believe that the converted statement is true. Those who do not get in trouble with the police are not necessarily those who obey the law; they may simply be very clever or, for whatever reason, they just don't get caught.

6. Undistributed middle term. The first and second premises are I statements. *Most* is translated as *some*, because it is *less than all*. In an I statement, neither term is distributed, which means that the middle term *nonviolent acts* is undistributed. An argument with an undistributed middle term violates the structural criterion of a good argument, because it violates a well-established rule of deductive logic.

7. Denying the antecedent. Sarah argues by means of a conditional argument that if Sherry's mother saw Sherry go into an X-rated movie this weekend, Sherry would be very embarrassed. Sarah then denies the antecedent by claiming Sherry's mother will *not* see her go into the movie, because her mother is out of town for the weekend. She then concludes that Sherry will therefore *not* be embarrassed. Such a move violates a rule governing conditional reasoning that says that one cannot deny the antecedent of a conditional statement and then conclude the denial of the consequent. Doing so would violate the structural criterion of a good argument, because the argument employs a structurally flawed argument form. The formal flaw in this particular argument precludes Sarah from considering things other than Sherry's mother seeing her that may cause Sherry some embarrassment.

9. Affirming the consequent. This argument uses a conditional argument to determine that Esther has failed Philosophy 101. According to Esther's testimony, if she failed the course, she would drop out of school. By claiming that she has dropped out of school, the arguer has affirmed the consequent. The arguer then concludes the truth of the antecedent. This violates the rule against affirming the consequent in a conditional argument and concluding anything at all, because nothing follows from a claim that affirms the consequent. To do so violates the structural criterion of a good argument.

10. Illicit distribution of an end term. This argument violates the structural criterion of a good argument by using an argument that is structurally not well-formed. It violates the rule of a valid syllogism that disallows the drawing of a conclusion with a distributed end term that is not distributed in one of the premises. The argument uses two A statements in the premises, each of which has a distributed subject term. The subject term of the conclusion, *readers of this book,* is the subject of an A statement and is thus a distributed end term, but that same term is not distributed in the second premise, where it is in the predicate position of an A statement and thus *not* distributed.

Chapter VI: Fallacies That Violate the Relevance Criterion

A. Fallacies of Relevance (p. 91)

1. Using the wrong reasons. None of the reasons given in the argument supports the conclusion that Ms. Cox should be hired for the position. She may have other relevant qualifications, but those are not mentioned. The argument violates the relevance criterion because the conclusion of a good argument must be supported by the *right* reasons.

2. Genetic fallacy. The arguer has assumed that a white dress still means that the bride is a virgin and then has drawn the conclusion that Debbie, who is not a virgin, should not wear white at her wedding. Since a white dress is no longer a sign of the sexual experience of a bride, the arguer's claim becomes irrelevant to whether she should wear white. The argument violates the relevance criterion because it falsely assumes that the meaning or quality of a thing in the past is always relevant to the thing in the present. Since in this case it is not, the conclusion does not follow.

3. Irrelevant authority. Dr. Chamberlain would perhaps be a relevant authority if she were testifying about another one of her clients. However, in this case, since she is a friend of the family of the accused, she is likely to be biased in her testimony about a member of that family. An authority who is likely to be biased cannot be a relevant authority. The use of her testimony in a defense argument would violate the relevance criterion of a good argument.

4. Rationalization. There is good reason to believe that the arguer is rationalizing. While there may be very fine articles that appear in *Playboy* from time to time, that is probably not the real reason the arguer subscribes to it. The argument violates the relevance criterion, because if fake rather than the real reasons for an action or belief are given in support of that claim, they cannot be relevant to the truth or merit of that claim.

5. Drawing the wrong conclusion. The two claims made about the relationship between good teaching and holding a Ph.D., even if true, do not lead to the conclusion that in this particular case a Ph.D. should not be hired in the chemistry department. Interestingly, the opposite claims could also be true—namely, "Many people *with* Ph.D.'s are much better teachers than people *without* them" and "Not having a Ph.D. doesn't make one a better teacher." If opposite sets of claims could both be true, it would appear to have little relevance in determining whether the argument's conclusion is true. The conclusion that should have been drawn from the premises is that it is not possible to determine the quality of teaching of a person based solely on whether that person has a

Ph.D. The argument violates the relevance criterion because the premises of a good argument must support or be relevant to the truth or merit of the claim at issue.

6. Appeal to common opinion. The fact that most women take their husbands' name when they marry is not relevant to whether or not that is a good practice. The argument violates the relevance criterion because what large numbers of people or even the majority of people do or believe about a thing is not relevant to whether that thing is worthy of doing or believing.

B. Irrelevant Emotional Appeals (p. 101)

1. Appeal to tradition. That fact that the speaker and his or her family has always, or traditionally, voted for and considered themselves Democrats should play no role when the evidence in a particular case suggests that there are good reasons to vote for a Republican. An appeal to tradition when there is the more important issue of citizenship responsibility at stake violates the relevance criterion of a good argument.

2. Appeal to force or threat. Dawn is being threatened by her mate. He says to her that if she intends to keep her own name if they marry, then he would not marry her. He is therefore using force or threat rather than good reasons to persuade her to take his name. An argument that uses force or threat in the place of evidence violates the relevance criterion of a good argument.

3. Appeal to self-interest. The appeal that is made in this argument is directed toward the personal interests of a fellow Catholic—that is, whether or not their struggling Catholic schools will be assisted financially. No evidence is offered for the parochial school concept itself. An argument that appeals to the personal interests of another when there is a more important issue at stake violates the relevance criterion of a good argument.

4. Playing to the gallery. The broker is trying to create a feeling of shame in the potential customer for accepting the enticements but not buying the product. But such enticements are offered with "no strings attached." There is no reason at all for the customer to feel shame. The attempt to persuade others by exploiting their emotions is a violation of the relevance criterion.

Chapter VII: Fallacies That Violate the Acceptability Criterion

A. Fallacies of Linguistic Confusion (p. 118)

2. Equivocation. The meaning of the word "feel" shifts in midargument. The first use has to do with a physical sensation, while the second use refers to a mental perception. Since the key word in the premises does not maintain its uniform meaning throughout the argument, the conclusion does not follow. A linguistically confusing premise violates the acceptability criterion of a good argument.

4. Distinction without a difference. The speaker is trying to make a distinction between lying and stretching the truth, and wants the hearer to conclude the less embarrassing latter interpretation. However, there is no distinction in substance between the two. Only the words are different. Hence, the hearer should not draw the less troublesome conclusion. An argument that, in this case, uses a deliberately confused key premise cannot be a good one, for a confusing premise violates the acceptability criterion of a good argument.

5. Illicit contrast. From the claim that Dave feels good today, Dan has no right to infer that Dave had not been feeling good before. Dan has improperly placed an emphasis on Dave's last word and has then illicitly drawn an unstated contrasting claim. A case of improper emphasis placed on a speaker's words creates a confusing and therefore unacceptable premise, the use of which is a violation of the acceptability criterion of a good argument.

8. Argument by innuendo. Lisa does not say that Valerie is not helping with the charity show, but by her carefully worded response she suggests but does not assert that claim. An argument that bases its conclusion on a premise that is suggested by innuendo is using a confusing and thereby unacceptable premise, which is a violation of the acceptability criterion of a good argument.

10. Misleading accent. The headline accents the words "doctors" and "patients" in a way that would cause the reader to draw the unwarranted conclusion that there may be a shortage of medical personnel serving the human population in the county. A claim that is confusing by virtue of its being improperly accented is a violation of the acceptability criterion of a good argument.

13. Misuse of a vague expression. The arguer misuses the vague word "liberal" by arbitrarily assuming that if Ron Diss is a liberal he would be critical of the military, and there is no reason to believe that the term necessarily has that range of application. A premise that arbitrarily assigns a precise meaning to a vague word is an unacceptable one, and using an unacceptable premise violates the acceptability criterion of a good argument.

14. Ambiguity. Since it is unclear which of two meanings Roman intended by the term "couldn't," no conclusion can be drawn. The term could mean "unable because of other commitments on his time" or it could mean "is unable because he does not know how to do it." Sela appears to arbitrarily choose one of those meanings, but she probably has no basis for doing so. The use of an ambiguous premise in an argument is a violation of the acceptability criterion of a good argument.

B. Unwarranted Assumption Fallacies (p. 136)

1. Faulty analogy. This arguer compares coffee and alcohol and finds superficial similarities but ignores serious differences when drawing a conclusion. The argument violates the acceptability criterion because it uses the unwarranted assumption that things that are alike in one respect are alike in another.

2. Misuse of a principle. This arguer attempts to disprove or reject the principle that lying is wrong by citing unusual exceptions to the rule. The argument violates the acceptability criterion of a good argument because it employs the unwarranted assumption that a principle has no exceptions.

4. Fallacy of composition. The arguer commits the fallacy of composition because he or she falsely assumes that if every event or incident in the novel sounds plausible, the whole novel will sound plausible. The argument violates the acceptability criterion of a good argument because it makes the unwarranted assumption that what is true of the parts will be true of the whole.

5. Fallacy of the continuum. The arguer commits this fallacy by falsely assuming that it is arbitrary to make distinctions or cutoff points on a continuum between humans and other animal species and draws a conclusion based on that assumption. The argument violates the acceptability criterion of a good argument because it makes the unwarranted assumption that small differences along a line between extremes are insignificant.

6. Fallacy of division. This arguer commits the fallacy of division by falsely assuming that if the University of Virginia is one of the best universities, than one of its parts, the philosophy department, will be among the best. The argument violates the acceptability criterion of a good argument, because it makes the unwarranted assumption that what is true of the whole is true of each of its parts.

7. **False alternatives.** This arguer falsely assumes that there are only two options available concerning the future of the football program and that one of them must be chosen. The argument violates the acceptability criterion of a good argument because it assumes unwarrantedly too few options and that one of them must be the right one.

8. **Is-ought fallacy.** Eugene commits the is-ought fallacy by assuming that since the typical manner in which people deal with sex is not through rational reflection, then that is the way it should be. The argument violates the acceptability criterion of a good argument because it uses the unwarranted assumption that the ways things are is the way they should be.

9. **Wishful thinking.** The arguer commits this fallacy by falsely assuming that in the absence of proof for the existence of God, one can simply make God a reality by "accepting" his reality. Believing or wanting it to be true that God exists is not sufficient to produce that reality in one's life. The argument violates the acceptability criterion of a good argument because it uses the unwarranted assumption that what one wants to be true, is or will be true.

10. **Fallacy of the mean.** The judge in this example commits the fallacy of the mean, since there is no good reason to suggest that the truth is to be found somewhere between the two testimonies. This argument violates the acceptability criterion of a good argument because it uses the unwarranted assumption that the moderate position between extremes is the best or correct one, simply because it is the middle position.

Chapter VIII: Fallacies That Violate the Sufficiency Criterion

A. Fallacies of Missing Evidence (p. 155)

1. **Special pleading.** The student is asking to be an exception to the professor's rule but gives no argument for it other than mentioning considerations that might be just as descriptive of the other students. Since sufficient evidence on behalf of the claim for exceptional status is completely missing, the argument fails the sufficiency criterion.

2. **Insufficient sample.** One experience of eating bad or not so good food in one cafeteria would not be sufficient to infer anything about the quality of food in all institutional cafeterias. Since one such experience would not constitute sufficient evidence for the general claim, the argument would fail to satisfy the sufficiency requirement.

5. **Omission of key evidence.** The key pieces of evidence in the decision to buy a timeshare are the initial price of the timeshare and the amount of the annual maintenance fee, and they are totally absent from the argument. Since the key evidence is missing from the argument, the argument violates the sufficiency criterion of a good argument.

6. **Contrary-to-fact hypothesis.** There is no way of knowing whether having a college degree would have precluded one's being jobless at the present time. Since evidence relevant to a past event that did not occur is unavailable or impossible to obtain, the argument violates the sufficiency criterion.

8. **Arguing from ignorance.** Nothing can be inferred from no evidence at all. The fact that there have been no expressions of concern or no complaints is not evidence that there is satisfaction with the status quo. An argument that draws a conclusion based on the absence of evidence is a violation of the sufficiency criterion of a good argument.

13. Unrepresentative data. Even if the sample is a representative sample of New York City residents, it is not representative of Americans. People who live in an urban area the size of New York are not likely to even have the opportunity to spend their leisure time hunting. Unrepresentative evidence does not provide sufficient evidence to draw a conclusion and is thus a violation of the sufficiency criterion of a good argument.

14. Fallacy of popular wisdom. Since there are many ways to discipline children short of spanking them, the appeal to the spanking proverb appeals to questionable wisdom rather than to evidence. An argument that appeals to the nonevidence of folk wisdom is a violation of the sufficiency requirement of a good argument.

B. Causal Fallacies (p. 168)

1. Causal oversimplification. This argument oversimplifies the factors that cause colds. One cannot get a cold simply from not wearing a hat in cold weather, unless the cold germs are already present. Since the argument oversimplifies the causal antecedents of an event, the sufficiency requirement is not met.

2. *Post hoc* fallacy. The arguer here has inappropriately determined that there is a causal relationship between two events based solely on the temporal priority of the event of the Senator's meeting with the president to the event of the Senator's coming out in favor of the budget bill. Since temporal priority is not a sufficient reason for drawing any conclusion about a causal relation between events, the argument fails the sufficiency requirement of a good argument.

3. Confusion of a necessary with a sufficient condition. Controlling one's temper in this argument is stated as a necessary condition of making new friends—not a sufficient condition. Since the argument confuses a necessary condition with a sufficient condition, it fails to provide sufficient evidence for the conclusion. Therefore, the argument violates the sufficiency criterion of a good argument and the conclusion does not follow.

4. Domino fallacy. This argument fails to provide evidence that shows how each event is causally related to the next in the series. Since the argument does not provide sufficient evidence for its claim, it fails the sufficiency criterion of a good argument and the "freaked out" conclusion does not follow.

5. Gambler's fallacy. If shooting a deer can be construed as a chance event, and it appears to be the case that it can be so construed, the arguer has committed the gambler's fallacy, because the lack of luck in the past three seasons is not causally related to the next season and thus will not affect the outcome in any way. Since the claim about this season's outcome is based on a faulty causal analysis, the argument violates the sufficiency criterion of a good argument and no reliable conclusion can be drawn.

6. Neglect of a common cause. Rather than assuming that a large vocabulary ensures business success or even that business success leads to a larger vocabulary, it is more likely to be the case that some other common factor leads both to business success and a large vocabulary. Since the argument fails to recognize the probable common causal factor in this context, it violates the sufficiency requirement of a good argument and the argument's conclusion does not follow.

7. Confusion of cause and effect. The arguer has confused the cause with the effect in this argument. It is more likely the case that the irritability has caused the fewer number of tips rather than that the fewer number tips has caused the irritability. Since the argument confuses the cause with the effect of an event, it violates the sufficiency criterion of a good argument and the conclusion should not be embraced.

Chapter IX: Fallacies That Violate the Rebuttal Criterion

A. Fallacies of Counterevidence (p. 176)

1. Denying the counterevidence. This argument doesn't even make an effort to minimize or explain away the evidence in the Commission report. It simply denies the evidence altogether. An argument that has no rebuttal premises and refuses even to consider counterevidence to a position held violates the rebuttal criterion of a good argument.

2. Ignoring the counterevidence. This arguer totally ignores the factor of the "sheer thrill of it all" in assessing the worthwhileness of the climb. The arguer may not give the thrill factor much weight, but the argument makes a judgment for all potential climbers. An argument that ignores important evidence against the position defended violates the rebuttal criterion of a good argument and the conclusion of the worthlessness of the climb does not follow.

B. *Ad Hominem* Fallacies (p. 182)

1. Two-wrongs fallacy. In this short exchange Mike points out that Claudia, by her crying, is doing something that is similar or at least has the same effect as Mike's yelling, but does not address her proposal. Because of Mike's "you do it, too" thinking, he feels justified in ignoring Claudia's proposal and thus violates the rebuttal criterion of a good argument.

2. Poisoning the well. The parishioner poisons the well of the priest and refuses to listen to his advice about or criticisms of his or her marriage, but there is no reason why a priest might not have some very good ideas about how to salvage a marriage, even though he may never have been married himself. The parishioner violates the rebuttal criterion of a good argument, because he or she does not attempt to assess the merit of the priest's actual advice or proposal.

5. Abusive *ad hominem*. Rather than respond to the charge that he lied about his legislative attendance record, Mr. Abbott abusively attacks Ms. Phillips about her earlier stay at a mental hospital. By refusing to address the substantive issue, the arguer has violated the rebuttal criterion of a good argument.

C. Fallacies of Diversion (p. 190)

1. Red herring. The professor totally ignores the student's argument about student involvement in governance and tries to shift attention to faculty involvement in governance. The professor violates the rebuttal principle by shifting the discussion to a different issue rather than addressing the question at issue.

2. Resort to humor or ridicule. Rather than answer Diana's concern, Dan uses humor to shift attention away from a serious domestic issue. It is a violation of the rebuttal principle to inject humor in the place of a serious assessment of the criticism or argument.

3. Trivial objections. Professor Reid attacks a very minor point in Professor Lang's proposal. Even if Professor Reid's claim were true, it would do no damage to Professor's Lang position. Professor Reid fails to satisfy the rebuttal criterion of a good argument because he does not address the strongest arguments or supports for the proposal.

6. Attacking a straw man. The mother prefers to distort or misrepresent the argument or concern of her daughter. To misrepresent an argument for the purpose of making it easier to attack is a violation of the rebuttal criterion of a good argument.

Index